ISIS and the Yazidis

ISIS and the Yazidis

*How American Action
Stopped a Genocide in Iraq*

BENJAMIN WOOD

McFarland & Company, Inc., Publishers
Jefferson, North Carolina

Library of Congress Cataloguing-in-Publication Data

Names: Wood, Benjamin, 1964– author.
Title: Isis and the Yazidis : how American action stopped a genocide in Iraq / Benjamin Wood.
Other titles: How American action stopped a genocide in Iraq
Description: Jefferson, North Carolina : McFarland & Company, Inc., Publishers, 2023 | Includes bibliographical references and index.
Identifiers: LCCN 2022060928 | ISBN 9781476690650 (paperback : acid free paper) ∞ ISBN 9781476648491 (ebook)
Subjects: LCSH: Yezidis—Crimes against—Iraq—History—21st century. | Yezidi women—Crimes against—Iraq—History—21st century. | Genocide—Iraq—History—21st century. | IS (Organization) | United States—Military relations—Iraq. | Iraq—Military relations—United States.
Classification: LCC DS70.8.Y49 W66 2023 | DDC 956.7044/3—dc23/eng/20230124
LC record available at https://lccn.loc.gov/2022060928

British Library cataloguing data are available

ISBN (print) 978-1-4766-9065-0
ISBN (ebook) 978-1-4766-4849-1

© 2023 Benjamin Wood. All rights reserved

No part of this book may be reproduced or transmitted in any form or by any means, electronic or mechanical, including photocopying or recording, or by any information storage and retrieval system, without permission in writing from the publisher.

Front cover: (top to bottom) ISIS flag and the ruins of Sinjar (Levi Clancy/Shutterstock); Iraqi girl with her family at Newroz refugee camp (Rachel Unkovic/International Rescue Committee); Launch of an F/A-18F Super Hornet (Mass Communication Specialist 3rd Class Alex Corona/U.S. Navy)

Printed in the United States of America

McFarland & Company, Inc., Publishers
 Box 611, Jefferson, North Carolina 28640
  www.mcfarlandpub.com

For the Yazidi people who have suffered terribly,
and for all those who fought to destroy ISIS.

Table of Contents

Preface	1
Introduction	5
1. Tribalism, Saddam Hussein, and the Genesis of ISIS	7
2. ISIS Devastates the Yazidi Community	29
3. Genocide in the Middle East through the Ages	60
4. Yazidi Stories of Survival and the War Against ISIS	93
5. Fighting the Islamic State in the Chaos of Syria	118
6. A Complicated Part of the World	140
Chapter Notes	163
Bibliography	171
Index	177

Preface

Like millions of Americans, I first heard of the Yazidis of Iraq in 2014. In the summer of that year the world's media was covering the fast-moving events in northern Syria and Iraq. Islamic fundamentalists of the newly created Islamic State of Iraq and Syria (ISIS) were conquering territory at a breathtaking pace. What shocked me most was not that these religious extremists sought to create a society modeled on a strict interpretation of Islam, as we have seen theocracies before, but rather the brutality with which minorities were treated in their new state. Those slated for second-class status included ethnic groups such as the Turkmen and Kurds as well as religious minorities including Christians, Jews, and Shia Muslims. The new entity was to be an austere society modeled on that of the Islamic caliphates of the seventh and eighth centuries. Anyone who did not belong to the Sunni form of Islam was viewed as a threat, but special vitriol was directed at adherents of the ancient Yazidi religion. The Islamic State decreed that any Yazidi man who would not convert to Islam was to be executed. Yazidi men were marked for death, while the women and children were to be enslaved.

I watched the news closely as tens of thousands of panic-stricken Yazidi families fled their homes as ISIS militants approached the Iraqi city of Sinjar. They rapidly moved to the highest ground in the area, Mount Sinjar. Thousands found themselves trapped on the slopes while ISIS fighters surrounded the base of the mountain. Media reports indicated that the Iraqi government was utterly incapable of dealing with the crisis. It could neither defeat ISIS militarily nor protect its citizens. As the encircled Yazidis desperately called for help, I remember hoping the United States might take action to avert a massacre. This seemed unlikely since the United States had withdrawn all combat forces from the country only two and a half years earlier, and Americans had turned their attention to the war in Afghanistan.

As a U.S. history teacher at the high school level I have always encouraged my students to read and watch the news. This simple act allows young

Preface

people to gain a sense of what is happening around them, locally, nationally, and internationally. In class we have had many discussions as to what America's role should be in the world. Our debates have often centered upon whether we, as a nation, should become more isolationist or continue to occupy an active leadership position in international affairs. Most of my pupils tend to favor the latter, as do I. To that end, I must say I was elated when President Barack Obama ordered the U.S. military to aid the besieged Yazidis and lead the efforts to save an entire people from annihilation.

In late August 2014, as the news cycle inevitably moved on to other stories, the term "Yazidi" vanished from the headlines. My interest, however, had been sparked, and I was determined to learn more about these remarkable people and a religion that is all but unknown in the West. To that end I began my research. This included analyzing media reports, as well as conducting both telephone and one-on-one interviews with average Yazidis. As I gathered information, it became painfully clear that while the Yazidi community has endured scores of attacks over the centuries, nothing compared to the sheer size and scope of the ISIS onslaught.

In mid–2019 I traveled to Nebraska in order to visit the largest Yazidi community in the United States. As I spoke to survivors, I found them to be friendly and eager to relate the details of their harrowing ordeals. In order to escape the Muslim extremists they had been forced to leave their homes with very little notice and few possessions. Subsequently, hoping to find safety, they, along with their families, had immigrated to the United States. As my family had also come to America more than a century ago to escape religious persecution, I could empathize. The decision to leave the Middle East, although clearly necessary, was painful in that it meant they might never again return to their homeland. Yazidis have lived in what is today northern Iraq for more than two millennia. Like millions of immigrants before them, however, those I interviewed expressed gratitude toward the United States for the opportunity to begin a new life in this country.

I wrote this book because it is a story that needed to be told. The American effort to save the Yazidis was motivated by humanitarian concerns. It was done simply to prevent a genocide. In an address to the nation on August 7, 2014, President Obama expressed his belief that it would be morally wrong for the United States to stand by and allow a massacre to occur when we had the capacity to stop it. One of my interviewees echoed the president's sentiments when he stated that, during the crisis, he felt that if the Americans would not intervene to save his people, then no one

Preface

would. A cynic, or a student of realpolitik, might argue that the president had ulterior motives. I reject this view. The Yazidis had no political power, nor did their lands contain vast amounts of oil or other valuable natural resources. They were simply a people who had been abandoned by their government and left to fend for themselves against a powerful, merciless enemy.

The war that followed, led and coordinated by the United States, was fought to destroy the Islamic State. It was as necessary as that waged to defeat Nazi Germany. It is not an oversimplification to say that the conflict against the Islamic State of Iraq and Syria, like the Second World War, was a case of good versus evil. Any state in which minorities are to be eliminated, religious deviation forbidden, women treated as chattel, and slavery condoned should rightly be categorized as evil. What was accomplished over the course of a few days in 2014 was remarkable. The United States and its allies confronted a brutal, intolerant terrorist army and rescued thousands of persecuted people. The fact that our country refused to allow a genocide to take place unchecked, even though it was occurring on the other side of the world, is laudable. The taking of swift and decisive action to save vulnerable men, women, and children not only demonstrated courage on the part of the Obama administration but showed America at its best.

Introduction

In the spring of 2014, an army of terrorists swept out of Syria and across northern Iraq. Within weeks it had conquered thousands of square miles and subjugated millions of people to its extreme interpretation of Islam. The militants represented the Islamic State of Iraq and Syria (ISIS), an organization that the world would come to see as the embodiment of cruelty and intolerance in the name of religion. The Yazidis, a small religious minority, would suffer more than any other group at the hands of these fanatics. Theirs is an ancient religion, predating Christianity and Islam by centuries.

In August, as ISIS fighters approached the Iraqi city of Sinjar, panic gripped its Yazidi citizens. Those who were captured were robbed and beaten: the men were murdered, the women and children literally enslaved. Approximately fifty thousand men, women, and children desperately sought refuge on nearby Mount Sinjar. ISIS militants soon surrounded the base of the mountain, and with little food and water thousands suffered on the barren mountainside in the intense heat of the summer. People, including young children, began to die. It was at this point that President Barack Obama ordered the U.S. military to act in order to prevent a genocide.

When one thinks of genocide, the Holocaust comes readily to mind. Because of the staggering number of innocent people murdered this is to be expected, but incidents of mass killings (albeit on smaller scales) have been all too common in world history. The Middle East is no exception. This part of the world has seen its share of mass murder, from the Roman-Jewish wars, to the Crusades, to the Armenian genocide of 1915. ISIS's genocidal policy directed at the Yazidis is just the latest example, and like the Crusades of a thousand years ago it is based on religious fanaticism and the quest for wealth and power. Now, as then, when towns and villages are attacked by an army intent on destruction, there is little the civilian population can do to defend itself. The Yazidis faced such a crisis in 2014.

What the world has learned through painful lessons is that genocide can be avoided if men have the will to come to the aid of those in need

ISIS and the Yazidis

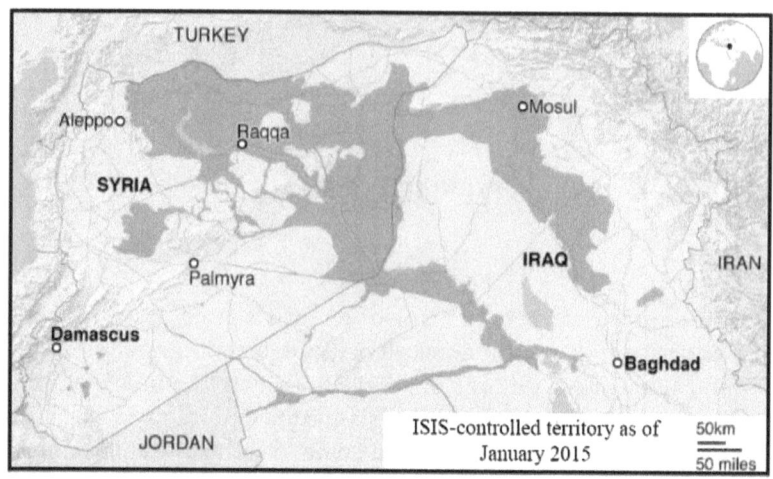

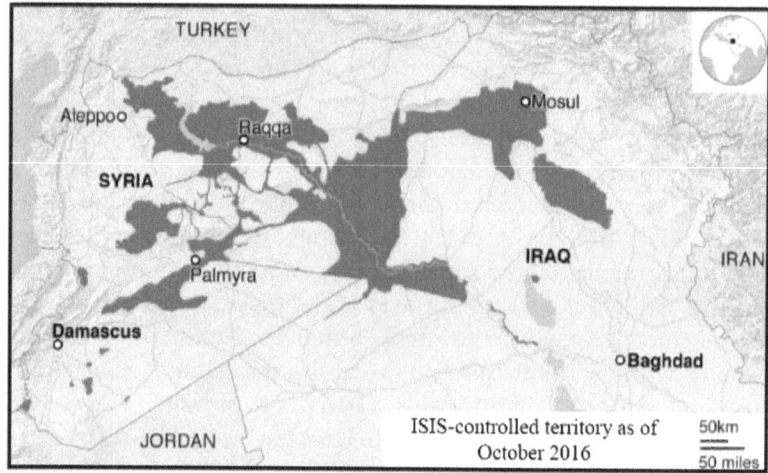

Source: IHS Conflict Monitor

Two maps of ISIS-controlled territory in 2015 and 2016 (Conflict Monitor by IHS Markit).

and nations band together to take action to stop the perpetrators. This was exemplified by the international coalition of countries that formed under American leadership to defeat the Islamic State of Iraq and Syria. The fact that these extremists failed to annihilate the Yazidis and their culture is due to the bravery of Kurdish fighters in Syria and Iraq, the U.S. military, and the Yazidi people themselves.

1

Tribalism, Saddam Hussein, and the Genesis of ISIS

When the assault on Sinjar city was launched by ISIS terrorists in the early morning hours of August 3, 2014, it was not totally unexpected, but it was nonetheless shocking and terrifying. The Islamic militants came from Syria to the west and from the northern Iraqi city of Mosul to the east, which they had captured almost two months earlier. In June Iraq's second largest city had been taken by a mere three thousand ISIS fighters. After a brief military engagement in which twenty-five hundred Iraqi soldiers had been killed or wounded, some twenty-five thousand Iraqi troops in the area had withdrawn. The Iraqi military had undoubtedly been intimidated by stories of the fanaticism and brutality of the militants. The same scenario was about to play out in Sinjar with devastating consequences for the Yazidis. In the predawn hours eighteen thousand Peshmerga soldiers, part of the Kurdish defense forces that had been stationed nearby to protect the Yazidis, also abandoned their posts. The civilian population was left defenseless and alone to deal with a ruthless enemy.

The Yazidis

The Yazidis are not Arabs; they are ethnic Kurds. While there has always been religious tension between Kurdish Muslims and Yazidis, they acknowledge one another as kin. Approximately four hundred thousand Yazidis live in Nineveh province in northern Iraq. Their population is estimated to be only one million worldwide.[1] Yazidis speak Kurdish: the most widely spoken dialect is Kurmanji, which is used by people around Sinjar (Shingal in Kurdish) in neighboring Syria, and by most Kurdish Muslims in Kurdistan. Some Yazidis who live farther east along the Iran-Iraq border, however, speak the Sorani dialect. In addition to their primary language, most Yazidis also speak some Arabic.

ISIS and the Yazidis

Theirs is an ancient religion. Most historians believe it emerged from Zoroastrianism, although elements of Judaism, Christianity, and Islam (e.g., monotheism, circumcision, baptism) have influenced the faith over the centuries. The ancient Persian philosopher Zoroaster spread the ideas of free will, charity, caring for others, and that people will be judged by God after death. Since Yazidis rely on an oral tradition, it is almost impossible to trace their exact origin; the first written mention of them did not appear until the twelfth century. It is a "closed" religion in that one must be born to it, conversion is not allowed, and, should a Yazidi marry outside the faith, he/she would be shunned by the community.

According to Yazidi religious beliefs, after God created the earth, He made seven angels led by the Peacock Angel, Melek Taûs. This chief angel rebelled against God and was, as a result, cast out of heaven. Unlike Lucifer in the Christian religion, however, Melek Taûs showed true repentance and was eventually forgiven. Having regained God's favor, the Peacock Angel was placed in charge of the worldly affairs of man.[2] As this celestial being is considered an intermediary between humans and the Almighty, people pray to him. It is extremely rare for Yazidis to pray directly to God. In this sense it is much like Catholics praying to the Virgin Mary rather than to God Himself. This story of Melek Taûs is the basis for the mistaken belief among many Muslims that the Yazidis worship the devil. As the power of ISIS spread, its fighters would contemptuously refer to the Yazidis as "devil worshipers."

Yazidis tend to marry young, most in their middle teens, and have large families: five or six children is not uncommon. A girl is expected to be a virgin until her wedding day. Arranged marriages have been the norm for centuries and are orchestrated by the fathers of the young couple. The family of the groom is expected to pay a "bride price" to the bride's family. The amount is based on the beauty of the young woman and her family's social standing.

People pray individually. While daily prayers are not compulsory, this act, along with kissing the hands of holy men and visiting revered shrines, demonstrates devotion to the faith. Even when Yazidis gather in temples, they may pray in whatever way suits the individual. Prayers are offered three times a day: at sunrise, later in the morning, and at sunset. Especially pious men and women pray four times a day. In the morning ritual, one prays with open hands facing the rising sun. Yazidis revere both fire and the sun as symbols of light, warmth, and the creative power of God.

In the long history of the Yazidis there is no more renowned figure than Sheikh Adi ibn Musafir. Known as Sheikh Adi, he arrived in

1. Tribalism, Saddam Hussein, and the Genesis of ISIS

northern Iraq in the twelfth century. Born a Muslim in Lebanon's Beqaa Valley, he studied in Baghdad and was drawn toward Sufism (Muslim mysticism). This spiritual man moved to the mountains of northern Iraq to live a contemplative life. Well-liked by both the local Arabs and Kurds, he soon developed a following. As a teacher he earned the respect of his pupils due to his patience and ascetic lifestyle. Denying himself worldly pleasures, he never married and had no children. It was said he could work miracles such as returning sight to the blind and communicating with the dead.[3] After having been accepted by the Yazidis, he reorganized their society and would become their most influential and revered spiritual leader. When he died in 1163 CE, he was buried at Lalish. Yazidis consider his tomb, which is easily identifiable by its three cone-shaped cupolas, as their holiest site.

The valley of Lalish, some 40 miles north of Mosul, is at the heart of the religion. As Jews view Jerusalem as their holy city and Muslims revere Mecca in the same way, so too Yazidis see this valley as their most sacred site on earth. It is the center of their spiritual and cultural life. Lalish contains a multitude of shrines to Yazidi saints as well as two sacred springs—Zamzam and Kaniya Spî. The valley is considered semi-divine land that descended in one piece from heaven. If possible, every member of the faith is expected to make a pilgrimage to Lalish at least once in his or her lifetime. Once in the valley, Yazidis, as well as people of other religions, are expected to remove their shoes as a sign of respect. On the first Wednesday in April, throughout the valley, Yazidis celebrate the new year by lighting 365 lanterns, a custom designed to usher in the new year with light. It is known as Red Wednesday since people decorate their doors with red flowers. The largest religious festival at Lalish is the annual Festival of the Assembly. In September, those Yazidis living in the region gather for this weeklong celebration. Events include the performing of baptisms, the reciting of hymns, and the lighting of oil wicks that are placed near holy sites throughout the valley. All week pilgrims sing and dance (accompanied by flutes and tambourines), and on the fifth day all enjoy an enormous feast. On the last two days of the week a special ceremony takes place to honor Sheikh Adi.

For centuries, most Yazidis in the Middle East have been farmers. In the Sinjar area small farms are ubiquitous. The farmers raise a variety of crops, foremost among them wheat and barley. In addition, Yazidis also raise chickens, sheep, goats, and honeybees. Like subsistence farmers across the globe, Yazidis use what is produced to support their families, while any surplus is sold in larger markets, generally in Sinjar.

ISIS and the Yazidis

All Yazidis belong to one of three castes: they are Sheikhs, Pirs, or Mirids. It is forbidden for an individual to move from the caste into which he or she was born to another. Intermarriage between members of different castes is also prohibited. Most people fall within the Mirid class; they are just average people with no special religious or political roles within the community. Members of the Pirs caste are religious leaders: they perform ceremonies such as marriages and baptisms. They also maintain the various shrines, are the keepers of holy places such as small rural mausoleums, and confer blessings upon individuals.

The Sheikh caste is the most prestigious in that it provides the three leaders of the Yazidi community. The most important of these is the baba sheikh (father sheikh). This is a hereditary role that passes from father to eldest son. This man is viewed as the spiritual leader of all Yazidis. He leads a pious life of austerity, fasting for at least 80 days a year and consuming no alcohol. He is essential to the rituals conducted at Lalish and is easily identified by his white turban and large black belt. He and his family live off the donations given at feast days and by contributions given by those visiting the sacred valley.

The mîr (prince) is seen as the central political figure. This position is, like the baba sheikh, hereditary. His responsibilities include serving as a representative of the people to Muslims and Christians and settling disputes among Yazidis. The pesh imam (chief imam) presides at weddings and sets the "bride price." He is appointed by the mîr, accompanies the baba sheikh on his travels, and is at his side during all religious ceremonies.

Iraq's Two Main Ethnic Groups

While most of Iraq's population is Arab and Muslim, the Kurds—a smaller group whose members have their own language, history, and culture—inhabit the north of the country. Despite the fact that the Kurds are fellow Muslims, tensions have always existed between the two communities. At times, this low-level hostility has erupted into open warfare. This was especially true under the dictatorship of Saddam Hussein (1979–2003).

The Kurdish population of twenty-five million is distributed across the modern countries of Turkey, Syria, Iraq, and Iran. For centuries, the Kurds have longed to establish their own nation, and to this day they are one of the largest ethnic groups in the world without a country of their own. Kurds within the Ottoman Empire (today's Turkey, Syria, Iraq,

1. Tribalism, Saddam Hussein, and the Genesis of ISIS

Jordan, Lebanon, Israel, and part of Saudi Arabia) hoped for an independent homeland at the end of World War I. In 1918 the Central Powers composed of Germany and the Austro-Hungarian and Ottoman Empires, having been defeated in that devastating war, were to be humbled and the two empires broken apart. In the wake of the Great War, the victorious Allies—Great Britain and France—created the 1920 Treaty of Sèvres to deal with the partition of the empire that stretched across the Middle East.[4] One of the provisions of the treaty called for a referendum to decide the question of a Kurdish homeland. When the new Turkish Republic replaced the old imperial government, however, the idea of an independent Kurdistan was abandoned. The 1923 Treaty of Lausanne, which annulled the Treaty of Sèvres, made no mention of Kurdish autonomy or independence.

In the late 1970s a Kurdish movement emerged in the modern nation of Turkey and demanded independence. The PKK (Kurdistan Workers' Party) launched armed attacks against the Turkish state and other acts of violence in order to achieve its goal. It was immediately labeled a terrorist organization by the Turkish government. Three decades later across Turkey's southern border in Syria another group, the YPG (People's Defense Units), was formed to defend Kurds in that country. It too sought independence for the predominately Kurdish region in the north of Syria. Due to its close ties to the PKK, Turkey also viewed the YPG as a destabilizing force in the region. These two organizations with their armed militias would later prove essential in rescuing the Yazidis from ISIS militants in the summer of 2014.

During the Iran-Iraq War (1980–1988) Iraqi Kurds sided with the Iranian regime of Ayatollah Khomeini in the hope that an Iranian victory might lead to an independent Kurdish state. Kurdish leaders allowed Iranian troops to cross their land in the north in order to fight the Iraqi army. In 1983, during this long-running war, the Kurds rebelled against the central government in Baghdad. A furious Saddam Hussein retaliated by initiating the Anfal campaign. Between 1986 and 1989 the Iraqi army killed tens of thousands of Kurds. As part of this military operation thousands of civilians were driven from their homes, which were then looted by Iraqi troops. An "Arabization" effort was begun to replace Kurdish residents with Arabs from the south. The government enticed low-income Arabs from all over the country to relocate to Kurdish towns and cities such as Kirkuk with promises of cheap housing and land.

The man personally responsible for these outrages was Saddam's cousin Ali Hassan al-Majid (nicknamed Chemical Ali). The world was shocked when, on March 16, 1988, as commander of Iraqi forces in the north of the country, he gave orders for the air force to drop bombs filled with mustard gas and other nerve agents on the Kurdish town of Halabja. Approximately five thousand men, women, and children died agonizing deaths, and some ten thousand people suffered injuries. Many years later, after the fall of Saddam, "Chemical Ali" was finally brought to justice in an Iraqi court. In 2007 he was convicted for his role in the Anfal campaign and sentenced to death. In 2010 he was also found guilty of ordering the Halabja massacre. He was hanged on January 25, 2010.

Despite Saddam's best attempts to crush their spirits, Iraqi Kurds would not be dissuaded from their dream of independence. In March 1991, shortly after the end of the Gulf War, Kurds saw another chance for freedom. A new uprising was launched to take advantage of the dictator's weakened position and the turmoil within Iraq's military after having been expelled from Kuwait by an American-led alliance of nations. In order to aid the Kurds, the United States and Great Britain established and enforced a no-fly zone in the north; the Kurds were finally able to negotiate a measure of autonomy. The next year the two main Kurdish political parties, the Kurdistan Democratic Party (KDP) and the Patriotic Union of Kurdistan (PUK), agreed to work together and established the Kurdistan Regional Government (KRG). In 1994 the two rival groups, each seeking to increase its influence and power, ended their cooperation and a civil war erupted. The conflict lasted four years; hostilities finally ceased with the signing of the Washington Agreement in 1998. From its founding, the KRG has relied upon its vaunted military force known as the Peshmerga, Kurdish for "those who face death." In 2003, following the U.S. invasion of Iraq, this force worked with the Americans to drive Saddam's troops from the northern regions of the country. Following the dictator's ouster, a new constitution was written that formally recognized the Kurdistan Regional Government. From the time American troops first arrived in Iraq in the wake of the 9/11 attacks until their departure in 2011, Kurdistan was by far the most stable area in the entire country.

In the southern three quarters of Iraq, the people are Arab and Muslim. Though Islam is their common religion, it has also divided Arabs for centuries. There are some 1.7 billion followers of Islam worldwide,[5] 85 percent of whom are Sunni and 15 percent Shia. Shia majorities exist in Iraq, Iran, Bahrain, and Azerbaijan, while Sunnis are in the majority in all other countries of the Muslim world. In Iraq approximately 60 percent of the population is Shia and 32 percent Sunni.[6]

1. Tribalism, Saddam Hussein, and the Genesis of ISIS

The division within Islam has often been compared to the Protestant-Catholic schism in Christianity. Of course, there are major differences. The split in Islam occurred over who should lead the faithful in the first few years after the birth of the religion, whereas the rupture in Christianity took place more than a millennium after its founding. Early Protestant leaders of the sixteenth century—such as Martin Luther and John Calvin—"protested" against the abuses and corruption of the Church and sought fundamental reforms. While criticizing the lavish lifestyles of popes and the hypocrisy of the clergy, they also stressed a one-on-one relationship with God and no need of a church hierarchy. As these revolutionary ideas spread, European monarchs were forced to choose between remaining loyal to the Catholic Church or adopting a new interpretation of Christianity. Most northern European countries became Protestant while those in the south remained Catholic. As a result, centuries of religious warfare followed (although power politics and economics also played their parts).

Soon after the death of the Prophet Muhammad in AD 632 there was disagreement about who should succeed him as leader of the Islamic community (*Umma*). Most people felt the community should choose the successor. They became known as Sunnis, from *sunna* or tradition, and rallied around Abu Bakr, a close friend of Muhammad. A minority, however, believed leadership should pass to a member of Muhammad's family, and be hereditary. They looked to Ali, the prophet's cousin and son-in-law. These people were known as the followers of Ali (*Shiat Ali*) or Shias. Eventually the Sunnis prevailed, and Abu Bakr became the first caliph, or successor. Ali went on to become the fourth caliph, but as the struggle for power continued, he was assassinated in AD 661 while praying at the Great Mosque in Kufa.

In AD 680 Ali's son Hussein journeyed with his family and supporters from Mecca to Karbala, in present-day Iraq. His group was attacked by an army loyal to the Sunni caliph Yazid. Hussein and most of his family were killed and the survivors sent to Damascus as prisoners. To this day Shias commemorate the battle and the martyrdom of Hussein in a yearly ceremony. The importance of this event cannot be overstated in Shia culture and history. Although each group held a deep mistrust and suspicion of the other, Sunnis and Shias managed to live together in relative harmony for centuries. This state of affairs ended, however, with the 1979 Iranian revolution. That year saw a new militant form of Shia Islam emerge. Although Iran is not an Arab nation (the people are Persian and speak Farsi, not Arabic), it has considerable influence with Shias in Iraq and has sought to compete with conservative Sunni dominated Saudi Arabia for power and influence throughout the Middle East.

The Fall of a Tyrant

Saddam Hussein was a ruthless dictator who ruled Iraq with an iron hand for more than two decades. Throughout the 1970s, even before he officially became "president" of Iraq, he was the "power behind the throne." Saddam greatly admired Joseph Stalin and Adolf Hitler for their skills as politicians. Like Stalin he schemed and made temporary alliances with others, in his case members of the Ba'ath Party, to ensure his rise to power. In 1979 he forced out the ailing president, Ahmed Hassan al-Bakr and assumed direct control of Iraq.

Saddam lived a lavish lifestyle: even as the common people suffered during the wars he began, he continued to build numerous palaces for himself throughout the country. As with all dictators, he amassed a huge personal fortune, appointed sycophants to government positions, and imprisoned anyone who opposed his rule. Not surprisingly, he and his family were above the law. His two sons, Uday and Qusay, were considered "untouchable" by the authorities. Over the years the two brothers literally got away with murder. Uday, the elder of the two, was the more sadistic. He was known to frequently beat his servants for the slightest misstep, as well as anyone else who displeased him. He was a sexual predator who instructed his bodyguards to kidnap young women off the street he found attractive. After raping the woman, he would threaten the traumatized victim that should she speak out against him, she and her entire family would be killed.[7]

In 1980 Saddam launched an invasion of Iran. Hoping to benefit from the internal chaos unleashed by the Iranian revolution, the Iraqi leader sought to overrun the oil fields along the Shatt al-Arab River. In Saddam's mind, these lands, which had long been a point of contention between the two nations, would be easily taken. He miscalculated badly. The Iranians counterattacked, and over the next two years the war ground to a stalemate. In desperation, both sides shelled civilian cities behind the front lines. The Iraqi military dropped nerve gas on enemy soldiers, while the Iranians, with their superior numbers, mounted multiple waves of suicide attacks by fanatical young soldiers. These assaults were not unlike the banzai charges of the Imperial Japanese Army in World War II. Infused with the spirit of the revolution, thousands were determined to become

1. Tribalism, Saddam Hussein, and the Genesis of ISIS

Shia martyrs. By 1988, as both nations neared exhaustion, a ceasefire was finally negotiated. In the end, Saddam's first war cost the lives of some seven hundred thousand people,[8] while the figure for those wounded is between one and two million.

Having failed to conquer territory to the east, the dictator waited only two years before attacking his small yet very wealthy southern neighbor, Kuwait. On August 2, 1990, Saddam's army invaded the Gulf Arab state on the pretext that the Kuwaitis were using slant drilling along the border, thereby stealing Iraqi oil. His actual reasons were quite different: by conquering Kuwait, he could control a greater share of the world's oil supply, and, equally as important, he would not have to repay the $14 billion the Kuwaitis had lent his government to fight Iran. Again he miscalculated. He underestimated the world's outrage at this naked aggression. A few months later the Gulf War erupted as 32 nations joined forces to oppose his blatant territorial expansion.

Shortly after Iraq's invasion of his country, Kuwaiti Ambassador to the United States Saud Nasser al-Sabah appeared on television pleading for the United States to take military action to free his country. Saddam quickly announced that the nation of Kuwait had ceased to exist and was now the 19th province of Iraq. In response, The United Nations imposed economic sanctions, and the United States set a deadline of January 15, 1991, for the withdrawal of all Iraqi troops. With the approval of the United Nations, the military forces of several countries, led by the United States, were assembled. American soldiers began arriving in Saudi Arabia as part of Operation Desert Shield. When Saddam ignored the deadline, Desert Shield morphed into Operation Desert Storm. An air campaign commenced against Iraq that lasted six weeks. On February 24, the ground war began as some seven hundred thousand troops, the majority of whom were American, attacked from Saudi Arabia.[9] Despite Saddam's rhetoric that this would be the "mother of all battles," the Iraqis were clearly outmatched; the war lasted a mere one hundred hours. As the Iraqi army retreated, soldiers set fire to more than six hundred Kuwaiti oil wells, filling the sky with thick black smoke. While this action was taken partially to hinder U.S. air operations, it also revealed Saddam's vindictive nature. Despite his bluster and threats, American forces moved forward, and Kuwait was liberated on February 28, 1991, after only four days of fighting. President George H.W. Bush, having no desire to invade Iraq or occupy a foreign land, announced that his goals of deterring aggression and liberating Kuwait had been achieved and declared an end to hostilities.

Economic sanctions were to remain in place until Saddam

surrendered all surface-to-surface missiles, dismantled his chemical weapons facilities, and destroyed any weapons of mass destruction (WMDs).[10] The dictator refused to comply. As a result, the economy went into a free fall, and ordinary Iraqis endured tremendous hardships. The UN offered to allow Iraq to sell oil on the international market for credit that could only be used to buy food and medicine. Once again Saddam's pride would not allow him to agree to this deal. As a result thousands of Iraqis suffered and died. He finally relented in 1995. His arrogant and obstinate manner continued, however, and in 1998 his government expelled UN weapons inspectors and most sanctions remained in place.

On September 11, 2001, the United States was attacked by 19 terrorists. The men, all from the Middle East, had hijacked four civilian airliners and flown three of them into the Twin Towers of the World Trade Center, and the Pentagon. (Brave passengers aboard the fourth aircraft overpowered the hijackers, and the airplane crashed in a field in Pennsylvania short of its objective.) Speculation as to the last plane's target centers on either the White House or Capitol Hill. Almost three thousand people were killed, and 9/11 became seared into the American consciousness.

A shocked nation soon learned that the man responsible for the horrendous attack was Osama bin Laden. The son of a wealthy Saudi family, bin Laden headed al-Qaeda, a group dedicated to jihad, or holy war against the West. Within weeks the United States struck back at Afghanistan, the nation that harbored the terrorist organization. The United States, along with the other NATO (North Atlantic Treaty Organization) countries, committed tens of thousands of soldiers to the war effort in Afghanistan to combat al-Qaeda and the Taliban. After years of searching, the United States found bin Laden hiding in Abbottabad, Pakistan, and killed him in 2011. Subsequently, U.S. troop levels were reduced to approximately fourteen thousand in Afghanistan.

Bin Laden and his extremists had found haven in a country ruled by the Taliban, a radical Pashtun group that had taken power in Afghanistan in 1996. Although this Islamic fundamentalist government was toppled by the U.S. invasion of 2001, even today the Taliban has not been totally eradicated. Over the past two decades many of its fighters have found sanctuary in the tribal areas of neighboring Pakistan. Since U.S. forces and the Afghan National Army are not permitted to follow, Taliban militants have been able to regroup and venture back across the border. They continue to exercise varying degrees of political and military control over approximately half of Afghanistan.

After the 9/11 attack, President George W. Bush and his senior

1. Tribalism, Saddam Hussein, and the Genesis of ISIS

advisors believed that Saddam Hussein had ties to terrorist groups, including al-Qaeda. In addition, two years later the Bush administration asserted that intelligence reports showed Saddam possessed weapons of mass destruction (WMDs). This claim later proved to be false.[11] The fact that WMDs could have been used against the United States led directly to the U.S. invasion of Iraq. President Bush ordered the military to prepare for war; their mission was to replace Saddam's regime and locate any WMDs (although none were ever found). On March 20, 2003, more than one hundred thousand U.S. troops, joined by almost fifty thousand British soldiers, attacked Iraq from Kuwait. Kurdish militias in the north also aided in the war effort.

Only three weeks after the fighting began, U.S. troops entered Baghdad. On April 9, the iconic image of Americans pulling down a bronze statue of Saddam in Baghdad's Firdos Square was shown around the world. The dictator's brutal 24-year rule was at an end. While average Iraqis destroyed the ubiquitous paintings and posters of Saddam in cities and towns all over Iraq, the man himself went into hiding. He was finally captured on December 13, literally hiding in a hole in Ad-Dawr near his hometown of Tikrit. The now ex leader of Iraq was turned over to an Iraqi special tribunal and charged with crimes against humanity. After a year-long trial, a verdict of guilty was handed down on November 5, 2006. Saddam was given the death penalty. He was hanged on December 30 at the appropriately named Camp Justice, a joint U.S.–Iraqi army base in a suburb of Baghdad. Iraq's strongman outlived his sons by three years. The brothers were killed in a firefight with American soldiers of the 101st Airborne Division in Mosul on July 22, 2003.[12]

While ousting Saddam had been relatively simple, occupying the country proved to be a much more daunting task. U.S. government officials underestimated the political and social complexities of the newly defeated nation. As a result the Iraq War lasted from 2003 until 2011. The United States hoped to establish a democratic form of government in a nation of competing political factions, tribes, and an intense Sunni-Shia rivalry. Saddam had kept sectarianism in check, in large part, by ruling through extreme brutality and fear. Once he was gone these forces were unleashed in much the same way as in Yugoslavia in the mid–1990s, following the death of Tito. In the case of that nation, Serbs, Bosnian Muslims, and Croats fought one another for much of the decade, as Europe witnessed massacres and episodes of ethnic cleansing not seen since World War II. In the end Yugoslavia was torn apart and ceased to exist. In its place the independent nations of Serbia, Croatia, Slovenia, and Bosnia-Herzegovina emerged based solely upon ethnic identity.[13]

ISIS and the Yazidis

The occupation of Iraq proved to be incredibly difficult from the beginning. Anyone who had worked for the previous regime, especially at the national level, was viewed with suspicion. This, in turn, led to the dismissal of thousands of bureaucrats, which made governing all the more difficult. During the Saddam years Sunnis, who were a minority in the country, had held political power; henceforth Shias, who were Iraq's majority population, would occupy the top positions in the government. Not surprisingly, sectarian tensions increased dramatically. Unfortunately, a change in leadership did nothing to end the corruption and cronyism that were endemic within the Iraqi government.

As part of the restructuring plan the Iraqi army was dismantled, and a new military force was created in its place. As the military was being reconstituted tens of thousands of men found themselves without jobs. Many ex-soldiers grew angry and resentful that their incomes were no longer secure and that a foreign power was wielding immense power within their homeland. Some men expressed their frustration by joining Sunni extremist groups. These terrorists targeted U.S. troops, Shias, and religious minorities such as Christians and Yazidis.

Over their long history the Yazidis have endured multiple attacks directed against their people. From AD 637 to 1917 scores of massacres and attempted genocides were perpetrated by Mongols and Muslims, be they of Persian, Ottoman, Kurdish, or Arab ethnicity. Nothing, however, prepared the community for the catastrophic onslaught that was launched by ISIS in the summer of 2014. By the middle of that year what had begun as a small group of Sunni Muslim extremists had grown into an army of religious fanatics. Their goal was nothing less than to kill or convert all those who did not agree with their radical fundamentalist view of Islam.

Al-Zarqawi and the Rise of ISIS

The founder and first leader of what would become ISIS was the Jordanian-born Ahmad Fadhil Nazzal al-Khalaylah. He is better known by his nom de guerre, Abu Musab al-Zarqawi. The man who would one day lead a bloodthirsty army that would cause so much misery took his name from Zarqa, a small Jordanian town north of Amman, where he was born. In his youth he was known as a bully and a thug. He was easily identified at this time by the numerous tattoos on his arms, which, as he became more religious, he removed by cutting out chunks of his own flesh with razors. Tattoos, like the consumption of alcohol, are considered

1. Tribalism, Saddam Hussein, and the Genesis of ISIS

haram (forbidden) in Islam, as opposed to *halal* (that which is permissible). While attending religious classes in Amman, al-Zarqawi was exposed to the Islamic ideas of Salafism. This strain of Islam, which first emerged in Egypt in the nineteenth century, originally focused on the twin goals of driving the Turks out of the region and returning to the original principles espoused by the Prophet Muhammad. Following the collapse of the Ottoman Empire, later adherents directed their animosity toward what they viewed as the corrupt and repressive governments in Jordan, Iraq, Syria, and Egypt.

The Salafists opposed all forms of Western influence in the Middle East, and al-Zarqawi himself was furious that the Jordanian government made accommodations with Israel. Like most fundamentalists, he viewed the Jewish state as illegitimate and an outpost of the West. Wahhabism is the better-known Saudi equivalent of Salafism, although the latter predates the Arabian form by a century. Named after Muhammad ibn Abd al-Wahhab (1703–1792), it objects to the elevation of anyone or anything that might detract from the worshipping of God, including the veneration of shrines or imams (religious leaders). Today most Sunni Muslims reject this puritanical form of Islam, and view Wahhabism as a sect. Al-Zarqawi was also drawn to the idea of *takfirism*, the belief that fellow Muslims could be excommunicated for their supposed heresy.[14] This concept was primarily directed at the Shia community and was later used by ISIS adherents to justify the murder of thousands of fellow Muslims.

In late 1989 al-Zarqawi journeyed to Afghanistan to wage jihad against the Soviet-supported Afghan government. Upon returning to Jordan in 1993 he began to acquire weapons on the black market and assemble several likeminded men whose goal was to overthrow the secular Jordanian government. Before he was able to act, however, he was arrested in 1994 by Jordanian security agents and charged with illegal weapons possession and terrorism. Although sentenced to 15 years in prison, the religious zealot served less than half his time. When King Hussein died, his son Abdullah II succeeded him to the throne. The new Western-educated monarch issued a general amnesty in 1999 that led to the release of some three thousand prisoners, including al-Zarqawi.

The next year, the now committed jihadi returned to Afghanistan to set up a training camp at Herat, with the assistance of a $200,000 "loan" from al-Qaeda.[15] ISIS went through a series of name changes over the years; at this point it was known as Jund al-Islam (soldiers of Islam). The U.S. invasion of Afghanistan put al-Zarqawi and his group on the run. After he was injured in a NATO airstrike in Kandahar, he decided to flee the country. Though he traveled extensively throughout the region, networking and recruiting potential members to his cause, he decided to settle in Iraq. It was in this country that he, and his organization, would wreak the greatest havoc.

In the aftermath of the U.S. invasion, al-Zarqawi found a large reserve of angry, demoralized men ready to join his movement. Shortly after Saddam Hussein was ousted, the United States created the Coalition Provisional Authority. Headed by President Bush's appointee, Ambassador L. Paul Bremer (Bremer was known by this title as he had formerly been U.S. ambassador to the Netherlands), this body served as a temporary transitional government established to retain power until free and fair democratic elections could be held. It existed from April 2003 until May 2004.

Bremer, not only disbanded and reorganized the military, but also initiated a "de-Ba'athification" policy. The Ba'ath Party, which Saddam had led for years, had dominated the political scene. After the dictator was deposed, Bremer felt Ba'athists at all levels of government could not be trusted, and thousands of party loyalists were fired from their jobs. The unintended consequence from this well-meaning action was to drive many now bitter ex-government employees into the arms of jihadi groups. As his numbers grew al-Zarqawi set about developing plans that would allow him to strike back against the Western occupiers of Iraq.

Abu Musab al-Zarqawi's strategy in Iraq was to employ car bombs against his enemies in order to maximize casualties and destabilize the society. In early August 2003, a van filled with explosives was detonated outside the Jordanian embassy in Baghdad, killing 17 people. Later that month a second explosion in front of United Nations headquarters killed Sérgio Vieira de Mello, the UN's special representative to Iraq, and 21 others and injured some two hundred.[16] The terrorist leader next turned his attention to the Shias, masterminding two more car bomb attacks at the Imam Ali Mosque near the city of Najaf. The carnage resulting from these operations was massive: one hundred men, women, and children dead and approximately five hundred wounded. Al-Zarqawi reasoned that he could achieve two goals by disrupting normal life the country. Not only would this show that the Americans were incapable of maintaining order, but such attacks would also undoubtedly lead to reprisals on the part of Shias. This in turn could lead to civil war (Sunni versus Shia), which would leave him in a position to present himself as the defender of Sunni rights and allow the establishment of an Islamic caliphate.

Al-Zarqawi was not above committing cold-blooded murder himself. In 2004, foreshadowing what would become an all-too-common event in

1. Tribalism, Saddam Hussein, and the Genesis of ISIS

later years, he executed a captured American contractor, Nicholas Berg, by cutting his throat. He not only decapitated Berg, but had the gruesome spectacle videotaped; it was then posted online for millions to view around the world. ISIS would continue to use such shocking tactics to spread fear among civilians and intimidate armed opponents over the next decade.

One component of the terrorist leader's grand scheme was to keep pressure on the Shias in order to stifle their bid for political power. He not only despised their interpretation of Islam but saw them as mere proxies of the Shia government of neighboring Iran. He also hoped one day to reverse the semi-autonomous status of the Kurds in the north and appropriate their land. In his mind, the achievement of such goals would usher in a new "golden age" in Muslim history. First, of course, al-Qaeda in Iraq would have to drive out the Americans.

Like insurgents the world over, when facing a more powerful military force, guerrillas most often will choose to use hit-and-run tactics. The militants in Iraq were no exception. Their methods included the planting of roadside bombs and the use of snipers in order to demoralize American troops and those of the newly reorganized Iraqi army. During this chaotic time, while other radical groups formed, merged, frequently changed their names, and often fought against one another, al-Qaeda in Iraq continued to be among the most notorious and deadly.

In 2004 al-Zarqawi's militants, along with Ba'athist insurgents, fought pitched battles with U.S. forces in a bid to control some of Iraq's major cities. Fallujah was the site of two such clashes, the second of which was the largest and bloodiest battle of the Iraq war. Fought from November 7 until December 23, the struggle for Fallujah pitted more than ten thousand U.S. soldiers and marines, 850 British troops, and two thousand Iraqis against between four thousand and five thousand well-entrenched insurgents. Simultaneously, al-Qaeda in Iraq launched an attack against Mosul in the north. While militants briefly captured the city, they were soon forced to withdraw. Although both battles were ultimately U.S. tactical victories, they were costly. In Fallujah, some 1,350 militants were killed, while U.S. casualties totaled 51 killed in action and 425 wounded.[17]

American military leaders on the ground not only had to deal with the Sunni insurgency, but also had to walk a fine line when it came to the Shias. Though happy to be rid of Saddam, many Shias did not relish having Western soldiers in their country. Muqtada al-Sadr, a religious leader from the Sadr City section of Baghdad, posed a particularly serious threat to American efforts to maintain peace. Sadr City is a teeming, low-income suburb of the capital with a population of two million. It had previously been known as Saddam City, but the name was changed to honor the cleric's father, Sadeq al-Sadr. The elder al-Sadr was a revered Shia leader who had been killed by Saddam in 1999.

Shortly after the U.S. invasion, Muqtada al-Sadr formed a powerful militia dubbed the Mahdi Army (Jaysh al-Mahdi). The name refers to the 12th Imam or "guided one." Shias believe that a messianic figure will appear and drive evil from the world as a prelude to the day of judgement. As sectarian violence gripped the nation, the Mahdi Army and other Shia militias kidnapped, tortured, and brutally murdered Sunnis. When Sunnis retaliated, a cycle of revenge killings developed in which every day bodies were left on the streets of Baghdad bearing the marks of torture and a hideous death.

This new militia did in fact have links to Iran. Many of its weapons, including roadside bombs, were supplied by the Iranian Revolutionary Guard Corps' Quds Force. This division of Iran's military oversaw external clandestine operations. Its commander, General Qasem Soleimani not only provided funds to the various Shia militias but also acted as their advisor and a liaison to the Iranian leadership. For the next 17 years Soleimani, who preferred to keep a low profile, increased Iran's influence in the region. Incredibly, at the same time, the Iranian was not above aiding anti–Shia groups such as al-Qaeda. By adding to Iraq's instability, he hoped to erode American resolve, which in turn would lead to a U.S. withdrawal from Iraq.[18] Should his plan bear fruit, Iran would be in a much more powerful position vis-à-vis its war-torn neighbor. His interference in the affairs of other nations was not limited to Iraq. Once civil war erupted in Syria in 2011, he also made numerous trips to that country to help shore up the faltering dictatorship of Bashar al-Assad. The general's shadowy activities finally came to an end when he was killed in a U.S. missile strike on January 3, 2020, at Baghdad's international airport.

As Sunnis and Shias vied for power, American troops adopted a position of neutrality. Caught between these competing factions, both civilian populations resented this policy. American servicemen also found themselves under attack in Shia-controlled areas outside of Baghdad. Five Americans were killed in an ambush in Karbala that was carried out by the League of the Righteous (Asa'ib Ahl al-Haq), a group that had split from the Mahdi Army. In Sadr City itself, a convoy was ambushed on April 4, 2004, by militiamen armed with machine guns and rocket-propelled grenades (RPGs). Eight American soldiers were killed and 65 wounded. This type of urban combat proved to be extremely challenging as the streets are narrow and favored the fixed defensive positions of the militiamen. Over

1. Tribalism, Saddam Hussein, and the Genesis of ISIS

the next four years Sadr City saw almost constant combat. Ceasefire agreements were repeatedly made, held for short times, and then were violated until, finally, in May 2008, Iraqi security forces with the assistance of U.S. troops took control of Sadr City.

The U.S. military was, naturally, still searching for al-Zarqawi, but had lost track of him after the Second Battle of Fallujah. In early 2006 both the Joint Special Operations Command (JSOC) and the British Special Air Service (SAS) began to close in on the terrorist mastermind. By interrogating mid-level al-Qaeda in Iraq operatives the two military organizations learned the name of al-Zarqawi's "spiritual advisor," one Abd al-Rahman.[19] By tracking al-Rahman's movements, as well as those of the intermediaries carrying messages between the two men, they were able to pinpoint his location. On June 7, 2006, a U.S. drone confirmed that the men were meeting in the village of Hibhib, 35 miles northeast of Baghdad. Two U.S. Air Force F-16s were dispatched. Targeting the safe house, the lead plane dropped two 500-pound laser guided bombs. Abu Musab al-Zarqawi and seven of his aides were killed in the airstrike. Though al-Zarqawi's death was a blow to the organization he created, his devoted followers defiantly continued their murderous activities.

An Egyptian named Abu Ayyub al-Masri assumed control of al-Qaeda in Iraq (AQI) and changed the name to the Islamic State of Iraq (ISI). While the name may have changed, the goals remained the same. In the northern city of Mosul, Christians and Yazidi minorities were targeted. Despite an increased American presence, militant attacks continued. In October 2008, 14 Christians were murdered, which led some thirteen thousand to flee the city. The situation was summarized in a Defense Department report presented to Congress in September, which read: "During the past few years, Mosul has been a strategic stronghold for [al-Qaeda in Iraq (AQI)], which also needs Mosul for its facilitation of foreign fighters. The current sustained security posture, however, continues to keep AQI off balance and unable to effectively receive support from internal or external sources, though AQI remains lethal and dangerous."[20]

Violent attacks were also directed against the Yazidi population. It had long been common for some young Yazidi men to move to Mosul in search of jobs. After securing employment, they were able to send money home to augment the income of their families. On April 22, 2007, gunmen stopped a bus near Mosul and proceeded to identify 23 Yazidi men by checking their credentials (the bearer's religion is printed on Iraqi identity cards). After releasing the other passengers, the Yazidis were driven to eastern Mosul where they were forced off the bus and shot.[21] Following this murderous act, militants attempted to intimidate the Yazidis of the city into leaving by posting leaflets and sending anonymous letters denouncing them as "infidels" and promising more violent acts in the near future.

Yazidis also felt intimidated and besieged in Sinjar itself. The Sinjar region has a mixed population of Arab Muslims and Yazidis. A plebiscite was to be held in late 2007 to decide whether the area would remain part of Iraq proper, which most Muslims favored, or would join the Kurdish semiautonomous region. As the year wore on tensions increased between the two populations. Members of the U.S. Commission on International Religious Freedom who met with Yazidis reported that many were fearful of travelling outside their communities to conduct business. This, in turn, forced some farmers to employ Arab middlemen in order to get their crops to market. On August 14, 2007, Muslim extremists committed one of the most shocking acts aimed at civilians since 9/11. Four suicide bombers, using a fuel tanker and three cars, targeted the Yazidi towns of Qahtaniya and Jazeera. The massive explosions killed 796 men, women, and children, and wounded 1,562.[22] The two towns were utterly destroyed, leaving one thousand Yazidi families homeless. From the beginning AQI was suspected, and one Abu Mohammad al-Afri was considered to have masterminded the coordinated attacks. The U.S. military set about tracking him down. On September 3, just over two weeks after his murderous plan had been implemented, he was located 70 miles southwest of Mosul and, like al-Zarqawi, was killed in an airstrike

Islam, like all religions, contains those who hold intolerant and narrow-minded views when it comes to people of other faiths. While the vast majority of the world's 1.8 billion Muslims are peaceful, there are some who advocate violence against those who adhere to other religions. Even though suicide is considered a sin in Islam, there are, and always have been, religious fanatics who seek martyrdom. In recent decades, the West has come to associate suicide bombers with Islamic terrorists. These men, and in a few cases women, have chosen death for a variety of reasons. Some have written notes or made prerecorded messages before embarking upon their missions in which they declare their desire to defend the faith and punish those they see as heretics. In almost all cases the non-believers who have been targeted, such as the Yazidis, pose no actual physical or ideological threat to the followers of Islam.

Suicide bombers, such as the men who struck Qahtaniya and Jazeera, also expect, in exchange for their sacrifice, that they will be held in esteem by their communities and money will be paid to their surviving family members. Most important, however, is their belief that as martyrs they will go directly to heaven, where they will be richly rewarded. All manner of pleasures will be afforded, including the company of 72 virgins. Nowhere in the Koran, the holy book of Islam, does it mention anything about this generous form of compensation. This outlandish idea, which has endured through the centuries as an enticement for young men to give up their lives, can be traced back to the ninth-century Persian Islamic scholar al-Tirmidhi.

Iraq is not alone in having to deal with suicide bombers and the havoc caused in their wake. In the 1990s and early 2000s Israel suffered through a series of such attacks launched by Hamas and Islamic Jihad. Their intent, of course, was to inflict maximum carnage, and in many cases they did just that. Fortunately for potential victims, terrorist operations are not always successfully executed. Some years ago, a story was widely covered in the Israeli press that involved a suicide bomber whose explosive vest failed to detonate properly. While no bystanders were injured, the perpetrator was knocked unconscious. He awoke to find himself in a bed with a woman dressed in white standing over him. Looking up he stated, "You must be one of my 72 virgins." The woman, who spoke Arabic, replied, "You're not dead, idiot, you're in an Israeli hospital and I'm a nurse."[23]

Weakening ISI and the American Withdrawal

In January 2007 President George W. Bush announced he was ordering the deployment of an additional thirty thousand U.S. troops to Iraq to stem the violence. This new strategy became known as "the surge." In addition to more soldiers "in country," a plan was devised to persuade Sunni tribal leaders to abandon their allegiance to ISI and instead cooperate with the Americans and the Iraqi government. The program was begun by General David Petraeus, commander of all U.S. forces in Iraq at the time. It was dubbed the "Sons of Iraq" and succeeded for the most part in that many Sunni leaders who had actively opposed the U.S. presence increasingly came to view Iran and ISI as more of a threat than the Americans.[24] Money was used as leverage. Sunni tribesmen were paid by the United States government to man checkpoints in areas where ISI and other militant groups were active. General Petraeus was himself adept at working with Iraqis from his time commanding an army division in Mosul three years earlier, the contacts he made would serve him well in the future. At that time, he very adroitly had held conferences with ex-Ba'athists at which they aired their grievances. Additionally, upon hearing that former Iraqi military officers from Saddam's army were struggling financially to support their families, he offered many of the men salaried positions working with the U.S. Army within his area of operations.

Senior American officers also exploited the fact that some Sunnis resented the arrogant and bullying manner of ISI fighters living in their midst. The jihadis from foreign countries seemed to have been especially mean spirited. The militants often demanded that locals provide them with food and shelter, forbade them from smoking cigarettes or drinking alcohol, and, incredibly, forced some families to marry their daughters to suicide bombers.[25] The extremists' puritanical way of living, which was foisted upon Sunni communities, at times reached the realm of the absurd. In certain areas people were forbidden to carry or sell cucumbers and tomatoes at the same time because they resembled male and female genitals.[26]

The surge, coupled with increased raids conducted by JSOC, had the desired effect. By 2008 the level of violence had decreased significantly. In November of that year the American and Iraqi governments agreed to a timetable for a U.S. troop withdrawal. American soldiers and marines would be withdrawn from the major cities by the middle of 2009 and would leave the country by December 2011. The Bush administration had begun negotiations for a troop drawdown in part because, as the years wore on, the American public had grown tired of the conflict in Iraq. Economically it was expensive stationing troops on the other side of the world. More importantly, however, American soldiers were still dying in a land in which establishing a stable democracy was proving to be very elusive. President George W. Bush flew to Iraq to view the situation on the ground in late 2008. Despite the positive developments, tensions within the war-torn country continued to run high.

On December 14, the president and Iraqi Prime Minister Nouri al-Maliki held a joint press conference in Baghdad to announce the signing of two documents, the Strategic Framework Agreement and the Status of Forces Agreement. The actions of an Iraqi reporter, however, overshadowed the diplomatic niceties, and the "shoe throwing incident" made headlines around the world. An Iraqi journalist, Muntadhar al-Zaidi, threw his shoes, one after the other, at the president. As he did so he shouted he was acting on behalf of the widows and orphans of those killed in Iraq. President Bush was not hit by the shoes and, to lighten the mood, immediately joked that the shoes that flew past his face were size 10.[27] The assailant was hustled away by Iraqi security officers and severely beaten. Al-Zaidi was sentenced to three years in prison

1. Tribalism, Saddam Hussein, and the Genesis of ISIS

for assaulting a foreign head of state, although he was released after serving only nine months.

By the time of his press conference with George W. Bush, Nouri al-Maliki had been prime minister for two years. While he went on to serve until 2014, he was a controversial figure. A Shia who had opposed Saddam Hussein, al-Maliki had been forced into exile in 1979. He had not returned to Iraq until the U.S. invasion in 2003. Had he been a true reformer, he might have helped his country bridge its sectarian divide. Unfortunately, he was more interested in gaining and retaining personal power. At one point, in addition to prime minister, he also held the posts of acting interior minister, national security minister, and defense minister. He was criticized by many of his countrymen for showing favoritism to fellow Shias and moving too slowly to confront Shia militias. These actions naturally caused resentment among both Kurds and Sunnis and in the end made it more difficult to present a united front against ISIS in 2014.

By 2010, as the United States was in the process of withdrawing from Iraq, ISI had lost much of its strength. In June General Raymond Odierno, the top U.S. commander in Iraq, claimed in a briefing that American troops had "either picked up or killed 34 out of the top 42 al-Qaeda in Iraq leaders. They're clearly now attempting to reorganize themselves."[28] That same year Abu Bakr al-Baghdadi became the new leader of the organization. Over the next few years, he transformed ISI from a deadly terrorist group into a powerful and fanatical army that would change the map of the Middle East.

The last American combat troops departed Iraq as scheduled in December 2011. As they crossed the Iraqi-Kuwaiti border, they left behind a weak, divided nation and one in which ISI, though severely weakened, was already regrouping. Unfortunately, the chaos of the Syrian civil war would breathe new life into al-Baghdadi's organization. Only a few months earlier a rebellion had begun against the autocratic rule of Syrian dictator Bashar al-Assad. Beginning in 2013 al-Baghdadi's fighters began crossing into Syria to take advantage of the turmoil and to recruit new members. They found fertile soil for their activities.

While some rebels opposed to al-Assad's rule hoped to replace the regime with a democratic government, others fought to establish a conservative Islamic state. The extremists of the al-Nusra Front fell into the latter category. Their views coincided nicely with those of ISI. In Syria, as in Iraq, radical groups constantly shifted and formed new alliances. In late 2013 the al-Nusra Front split into two factions: one remained loyal to al-Qaeda, the other joined ISI. With this merger, al-Baghdadi announced

ISIS and the Yazidis

that his now larger, stronger organization would be renamed the Islamic State of Iraq and Syria (ISIS).[29] In the Middle East the group was known by the equivalent Arabic acronym Daesh. It was this name that struck panic and dread in the hearts of millions as ISIS militants emerged from Syria to terrorize anyone who did not share their vision of the future. While all minorities would suffer persecution in areas under ISIS control, one group in particular was marked for slavery and extinction, the Yazidis.

2

ISIS Devastates the Yazidi Community

In January 2014 ISIS fanatics took control of the northern Syrian city of Raqqa, which they designated as their capital. From this stronghold they quickly moved eastward to conquer territory stretching across northern Syria and Iraq. Within the first few months of the year, multiple Iraqi cities fell to the terrorist army. With lightning speed they captured Fallujah, which lies only 40 miles from Baghdad, and by June Tikrit and Mosul, Iraq's second largest city, had also been conquered. From the Great Mosque of al-Nuri in Mosul, Abu Bakr al-Baghdadi proclaimed the establishment of an Islamic caliphate on June 29, 2014, with himself as caliph. He called upon all Muslims to declare their loyalty to the new entity and accept him as their rightful ruler.

The men fighting for al-Baghdadi saw themselves as warriors waging

ISIS fighters celebrating the declaration of an "Islamic caliphate," June 30, 2014 (Stringer / Reuters Pictures).

ISIS and the Yazidis

jihad (holy war) against all those they deemed enemies of Islam. Clothed in this religious righteousness, over the next five years his men would commit multiple acts of mass murder. One of the first occurred near Tikrit. Camp Speicher was a former U.S. base that had become a training facility for Iraqi army recruits. After overrunning the area, the militants divided the young soldiers into two groups—Sunnis and Shias. The Shias were then taken in small batches to the edge of the camp and shot. Seventeen hundred men were executed.[1]

Those recruits who could escape desperately sought refuge in the nearby town of al-Alam. Many of the townspeople, including a middle-aged woman known as Um Qusay, sheltered the young men. In total 850 were saved. Putting her own life at risk, Um Qusay hid 58 men in her home, providing them with food and shelter for several days. When asked later why she aided the frightened men, she said simply that it was because they were fellow Iraqis. She added: "Someone had to stand against them [ISIS]. Without love the whole world would be killing each other."[2] The Iraqi government subsequently sent her a letter of gratitude in recognition of her courageous act.

Like the Mongols of the thirteenth century, ISIS spread fear to intimidate and dishearten both its military opponents and the local civilian populations. This strategy worked as well as it had eight centuries earlier. The Iraqi army abandoned its positions, and Mosul was captured by a relatively small force of a few thousand combatants. By September 2014, according to a CIA estimate, the army of the caliphate (which was then at the height of its power), numbered only between twenty thousand and thirty-one thousand combatants,[3] while the Iraqi army included some two hundred thousand men. Despite their numerical inferiority, however, by years end vast stretches of land in northern Syria and Iraq had come under al-Baghdadi's control.

The Abandonment of the Yazidis

The Iraqi army's failure to defend its positions came less than three years after the American withdrawal. This dereliction of duty left the country wide open to an ISIS invasion. The causes range from corruption at the senior level, to a lack of proper training of new soldiers, to the selling of military equipment on the black market.[4] Following the American departure the Iraqi military ended the policy of paying soldiers directly and returned to a system whereby the Ministry of Defense distributed

2. ISIS Devastates the Yazidi Community

money to commanders who in turn paid their soldiers. Unscrupulous officers found it easy to manipulate this process in order to line their own pockets. A variety of methods were employed by commanders, such as accepting bribes to allow their soldier to go on leave and failure to report men who were AWOL (absent without leave) in order to collect their salaries. ISIS propaganda was also remarkably effective at undermining the morale of Iraqi soldiers and officers alike. The terrorists let it be known that, should Iraqi soldiers be captured while fighting against the caliphate, they would immediately be executed, as would their entire families.

There are numerous examples of junior and senior officers either not at their posts on the front lines or having ordered their men to withdraw shortly after engaging in skirmishes with ISIS militants. As one soldier stated: "We felt like cowards, but our commanders were afraid of Daesh [ISIS]. They were too afraid to lead us."[5] Over the next few years some of these deficiencies were addressed, but in 2014 they severely hampered the government's ability to respond to the threat ISIS posed to the nation and its people.

In July, Mosul's Christian minority was targeted. Leaflets were distributed throughout the city demanding that Christians convert to Islam, leave, or pay *jizyah* (traditionally a "toleration" tax in Muslim countries aimed at Christians and Jews). The penalty for not taking one of these three options was death. As thousands of Christians fled, many reported having their possessions stolen and being physically assaulted at ISIS checkpoints.

Had almost all of Iraq's Jews not fled the country decades earlier, they would have been offered the same choices. Following the establishment of the state of Israel, Jews in Iraq were vilified by fellow Iraqis and portrayed as having divided loyalties and of serving as spies for the new nation. In 1951, as part of the "ingathering of Jews" the government of Israel airlifted some 130,000 Iraqi Jews to Israel during the aptly named Operation Ezra and Nehemiah.[6] Yazidis view Israelis as members of a fellow minority group, one that is also vastly outnumbered by Muslims in the Middle East. They admire Israel for its determination and ability to retaliate against Islamic extremists when necessary.

After the fall of Mosul, Yazidis throughout Nineveh province, already on edge, grew increasingly fearful as to where ISIS would strike next. People followed developments closely day and night on television and social media. Only the presence of the Peshmerga, the elite fighting force of Kurdistan, gave them comfort and reassurance that they would

ISIS and the Yazidis

be protected. When the Iraqi army disintegrated, the Kurdistan Regional Government was quick to deploy eleven thousand Peshmerga soldiers to Nineveh to resist ISIS and secure the province for Kurdistan.

The Peshmerga were held in the highest regard by all Kurds, be they Kurdish Muslims or Yazidis. Through the centuries the military prowess of this force had reached almost mythic status as it fought Arabs, Turks, and Persians on behalf of the Kurdish people. That is why it came as such a shock when, on the eve of an ISIS invasion of Nineveh, these legendary soldiers suddenly withdrew, leaving the civilians unprotected and defenseless. In the early days of August the Yazidis were confused and bewildered as to the reasons for the withdrawal, especially since the term *peshmerga* means "those who face death." Had they stood their ground, these Kurdish fighters would have been more than a match for ISIS.

In theory, the Ministry of Peshmerga Affairs in Erbil oversaw this organization. In reality, though, their military effectiveness was hampered by the fact that many units owed their primary loyalty to one of Kurdistan's two major political parties, the Democratic Party of Kurdistan (KDP) or the Patriotic Union of Kurdistan (PUK). The weapons possessed by the Peshmerga were adequate, but its fighters lacked the most up-to-date small arms. Officials in Baghdad had long banned Kurdistan from receiving the latest weapons and weapon systems, as it was feared these arms would be used against the central government in order to gain full independence.[7] As a result, the Peshmerga made do with older Soviet-made automatic rifles, either taken from the Iraqi army shortly after the American invasion or purchased from Iran. The Yazidis themselves had an array of personal weapons with which to protect themselves, including hunting rifles, handguns, and the odd AK-47, retained by those who had served in the military.

To this day it is still unclear why the Kurdish soldiers retreated. In some villages they did so after collecting all the weapons, assuring the Yazidis that they had no need of their guns as they would be well protected against any threat.[8] In a few cases they claimed to be leaving to obtain more ammunition, and then never returned. Those Peshmerga soldiers who did briefly fight ISIS militants on August 3 did not remain long on the battlefield. Some admitted that they ran out of ammunition and fled, while a general explained: "Many of our forces were mortared, killed, captured but we didn't have the reinforcements to send ... it was very hard at the beginning, it was a new fight.... ISIS had a lot of equipment from the Iraqi army."[9]

Yazidis today believe they were betrayed and sacrificed by the

2. ISIS Devastates the Yazidi Community

Peshmerga. Whether it was a "tactical withdrawal" or simply cowardice in the face of a terrifying enemy may never be known. Months later Kurdistan's president, Masoud Barzani, called for an investigation. He stated: "What happened in Sinjar did not happen to the Yazidis alone; it is an injury that has hurt us all. Those officials [military officers] should not have withdrawn; they should have sacrificed themselves in defense of the region." Despite this powerful statement, no senior military leaders were ever held responsible or relieved of command.[10] Eventually the Peshmerga regrouped and counterattacked, but the damage had been done. While the reputation of the Kurdish fighters was severely tarnished, it was the Yazidis who would pay the price with their lives.

ISIS's symbol is that of a black flag with white writing in Arabic across the top that states, "There is no God but God. Muhammad is the messenger of God." Black writing in a white circle at the center reiterates, "Muhammad is the messenger of God." As towns across northern Iraq fell to the extremists, the appearance of these flags meant a new force had come that would alter the lives of hundreds of thousands of people forever. ISIS members did not consider the Yazidis to be "people of the Book," meaning of the scriptures, i.e., Jews and Christians. Instead they were classified as *kufara*, a derogatory term for non-believers such as polytheists or pagans. Therefore, their options were either to convert to Islam or face death.

In Yazidi towns and villages those who refused to convert were slaughtered. Numerous reports began to reach the United Nations Assistance Mission for Iraq (UNAMI) and the Office of the High Commissioner for Human Rights (OHCHR) that the jihadis were committing massacres against civilians. Yazidi survivors told UN officials that, between August 3 and 6, "250–300 were killed (of whom at least 10 were beheaded) in the Hardan area, after ISIL [ISIS] promised them safety in exchange for giving up their weapons."[11] Others related how, after hastily leaving their homes, they had stopped in the village of Qiniyeh for water. ISIS fighters unexpectedly arrived and proceeded to separate the men from the women and children. After the people were robbed of their belongings, the men were taken outside the village, given shovels, and forced to dig a long ditch; they were then lined up alongside the trench and shot.

One of the worst atrocities was committed in the small village of Kocho, located 15 miles south of Sinjar City. On August 15, after a nearly two-week siege during which the jihadis demanded that the Yazidis renounce their religion and adopt Islam, the entire population was forced to assemble in the local school. Having been rebuffed in their efforts to convert the villagers, ISIS gunmen separated the Yazidis by gender and robbed them of their personal valuables. All men over the age of 10 were then loaded onto pickup trucks, driven a short distance outside the village, and shot. The women and children held in the school could hear the gunshots as their fathers, husbands, brothers, and sons were being killed. Four hundred men were murdered in cold blood.[12] The traumatized women and children were then taken away by the militants to be held as *sabaya* (slaves).

Nadia Murad, who survived the horrific events at Kocho and subsequent enslavement by ISIS, recounted her ordeal in a powerful book titled *The Last Girl: My Story of Captivity, and My Fight against the Islamic State*. In her account she relates what life was like prior to the ISIS attack and how her family and community were shattered by the Islamic fundamentalists. This shy, self-effacing young woman went on to become a human rights activist and winner of the Nobel Peace Prize in 2018. She shared the prestigious award with Denis Mukwege, a Congolese doctor. Both recipients were honored for their efforts to alert the world to the use of sexual violence as a weapon of war.

ISIS Captures Sinjar and Yazidis Flee to the Mountain

Sinjar City lies three miles from Mount Sinjar and only 20 miles from the Syrian border. In 2014 it was a city of some ninety thousand people, the majority of whom were Yazidis. While there has always been friction between Yazidis and Muslims in Sinjar, relations grew worse during Saddam Hussein's Arabization campaign, as Arabs from the south, with government assistance, relocated to the city. Political strife and economic competition further complicated matters. Under Saddam Arabs displaced Yazidis and assumed positions of leadership. Following the American invasion, however, the Peshmerga arrived, and Yazidis once again took control of the city's government. Not surprisingly, this shift in civic power led to resentment on the part of many Muslims. By the time Mosul fell to ISIS tensions between the two communities was palpable. While not all Arabs in Sinjar rejoiced that the forces of the caliphate were on the march, Yazidis noticed that some of their Muslim neighbors praised the militants' military successes, as well as their implementation of Sharia law. Another ominous sign was the fact that many young men in the city began to grow beards and attendance sharply increased at local mosques.[13] Yazidis worried that their

2. ISIS Devastates the Yazidi Community

Arab neighbors might welcome the arrival of the militants should they set their sights on Sinjar. Their concerns were not unfounded.

The attack upon Sinjar City began in the early morning hours of Sunday, August 3. At 3:00 a.m. the Peshmerga withdrew from their positions around the city, leaving it undefended and at the mercy of a vicious enemy. By 10:00 a.m. ISIS fighters began to arrive, panic set in, and thousands of Yazidis fled for their lives. Approximately half the city's population left that morning by any means available. People who had lived in this part of Iraq their entire lives now had only a few minutes to load their families into cars and depart. Those who did not own a car made their way out of the city on foot. Some had the foresight to pack food and water for the journey, but since all had only minutes in which to depart most carried little with them. Precious belongings and pets had to be left behind. This was, of course, most traumatic on the youngest Yazidi children, who could sense the fear in their parents' voices but who had no idea why they were leaving their homes.

For those who were unable or unwilling to flee, their ordeal was just beginning. As the terrorist army moved into the city, Yazidis were targeted, and a pattern emerged that would be repeated numerous times in smaller towns and villages. Men who refused to convert were shot on the spot and their wives and children abducted. In Sinjar, some five thousand Yazidi men were murdered, many simply executed in the streets. Those few men who did accept Islam in exchange for their lives were taken away under guard. They were assigned to work details digging trenches, sweeping streets, or tending livestock. The new converts were never fully accepted by the militants, and any who attempted to escape were immediately executed. Many local Arabs became collaborators. They aided ISIS fighters by pointing out the homes of prominent Yazidis who had been forced to run for their lives only hours earlier. Over the next few months these houses were looted by neighbors and then bulldozed by the jihadis.

The thousands who escaped the city felt they would be safe on high ground, so an enormous caravan made its way to the base of Mount Sinjar. The Sinjar Mountains run 62 miles east to west with Mount Sinjar rising to a height of forty-eight hundred feet. The climate in the mountains is semi-arid with little rainfall most of the year. The mountain itself is mostly barren, and rocky. At the higher elevation there is almost no shade as very few trees and shrubs grow in the dry soil. Like the desert Southwest of the United States, summers can be extremely brutal, with temperatures reaching 110 degrees. That August was no exception: as the sun climbed high in the sky, approximately fifty thousand people ascended the arid mountain.[14] ISIS fanatics soon surrounded its base, trapping those above. If help did not arrive soon, the frightened and exhausted people faced two choices: die a slow death from thirst and exposure, or risk descending the mountain and falling into the hands of the Islamic extremists.

Genocide and the Enslavement of Yazidi Women

Raphael Lemkin, a Polish-Jewish lawyer, coined the term "genocide" in 1943 as World War II raged and the Nazis were murdering millions of European Jews. At the time, the word "massacres" was used, but it was inadequate. A new term was needed that conveyed the sheer scale of the atrocities being committed by a regime Winston Churchill called "the foulest and most soul-destroying tyranny which has ever darkened and stained the pages of history."[15] In 1948 the United Nations Convention on the Prevention and Punishment of the Crime of Genocide defined Lemkin's new word in legal terms. The convention designated the crime of genocide to mean an attempt to annihilate a people including "acts committed with the intent to destroy, in whole or in part, a national, racial, ethnical, or religious group, as such."[16] The perpetrators' intent is key in determining whether murderous acts are considered genocide. If the goal is the complete destruction of an ethnic or religious group, then it is classified as genocide, regardless of whether the number of those killed is in the thousands, as with the Yazidis, or millions as in the Holocaust. Though genocide need not be state organized or implemented, traditionally nations have been the entities that have perpetrated such criminal acts. Governments have the power to direct negative propaganda aimed at vilifying minorities. They also have the ability to pass laws designed to demean and persecute targeted groups within their societies. In addition, it is the state that possesses the human resources, such as armies, militias, and police forces needed to implement genocidal policies.

In June 2016, the independent international Commission of Inquiry on the Syrian Arab Republic (known as the Commission) investigated ISIS's attacks against the Yazidis. The Commission interviewed 45 people and determined that the terrorist army had committed genocide, war crimes, and crimes against humanity. This evidence was turned over to the United Nations Human Rights Council. The report titled "'They came to destroy': ISIS crimes against the Yazidis" read in part: "ISIS has sought to destroy the Yazidis through killings, sexual slavery, enslavement, torture, and inhuman and degrading treatment and forcible transfer causing

2. ISIS Devastates the Yazidi Community

serious bodily and mental harm; the infliction of conditions of life that bring about a slow death."[17] It called for the UN to refer the matter to the International Criminal Court.

Muslim extremists had thoughts of annihilating the Yazidi people long before al-Baghdadi proclaimed his new state. It was the supporters and officials of that state, however, who would attempt to turn those ideas into deadly reality. One early strategy ISIS adopted was the kidnapping of Yazidi women. In the fourth edition of its online magazine *Dabiq*,[18] which ISIS used as a tool to recruit new members, an article appeared titled "The Revival of Slavery Before the Hour." It explicitly stated that pagan women and those of polytheistic religions can and should be enslaved.[19] The fact that Yazidis fit into neither of these categories made no difference to the militants. Labeled as "devil worshipers," captured women and girls were subject to enslavement in the minds of the jihadis. A few weeks after the article appeared, ISIS distributed a pamphlet to its adherents that detailed how these so-called "concubines" should be treated. It stated that they were to be regarded as property and therefore could be sold, traded, or given as gifts to fellow ISIS fighters.

Many women who could not reach Mount Sinjar or Kurdistan were quickly taken prisoner. It is estimated that approximately six thousand four hundred Yazidi women and children were kidnapped in 2014.[20] At this point boys under eight years old were allowed to stay with their mothers. At gunpoint, the women were robbed of their money, jewelry, and cell phones. They were rapidly loaded onto buses and driven to temporary "holding facilities" such as Badush prison outside Mosul and several sites in the city of Tal Afar. After a few days, the women were transported in large groups to Raqqa. During their ordeal, the terrified captives were given little food or water and no medicine of any kind.

Once they reached the ISIS capital the women were held in one of two facilities, an underground prison or a cluster of buildings surrounded by trees known as "the farm." The Yazidis were then sold to ISIS militants for between $200 and $1,500. The most beautiful were chosen first and sold for the highest prices. At the holding sites the jihadis entered the rooms to select the women and girls they wished to purchase. The Commission reported: "The selection of any girl was accompanied by screaming as she was forcibly pulled from the room, with her mother and any other women who tried to keep hold of her being brutally beaten by fighters. Yazidi women and girls began to scratch and bloody themselves in an attempt to make themselves unattractive to potential buyers."[21]

At first married women were separated from those who were single.

ISIS and the Yazidis

The action proved unnecessary as it made no difference in the way in which they would all be treated. This became evident when the ISIS guards callously informed those with husbands that their men were dead, and in any case their marriages had not been legal under sharia law. Therefore, they could be sold or given to ISIS fighters as if their marriages had never existed. Recalling her experience, Zahra (a pseudonym) said, "When we got to the farm, we saw four or five buses full of ISIS members with long hair and beards. They were like animals ... they came among us and started picking girls for themselves. Two or three of them would catch the girls, blindfold them, and take them by force into a car. The girls were crying and shouting and wailing but they didn't care."[22] Tragically, some women, unable to cope with the trauma of their capture and/or impending rape, committed suicide. Those who ended their lives did so either by cutting their wrists or hanging themselves with their own headscarves.

Once "purchased," the women were repeatedly raped and expected to become domestic servants in the fighters' homes. During the day they were forced to launder clothes and perform other forms of housework. As for those ISIS members who were married, their wives, incredibly, accepted the situation. Whether ISIS wives resented the presence of the women, or wholeheartedly approved of their husbands' actions varied from household to household. In most cases, the wives treated the new arrivals with contempt and often blatant cruelty. The Yazidis were also expected to supervise any children in the home. Generally their new responsibilities did not include cooking meals for the family, as ISIS philosophy derided Yazidis as "unclean" people.

Like their mothers, Yazidi children were treated with utter contempt by the militants. They were subjected to both physical and mental abuse. Not only were they psychologically traumatized by their ordeal, but the children were also given little to eat during their captivity. Young boys and girls were usually fed leftovers from the families' meals and were beaten if they cried out of hunger. The children were regularly insulted by being told that they and their mothers were dirty *kufara* (infidels). A woman who was held for 11 months and sold multiple times said of one of her captors: "When he would force me into a room with him, I could hear my children screaming and crying outside the door.... He beat and threatened to kill them. He forced two of them to stand outside in the snow until he finished with me."[23] Women that escaped also reported incidents that can only be described as depraved and heinous in which girls as young as nine were sexually assaulted.

Boys seven and eight years old were ruthlessly taken from their

2. ISIS Devastates the Yazidi Community

mothers and sent to ISIS training camps where they were forced to convert to Islam. At these facilities they were taught to use automatic weapons and, along with Sunni Muslim youths, were turned into child soldiers to fight for the caliphate. The Commission's report to the UN detailed how ISIS members often threatened Yazidi women with gang rape as punishment should they attempt to escape or refuse their "owners'" sexual advances. It read:

> One woman, bought by an ISIS fighter from Saudi Arabia and held in a village in Aleppo governorate, stated "[H]e raped me every day that I was with him.... He told me that if I did not let him do this thing to me that he would bring four or five men and they would all take turns raping me. I had no choice. I wanted to die." Another woman, held in Minbej (Aleppo) was told by her Syrian fighter-owner that if she resisted, he would throw her off the roof of his house. Some women also reported that ISIS members threatened to sell or beat their children.[24]

A woman named Zeina was captured by ISIS trying to leave Sinjar the day the city fell. She was sold to a Libyan militant who told her, "You are Yazidi, so it doesn't matter what we do with you."[25] She was later bought by a Syrian who held her for three months and raped her every night. During the day she was expected to wash the man's dishes and dirty clothes. Once, after a failed escape attempt, as punishment she was gang raped by the Syrian's commander and three other men. Zeina was sold again to an Iraqi who ultimately ransomed her back to her family for $2,000.

Women caught while attempting to escape were often severely beaten. Should a woman manage to slip away and elude her captor, before she could begin the arduous journey back to Sinjar or to the Kurdistan region, she would need to find aid among the locals. This often proved to be a difficult task. Most people were either ISIS sympathizers or feared retaliation should it be discovered that they had helped a Yazidi. Whether an escape was successful often came down to sheer luck. A woman on the run might knock on the front door of a house and find the inhabitants willing to give her food and shelter, or just as likely find the people within eager to report her presence to ISIS. Should the latter occur, the unfortunate woman would immediately be returned to slavery. Women with small children despaired and many contemplated committing suicide but dismissed the idea knowing that they had to live for the sake of their sons and daughters.

Nour, along with her two young daughters, was bought and sold seven times. As with Zeina, she too tried to escape. With her girls in tow, the trio frantically moved from house to house for hours in Palmyra, Syria.

No one would help them. Exhausted, they returned to the residence where they had been held; fortunately their captor had not discovered they were gone. Eventually she and her children were sold to a man from Raqqa who claimed to be a "slave trader." In reality, he was there to rescue her. As they drove away, he informed her that he was taking her back to her family. Nour recounted: "He looked like an ISIS militant—he wore their clothes, and had a beard and something covering his face. I told him I couldn't believe he wasn't ISIS, but he said: 'This beard is fake. I only wear it to save women and girls.'"[26]

Desperate Cries for Help from the Mountain

On Mount Sinjar the situation grew dire. With no food or water tens of thousands of people suffered in the stifling August heat. On Monday, August 4, ISIS fighters, having surrounded the base, cautiously began moving up the mountainside. In the first skirmishes some 30 Yazidi men were killed or wounded and, in what was becoming ISIS's *modus operandi*, several women abducted. Using their cell phones, people tried to stay in touch with relatives from whom they had been separated. Some reached out to UNAMI explaining their precarious situation. The next day The United Nations International Children's Emergency Fund (UNICEF) issued a statement that placed the number of children who had already died at 40.[27]

The men and women trapped on Mount Sinjar also called family and friends much farther away using WhatsApp on their cell phones. Yazidis in Houston, Texas, and Lincoln, Nebraska, were awakened in the middle of the night to panic-stricken voices informing them of ISIS massacres, the kidnapping of women, and the fact that thousands of their people were stranded on the mountain. Twenty-five families live in the Houston area, while approximately three thousand Yazidis have made their home in Lincoln, which has the largest concentration of Yazidis in the United States. The first immigrants arrived in Lincoln from Iraq in the early 1990s following the first Gulf War. Many had served as translators with the U.S. military in Iraq and came to this country with their families under a special visa program. A second group followed as the United States withdrew from the war-torn nation in 2011.

It is only natural for immigrants arriving in a new country to seek the company of their own ethnic or religious group. In the nineteenth century, Eastern European Jews escaping persecution journeyed to New York City

2. ISIS Devastates the Yazidi Community

and felt very much at home on Manhattan's Lower East Side. The same can be said of Italian immigrants hoping for a better life when they settled in the city's "Little Italy." In Boston, Irish arrivals created predominantly Irish neighborhoods beginning in the mid-nineteenth century. Lincoln proved to be an attractive and welcoming place for the newcomers. It is a mid-sized, midwestern city that serves as the state's capital. Additionally, it is a university town in which unemployment and crime rates are low, and housing is affordable.

The same day they received the frantic calls from friends and relatives in Iraq, the Yazidis in Lincoln sprang into action. Some five hundred people gathered in front of the governor's mansion. The demonstrators carried signs that read "Help the Yazidis," "They are killing us," and "Stop ISIS."[28] The local media took note and reported on the gathering. It was the first step in alerting the nation to what was taking place in northern Iraq. The next day, some two thousand Yazidis, including many children, marched to the office of Nebraska's congressman Jeff Fortenberry at the Cornhusker Marriott Hotel. The sympathetic lawmaker, after meeting with Yazidi community leaders and listening to their pleas for help, announced he would draft a letter to President Obama calling for action.

The congressman acted quickly. His letter, which he knew would carry more weight if it were bipartisan in nature, was co-signed by fellow Republican Frank Wolf of Virginia and Democratic Congresswoman Anna Eshoo of California. The document stated: "ISIS is waging a systematic and targeted campaign of religious and ethnic cleansing against minority groups, forcing thousands of innocent civilians from their ancestral homelands and triggering a refugee crisis that demands urgent international intervention."[29] It pointed out that Iraq's security forces had utterly failed to protect vulnerable minorities, and as a result the situation was desperate. The letter urged the president to take direct action to support the Kurdistan Regional Government in its efforts to aid refugees who had crossed into its territory. In an eloquent conclusion Fortenberry stated:

> The United States has always championed basic human rights and religious liberty—both at home and around the world.... Time and again throughout our history, the American people have spoken out for those who have no voice. As a maelstrom of violence ravages Iraq, we must empathize with the voiceless and act upon the cherished and transcendent ideals we seek to uphold ... the religious minorities of Iraq, many of them thousands of years old, are threatened with annihilation. If you were to speak directly to the situation, we believe this would be of great encouragement to the affected communities.

ISIS and the Yazidis

They also need immediate international humanitarian assistance. We ask that you stand with us as we stand with them in solidarity.[30]

A few days later Congressman Wolf, a longtime human rights advocate, sent a follow-up letter to the president. He cautioned the chief executive: "Much like President Bill Clinton has deeply regretted his failure to stop the genocide in Rwanda in 1994, I believe you will come to regret your inaction for years to come." He continued: "Tragically mass atrocities are happening again today—and on your watch. Genocide is taking place today in northern Iraq, where the Christian and Yazidi populations are being exterminated by the Islamic State of Iraq and Syria (ISIS)."[31] The Virginia representative went on to stress that families had been forced to flee with only the clothes on their backs. He then quoted from a speech the president had delivered at the Holocaust Memorial Museum in 2012 in which Mr. Obama had said: "And finally 'never again' is a challenge to nations. It's a bitter truth—too often, the world has failed to prevent the killing of innocents on a massive scale. And we are haunted by the atrocities that we did not stop and the lives we did not save." The congressman ended his letter with a prediction about what would happen if President Obama failed to act: "Your conscience will haunt you long after you leave office. Mr. President, say something; do something."[32]

The Yazidis in Lincoln knew that time was running out for the people trapped on Mount Sinjar. As much as they appreciated the work of Congressman Fortenberry and his colleagues, they felt that they had to go to Washington, D.C., themselves to press their demand for action. On Tuesday, August 5, some 60 Yazidis rented vans and planned to drive day and night until they reached the capital. The call went out, and others agreed to join them traveling from Michigan and Canada.

Approximately 30 Yazidis departed for Washington from Houston, among them Haider E., a former U.S. Army translator. For Haider, working with the American military had been a positive experience. The junior officers had been inclusive and kind, and the soldiers, both male and female, had impressed him with their professionalism. In 2003, when he first thought of working with the army, he was dissuaded by an incident that occurred on the way to his interview. During a taxi ride in Mosul, a cab driver told Haider what would happen if he took a job with the Americans: "My brothers in the Mujahedeen (al-Qaeda in Iraq) will kill you."[33] The intimidation tactic worked, but only temporarily. The next year Haider set his fears aside and began his job as translator. He assisted the army from 2004 until 2010. He then immigrated to the United States.

2. ISIS Devastates the Yazidi Community

As the Yazidis in America made their way toward the nation's capital, Vian Dakhil, one of only two Yazidi members of parliament, was preparing to address her fellow legislators in Baghdad.[34] The petite, auburn-haired Dakhil came from a wealthy family that valued education. Her father was a surgeon, and most of her eight siblings followed him into the field of medicine. Although she grew up in Mosul, the family had since moved to Erbil, the capital of Iraqi Kurdistan. Unlike her siblings she chose a career in politics. She joined the Kurdistan Democratic Party and was elected to the Iraqi parliament in 2010. Almost immediately she gained a reputation as an advocate for minority rights.

Obviously, she was well aware of ISIS's gruesome reputation and its attacks upon Yazidis. At that moment, however, she was desperately concerned about what would become of the thousands of people languishing on Mount Sinjar if help did not reach them within the next few days. On Tuesday, August 5, she rose in the Iraqi parliament to give the most important speech of her life. She began slowly, appealing to her colleagues' sense of justice and pointing out that ISIS was killing Yazidis in the name of Islam: "Mr. Speaker, we are being slaughtered under the banner of 'There is no god but God.'" Surrounded by supporters, she begged her government to take immediate action to save her people. Choked with emotion, she pleaded:

> For 48 hours, thirty thousand families are besieged on Sinjar Mountain without water or food. They are dying. Seventy babies have died so far from thirst and dehydration. Fifty old people have died from the deteriorating conditions. Our women are taken as slaves and sold in the slave market. Mr. Speaker, we demand that the Iraqi Parliament intervene immediately to stop this massacre. We are being slaughtered; we are being exterminated. An entire religion is being exterminated from the face of the Earth. Brothers, I appeal to you in the name of humanity to save us![35]

At that point Vian Dakhil, unable to continue, physically collapsed. Dakhil's heart-wrenching speech, which was videotaped, was almost immediately picked up by The Associated Press TV and Reuters TV. It appeared on You Tube soon thereafter and went viral on social media. For the first time, large numbers of people outside of Iraq became aware of the events unfolding on Mount Sinjar. Thanks to modern technology, people around the world could watch her powerful appeal for help.

In the weeks that followed, Dakhil continued to draw attention to ISIS's actions, including the kidnapping of Yazidi women. According to ISIS's tenets, women had no place in public life, as they were to assume a completely subservient position in society. In numerous instances ISIS members executed women professionals, including doctors and lawyers, who refused to give up their careers and return to the confines of the home. They seemed to have had a special hatred for female politicians. When the extremist organization issued a "death list" of its enemies, Dakhil's name was at the top. Undeterred, she stated in an interview: "I have received warnings from government intelligence that I am now IS's [ISIS's] most-wanted woman. If they capture me, they will execute me at once."[36]

In 2014 Iraq was not only militarily unprepared to deal with the devastating ISIS attack, but it was also politically paralyzed. Nouri al-Maliki, who, since 2006 had been the country's controversial and divisive prime minister, refused to step down at the end of his term in office. Despite a pledge in February 2011 not to seek a third term, al-Maliki balked at relinquishing power. When Iraq's president nominated the parliamentary speaker, Haider al-Abadi for the position of prime minister, al-Maliki sent the matter to the courts. He claimed the move was a violation of the Iraqi constitution, and therefore unlawful.

Months of political infighting followed between supporters and opponents of the embattled prime minister. For their part, American government officials, having grown tired of al-Maliki's corruption and accumulation of personal power, made it known that they favored al-Abadi to head the Iraqi government. An opponent of Saddam Hussein, al-Abadi had spent much of his life in exile. Educated in England, he had returned to Iraq following the American invasion. First elected to parliament in 2005, he had a reputation as a moderate, and a man free of corruption. Finally, on August 14, under enormous pressure from the international community as well as members of his own party, al-Maliki announced he was stepping down to make way for al-Abadi to become the new prime minister.

The United States Takes Action to Prevent a Genocide

On the evening of Wednesday, August 6, President Obama met with the chairman of the Joint Chiefs of Staff, Martin Dempsey. The general briefed the president on the situation in Iraq, including the fact that ISIS fighters were rapidly moving toward Erbil. General Dempsey warned the president that American consulate officials were now in harm's way. Barack Obama quickly convened a meeting with his top advisors to discuss military options. He had already decided that the United States would

2. ISIS Devastates the Yazidi Community

airlift food and supplies to the Yazidis on Mount Sinjar.[37] U.S. military action would also be needed in order to break the siege. The president was committed to protecting the consulate's staff and avoiding a repeat of the Benghazi incident that had occurred in Libya two years earlier.

The fall of Libyan dictator Muammar Gaddafi in 2011 left a power vacuum in that country, which, in turn, led to the formation of numerous militias. Armed groups fought with one another for power and influence. Ansar al-Sharia emerged as a dangerous and fiercely anti-Western, anti–American militia. On the night of September 11, 2012, its members attacked the U.S. consulate in Benghazi on the country's northwest coast. The American government was slow to recognize the seriousness of the situation and to react. In the assault, which lasted all night, Ambassador Christopher Stevens and three other Americans were killed, and 11 consular personnel were wounded.

Barack Obama was determined to act, both to aid the Yazidis and to halt the ISIS drive on Erbil. The problem was that America had limited manpower in-country at the time. In December 2011, after eight years of war, the United States had withdrawn the last combat units from Iraq. Americans were wary of being drawn back into a conflict in which, according to the Pentagon, 4,487 members of the American military had been killed and 32,226 wounded.[38] By 2014 only a few U.S. Army Special Forces soldiers (Green Berets) remained in Iraq as advisors, mostly located in Baghdad and Erbil. The president knew that whatever action was taken it must be limited in scope and could not include a large-scale deployment of "boots on the ground." The administration had been tracking the rising threat of ISIS, but, as with much of the rest of the world, underestimated the speed with which it conquered territory and the savagery of its adherents. In August and September, for example, ISIS began to post online the first of many gruesome beheadings of captives.

On Thursday, August 7, 2014, President Obama issued orders for the U.S. military to act in Iraq to aid the Yazidis and directly engage the forces of the Islamic State. At 9:30 p.m. he addressed the nation from the White House, outlining his strategy. He announced that he was authorizing two military operations in Iraq. The first involved airstrikes to halt the impending ISIS attack on Erbil, and to protect the U.S. consulate in the city. The second was to immediately send aid to the Yazidis trapped on Mount Sinjar. He stated:

> At the request of the Iraqi government we've begun operations to help save Iraqi civilians.... In recent days, Yazidi women, men and children from the area of Sinjar have fled for their lives ... tens of thousands are now hiding high

ISIS and the Yazidis

up on the mountain.... They're without food, they're without water. People are starving. And children are dying of thirst. Meanwhile, ISIL (ISIS) forces below have called for the systematic destruction of the entire Yazidi people, which would constitute genocide. So these innocent families are faced with a horrible choice: descend the mountain and be slaughtered, or stay, and slowly die of thirst and hunger.

.... When we face a situation like we do on that mountain—with innocent people facing the prospect of violence on a horrific scale ... when we have the unique capabilities to help avert a massacre, then I believe the United States of America cannot turn a blind eye.... Earlier this week, one Iraqi in the area cried to the world, "There is no one coming to help." Well today America is coming to help.[39]

On the same night of the president's speech, the U.S. Air Force, having received orders from the commander in chief, began a multi-day operation to deliver humanitarian aid to the Yazidis. On the first night two C-130 Hercules and one C17 Globemaster cargo aircraft dropped 72 pallets containing fifty-two hundred gallons of fresh water and eight thousand meals ready-to-eat (MREs).[40] Over the next week, as the number of airdrops increased, an additional C-130 and C-17 were assigned to the mission. According to United States Central Command (CENTCOM) the flights originated from "multiple bases" within its area of responsibilities—the countries of the Middle East, North Africa, and central Asia.

C-130 Hercules (U.S. Air Force photograph taken by Technical Sergeant Erin Hickok).

2. ISIS Devastates the Yazidi Community

The British quickly agreed to participate in this humanitarian effort. On August 9, two Royal Air Force C-130s flew from RAF base Brize Norton in England to Iraq. Their first pallets of supplies were dropped that same night. In just two days—August 11 and 12—they delivered 5,820 water purification containers filled with 7,600 gallons of fresh water; 816 solar lamps, which can also be used to recharge cell phones; and 528 shelter kits.[41] In total the United States supplied 114,000 meals and thirty-five thousand gallons of water to the Yazidis trapped on the mountain.

The mission to deliver supplies was remarkably successful. Shortly after operations began, Secretary of Defense Chuck Hagel addressed the situation at a press conference while traveling in India. When asked how much of the food and water was actually reaching the Yazidis he responded, "Well, on the efficiency of those airdrops, we have pretty solid information that of the 72 bundles that were dropped from the three aircraft, more than 60 got to … the people who were trapped up there. We have intelligence reports on that, as well as some on the ground reports."[42] When questioned about the United States taking direct military action against ISIS, the secretary stated that the terrorist army was well organized and armed and posed a significant threat to the stability of Iraq. He went on to reiterate the president's position that airstrikes would take place for "the protection of American citizens and our interests; also to protect those people trapped on the mountain."[43]

Less than 48 hours after the president's address to the nation the U.S. Navy engaged the forces of the Islamic State. On Friday afternoon at 1:45 p.m. local time, operations began as two Navy F/A-18 Hornets flew off the deck of the aircraft carrier USS *George H.W. Bush* in the Persian Gulf. The warplanes targeted a mobile artillery piece that ISIS had been using to shell the outskirts of Erbil. Later that day, an unmanned drone struck an ISIS mortar position. In a third wave that evening, four F/A-18 Super Hornets attacked an ISIS convoy of seven vehicles and another mortar position.[44]

On Saturday, August 9, as the Yazidis on the mountain, using only small arms, desperately sought to repel the ISIS fighters, U.S. Navy aircraft roared in to strike ISIS positions around Mount Sinjar. The F/A 18s using 500-pound laser-guided bombs were accompanied by EA-6B Prowlers tasked with jamming ISIS communications on the ground. By day's end Navy jets had flown five sorties against ISIS positions in the Sinjar area. Whenever U.S. warplanes appeared overhead the militants retreated. Unbeknownst to those on the mountain, a team of Green Berets had

ISIS and the Yazidis

Aircraft Carrier USS *George H.W. Bush* (U.S. Navy photograph taken by Mass Communications Specialist 3rd Class Nicholas Hall).

landed near the summit; from there they directed air operations. The soldiers worked from an abandoned airfield that was well known to special operations units as it had been used during the Iraq war.[45] From the mountain the Green Berets transmitted coordinates to Air Force Joint Terminal Attack Controllers (JTACs) of the special operations task force near Erbil. The JTACs coordinated and controlled airstrikes against ISIS targets. Credit must also be given to the few courageous Iraqi helicopter pilots who, braving fire from the ground, ferried supplies to the mountain and carried refugees off, two-dozen at a time.

As events unfolded in northern Iraq, the American Yazidis from Nebraska and Texas arrived in the nation's capital. On the first day of the supply drops half a world away, the small delegations met with officials at the State Department. That afternoon they, along with approximately 50 others including Hindus and Christians, demonstrated in front of the White House to draw attention to the dangers their relatives faced at that moment. Haider E. and his companions, who were in constant contact with their kin in Iraq, proved to be extremely helpful. Haider stated: "We talked to people on the mountain by cell phone. After President Obama

2. ISIS Devastates the Yazidi Community

The launching of an F/A-18 Super Hornet (U.S. Navy photograph taken by Mass Communications Specialist 3rd Class Alex Corona).

decided to act, we relayed information, such as ISIS positions, to people in the State Department by email."[46] They in turn sent the coordinates to the Pentagon, which passed them along to U.S. Central Command.

Even though U.S. military operations were proceeding rapidly, Yazidis were still, tragically, dying at the hands of ISIS fanatics. Haider's own brother Falah, after making multiple trips to the mountain on August 3 to aid friends and relatives fleeing Sinjar City, was himself killed in an ISIS ambush. Haider and several other men stayed in Washington, D.C., a total of three weeks. They not only continued to provide the government with vital information but Haider and his companions from Texas also co-founded Yazda, an organization dedicated to advocating on behalf of the Yazidi people.

Supplying Weapons to the Kurds

President Obama informed Congress on August 8 that the United States was reentering Iraq in order to fight ISIS. He did so in the form of a letter that not only explained his rationale for ordering combat operations, but also satisfied the requirement that a president must abide by the War Powers Act of 1973. This law, which was enacted during the Vietnam conflict (over the veto of President Richard Nixon), was designed to limit a president's power when it comes to waging war. It was meant to ensure that a president could not bypass Congress and take the country into another long, costly, undeclared war.

When it comes to combat situations, while the Constitution states that only Congress has the power to declare war, the president, as commander in chief of the armed forces, has the right to send soldiers into hostile territory if he deems it necessary and of vital interest to the nation. Lyndon Johnson did exactly that in Southeast Asia in 1965. According to this act a president must notify Congress within 48 hours of sending U.S. troops into action. It further limits the deployment to no more than 60 days (with an additional 30-day withdrawal period), without congressional approval or a formal declaration of war. In his letter the president repeated that this military action would be limited in scope. He further asserted that the airstrikes and humanitarian airdrops were clearly in the national security and foreign policy interests of the United States. He ended his communication with the assurance that he would keep Congress informed on the fluid situation in Iraq.

Four days after the president dispatched his letter, Secretary of Defense Hagel announced that the Pentagon was sending an additional 130 military advisors to Erbil. The soldiers were being deployed in order to ascertain how best to aid the Kurds in the struggle against ISIS. These troops were meant to augment the 90 advisors in Baghdad and the 160 in two operation centers—one in Erbil, the other in the Iraqi capital—already working with Iraqi security forces.[47]

The U.S. airstrikes continued around Mount Sinjar, totaling 17 over the next few days. To further increase the pressure on ISIS it was decided to send weapons directly to the Peshmerga. Previously both the Bush and Obama administrations had adhered to the "One Iraq" policy under which arms would only be supplied to the central government in Baghdad. It was feared that sending weapons to the Kurds would only encourage their drive for total independence and the fracturing of the nation. As the disgraced Peshmerga reorganized and prepared to attack the Islamic fighters they were in desperate need of arms. The Kurdish militias had long employed Russian-made weapons (mainly secured from Iran), including the durable AK-47. Therefore, they requested that particular type of automatic rifle as well as ammunition. Interestingly, the CIA, not the Pentagon, kept a stockpile of such weapons and quietly began shipping it to the Kurds.[48] Other munitions requested included long-range armor-piercing missiles, rocket-propelled grenades (RPGs), heavy machine guns, and Humvees.

Once the CIA's supply of AK-47s was exhausted the American

2. ISIS Devastates the Yazidi Community

government looked to other nations to procure the desired weapons. Albania and the Czech Republic each had large stockpiles of the semi-automatic rifles and were willing to cooperate. The two countries had formerly been part of the Eastern Bloc and had joined NATO following the collapse of the Soviet Union. CENTCOM set about purchasing the arms and ammunition. Together the two nations supplied thirty-two million rounds for the AK-47s, twenty thousand hand grenades, thirty-two thousand artillery shells, and five thousand warheads for RPGs.[49] The Kurds would use these munitions to great effect against ISIS over the next five years.

The move to provide arms to the Kurds was widely reported in the news media. Journalists also reminded the public of recent ISIS atrocities and the fact that the Kurds were the best hope for halting the advance of the terrorist army. The *New York Times* editorial board pointed out that the Kurds had been allies in the effort to overthrow Saddam Hussein and that "their semiautonomous region—peaceful, prosperous, reasonably well governed and an oil producer—has been the constant bright spot in Iraq's tumultuous post invasion history. It would be a huge blow for the Kurds, Iraq, Turkey, a NATO ally, if ISIS took over the region."[50]

As the Peshmerga was rearming and reorganizing Vian Dakhil returned to northern Iraq from Baghdad. One week after her dramatic speech in the Iraqi parliament, the persuasive legislator nearly lost her life in a horrific helicopter crash on Mount Sinjar. She had gone to the Kurdish military base at Fishkilbur and managed to talk her way aboard one of the few Iraqi relief helicopters flying supplies to Mount Sinjar. Late in the day she boarded an Mi-17 Russian-made transport helicopter together with five crew members, four other politicians, and four Western reporters. Two of the journalists were Alissa Rubin, the *New York Times* Paris bureau chief, and freelance photographer Adam Ferguson. The cargo consisted mainly of bread, as the priority was to deliver food to people that the airdrops had not reached. The pilot, Major General Majid Ahmed Saadi, was an experienced Iraqi air force officer. He had just returned from a flight to the mountain in which, after dropping off supplies, he had taken on as many refugees as his aircraft could carry. Rubin later wrote of the general:

> The pilot really made a big impression. You know, the Yazidis feel so betrayed by the Arab neighbors they had lived among for so many years; they all turned on the Yazidis when ISIS came. Many of the atrocities were carried out not by the militants but by their own neighbors. Yet here was General Majid, an Iraqi Arab himself, who was taking time off from his own job—he was in charge of training for the Iraqi air force—to help these people. He told me it was the

most important thing he had ever done in his life, the most significant thing he had done in his 35 years of flying. It was as if it gave his whole life meaning.[51]

Rubin described her impressions of the exhausted Yazidis: "One older woman's face sticks in my mind; it was very rough and tremendously sad. We were on the ground only about 10 minutes. The Yazidis were battered. Some older people were barefoot, legs swollen from walking; others were just totally dehydrated; and children sunburned. The kids—a lot of them—were crying, afraid and confused."[52] So many people scrambled aboard that the crew had to physically force some off or the helicopter would never have gotten off the ground. Still, the aircraft was terribly overloaded. General Majid attempted to take off, using the downward slope of the mountain to help generate momentum and lift. During this attempt, however, the helicopter struck a boulder and plummeted to the ground. Everyone was injured as people fell on top of one another and were thrown violently against the sides and floor of the chopper. Dozens of people slowly crawled or were helped from the wreckage. Alissa Rubin suffered a head injury, and both of her wrists were broken. Adam Ferguson, the photographer, managed to pull her out and stop the bleeding by tying a scarf around her head. Vian Dakhil's injuries were also severe, with both legs and several ribs broken. Tragically, Major General Majid was killed in the crash. He was the only fatality. As the sun set a rescue helicopter arrived and transported the injured back to the air base. From there both Rubin and Dakhil were evacuated to a hospital in Istanbul. Although it would take months, fortunately, both women recovered from their injuries.

The PKK, YPG, and the Breaking of the Siege of Mount Sinjar

Sitting in his prison cell in Turkey, Abdullah Öcalan, the head of the Kurdistan Workers Party or PKK, heard about what was happening to the Yazidis in Iraq and decided his organization had to act. In 1978 Öcalan had co-founded the leftist political and paramilitary organization, which was dedicated to the establishment of an independent Kurdish nation. Turkish leaders, not wishing to see their country divided, balked at the idea, prompting the PKK to go to war with the Turkish state. In 1984 it began a series of attacks against government security forces and assassinations of Turkish diplomats. Over the years, tens of thousands of Turks were killed in clashes with the PKK. As a result, it was labeled a terrorist group by

2. ISIS Devastates the Yazidi Community

Turkey, the United States, the European Union, and many other countries around the world.

From 1979 until 1998 the Kurdish leader directed operations against Turkey from across the border in Syria. When the Turkish government directly threatened its southern neighbor with war over the latter's support of the PKK, the Syrians expelled Öcalan. He was captured in Kenya in February 1999 by agents of the Turkish National Intelligence Organization (MIT). Öcalan was charged with treason, as he was technically a Turkish citizen. He was convicted by a military court and sentenced to death. In 2002, however, Turkey abolished capital punishment and his sentence was commuted to life in prison. After serving several years on the small prison island of İmralı in the Sea of Marmara, Abdullah Öcalan or Apo as he is known (Apo is short for both Abdullah and "uncle" in Kurdish), renounced violence. He has since advocated negotiating with the Turks to achieve Kurdish autonomy.

Despite being behind bars, upon receiving the news that thousands of Yazidis were besieged on Mount Sinjar, Öcalan ordered the PKK militia into action against ISIS. The complicated dynamics of Middle East politics can be seen in the fact that even though the United States considered the PKK a terrorist force, it simultaneously supplied those same Kurds with weapons. In theory, of course, such weapons were only to be used against ISIS.[53] To the south, in Syria, the PKK's sister organization, the People's Protection Units or YPG, also heeded Öcalan's call. Both Kurdish militias mobilized their troops and moved east into Iraq, one from Turkey the other from Syria.

The Kurds of the YPG, like their brethren in Turkey and Iraq, had a reputation as fierce fighters. This army had been formed in 2011 to protect their people living in northern Syria (known to Kurds as Rojava or western Kurdistan). Kurdish civilians were threatened not only by ISIS, but by the government forces of Bashar al-Assad as well. Unlike other armies in the region, however, both the PKK and YPG integrated women into their military units and treated them as equals. Öcalan had long been a champion for women's rights and equality. On April 4, 2013, the women of the YPG formed an all-female division known as the Women's Protection Units or YPJ. In the struggle against ISIS, they have proved themselves time and again to be excellent fighters. The YPG consisted mainly of light infantry and tended to favor quick hit-and-run tactics rather than long, drawn-out battles. YPG companies operated with a great deal of autonomy, which allowed them to rapidly mobilize their forces for combat and quickly adapt to changing battlefield conditions.

ISIS and the Yazidis

Three columns of Kurdish fighters attacked ISIS positions in the Sinjar area. While the PKK and YPG advanced from the north and south, respectively, the Peshmerga had reorganized and was moving in from the east. The assaults were uncoordinated, as the PKK and Peshmerga viewed each other as rivals, but were successful. On August 9, as U.S. Navy aircraft bombed ISIS targets from above, the YPG broke through to Mount Sinjar. They drove their SUVs and pickup trucks, displaying posters of Abdullah Öcalan on their sides, to the lower plateaus.[54] From these points the soldiers climbed the mountain on foot to reach the stranded refugees. By this time most of the Yazidis had been on the mountain for six days and nights.

Having broken the siege, some eight thousand Kurdish fighters established a safe corridor that ran between Mount Sinjar and the Syrian border through which the Yazidis could pass to safety. YPG troops aided the people as they descended, at times even carrying the elderly and children on their backs. As word spread that ground forces had finally arrived, people moved off the mountain by the tens of thousands. Upon reaching the base some walked, but most were helped into YPG vehicles for the short trip across the border. Many Yazidis noticed that the corridor was guarded by the highly disciplined women soldiers of the YPJ. It would take several days to move everyone off the mountain as they were scattered all along the slopes and some had hidden in isolated spots. The escape route remained open from August 9 until August 16,

Soldiers of the Kurdish People's Protection Units (YPG) breaking through to the besieged Yazidis on Mount Sinjar, August 10, 2014 (Rodi Said / Reuters Pictures).

2. ISIS Devastates the Yazidi Community

A female soldier of the Kurdish Women's Protection Units (YPJ) talks to Yazidis as they are led from Mount Sinjar to the Syrian border, August 10, 2014 (Rodi Said / Reuters Pictures).

by which time all those trapped on the mountain had been safely evacuated. Approximately 30 YPG soldiers lost their lives in the operation to liberate the Yazidis on Mount Sinjar.

Once safely inside YPG territory the refugees were transported to Camp Newroz. The small compound had originally been set up by the International Rescue Committee in 2013 to aid Syrians displaced by that country's civil war. The YPG dramatically expanded its capacity in anticipation of the influx of Yazidis. The International Red Cross, which provided the facility with food and medicine, was notified that thousands of people would soon need its services. As the multitudes of Yazidis began to arrive, it was clear they had to immediately be treated for dehydration, malnutrition, sunstroke, and shock. Additional aid organizations, including the World Food Program and UNICEF, rapidly sent supplies from their stockpiles in the nearby town of Derik.[55]

Most people remained in the camp only a few days. After they recovered their strength, the YPG drove the refugees to the town of Fishkilbur on the border. Families and friends who had been separated during the chaos of the initial ISIS attack were eager to locate one another. Once inside Iraq, those who could made their way to Dohuk or Erbil to search for relatives. After reaching Kurdistan, thousands of Yazidis were housed in refugee camps run by international aid organizations and the KRG. As Kurdistan is part of Iraq, technically the Yazidis were classified as displaced persons. This term refers to people who have been forced from their

ISIS and the Yazidis

A Yazidi mother walking with her children from Mount Sinjar toward the Syrian border, August 11, 2014 (Rodi Said / Reuters Pictures).

homes because of religious, racial, or political persecution but who remain within their own country. Although safe in the displaced persons camps, people were anxious to return to their previous lives and the homes that had been so violently taken from them by ISIS. Unfortunately, it would be years before any Yazidis could do so as Sinjar City remained occupied by the terrorists.

On Tuesday, August 12, 2014, 16 members of the U.S. Army's Delta Force landed near the summit of Mount Sinjar to evaluate the situation. They had flown from Erbil in V-22 Ospreys. These tiltrotor aircraft can take off and land like fixed-wing airplanes or like helicopters should the terrain warrant such maneuvers. The 1st Special Forces Operational Detachment–Delta (known as Delta Force) is the Army's elite counterterrorism unit. The soldiers immediately realized that the Yazidis had been evacuated. While on the mountain, they unexpectedly encountered several British SAS (Special Air Service) members conducting their own reconnaissance mission. The two units exchanged information and the Americans departed.

Unknown to the world at the time, the Obama administration was developing a backup plan to rescue the Yazidis should the Kurdish militias fail to break through ISIS lines. On October 7, General James Amos,

2. ISIS Devastates the Yazidi Community

the Marine Corps commandant, told *USA Today* that a massive evacuation operation, which fortunately never had to be implemented, had been in the planning stage. General Amos stated: "The plan was to pick everyone off the mountain ... it was going to be a round the clock operation."[56] It would have involved 24 Ospreys, some of which had been flown from Afghanistan to Kuwait, where their crews were placed on standby to await further orders. It would have been a complicated mission.

The marines would not only have had to secure a perimeter around the landing site but also control tens of thousands of people desperate to board the flights. Obviously limiting the number of people allowed on each aircraft would have been vital in order to avoid a crash like that in which Vian Dakhil and Alissa Rubin were injured. The Ospreys, once airborne, would also have been subject to ground fire from ISIS militants. Additional U.S. Navy and Air Force fighter jets would have been needed to protect the transport aircraft until they reached Kurdistan. Undoubtedly the U.S. military could have successfully accomplished this mission, but in the end the contingency plan proved unnecessary due to the success of the Kurdish militias.

After all that had befallen the Yazidis, it is understandable that many were eager to fight back. More than one thousand men soon joined the ranks of the YPG. Additionally, a Yazidi militia, the Sinjar Protection Force, was created. Over the next few months, the new militiamen were armed and trained at YPG bases in Syria. By 2019 the force numbered some seven thousand fighters. A smaller Yazidi militia, the Sinjar Resistance Units, which had been created earlier and supported by the PKK since 2007, also reasserted itself. Both fighting units took the battle to ISIS in the years after the devastating attack upon their homeland.

Those first American airstrikes to aid the Yazidis on Mount Sinjar would, by autumn, morph into Combined Joint Task Force–Operation Inherent Resolve (CJTF–OIR). In September 2014, the Global Coalition to Defeat Daesh (ISIS) was formed. Led by the United States, this alliance included Great Britain, Canada, several European nations, as well as such Middle Eastern countries as Iraq and Syria. Even as this force was coalescing, the president assured Americans that the country would not be drawn back into a ground war in Iraq. The additional 475 special operations soldiers who would soon be deployed were not on a combat mission. They were to act only as advisors to Kurdish and Iraqi troops, providing them with training, equipment, and intelligence. In a speech on the evening of September 10, 2014, President Obama explained why he believed the United States had to take further steps against ISIS:

ISIS and the Yazidis

As Commander-in-Chief, my highest priority is the security of the American people. Over the last several years, we have consistently taken the fight to terrorists who threaten our country. We took out Osama bin Laden and much of al Qaeda's leadership in Afghanistan.... We cannot erase every trace of evil from the world and small groups of killers have the capacity to do great harm.... One of those groups is ISIL [ISIS] ... these terrorists are unique in their brutality.

They execute captured prisoners. They kill children. They enslave, rape, and force women into marriage. They threatened a religious minority with genocide.... If left unchecked, these terrorists could pose a growing threat ... to the United States. Last month, I ordered our military to take targeted action against ISIL to stop its advances. Since then, we have conducted more than 150 successful airstrikes in Iraq. These strikes have protected American personnel and facilities, killed ISIL fighters ... and given space for Iraqi and Kurdish forces to reclaim key territory. These strikes have helped save the lives of thousands of innocent men, women and children.... This is American leadership at its best: we stand with people who fight for their own freedom; and we rally other nations on behalf of our common security and common humanity.[57]

In a powerful closing statement the president concluded his speech by referencing the Yazidis: "When we helped prevent the massacre of civilians trapped on a distant mountain, here's what one of them said. 'We owe

Iraq and Syria as of September 2014, showing 14 U.S.-led coalition airstrikes against the Islamic State's various military zones (RNGS Reuters / Reuters Pictures).

2. ISIS Devastates the Yazidi Community

our American friends our lives. Our children will always remember that there was someone who felt our struggle and made a long journey to protect innocent people.'"[58]

By 2020 the number of nations that had joined the coalition had grown to 83. Numerous countries deployed support units: some provided funds while others dispatched medical personnel and supplies. The United States continued to send military advisors and bomb ISIS targets from the air. By March 2017, the U.S. military had conducted almost fifteen thousand airstrikes in Iraq and Syria.[59] The ground war, however, was primarily waged by the Kurdish militias and Iraqi troops. Although the caliphate suffered a military defeat in the summer of 2014, it remained a formidable enemy and continued to cause untold suffering until eventually coalition forces were able to bring about its downfall.

3

Genocide in the Middle East through the Ages

The Yazidis are only the latest group to be the victims of genocide. Tragically, it has been a recurring occurrence throughout human history. One people deliberately attempting to annihilate another reaches far back in antiquity. The intent of the perpetrators is the key factor in determining whether acts of violence, such as massacres, are classified as genocide. History is replete with examples of ethnic groups or nations that have attempted to destroy the culture, society, and physical presence of others they view as rivals or threats to their civilizations. In the history of the Middle East three egregious cases stand out: the Roman–Jewish wars, the Crusades of the Middle Ages, and the Armenian genocide.

The Roman–Jewish Wars (AD 66–136)

In the long history of the Roman Empire rebellions against Roman rule were not uncommon. In the province of Judea revolts occurred in AD 66 and again in AD 132, both of which were suppressed with extreme brutality. As the empire expanded, it came to dominate the Mediterranean world militarily, economically, and politically. Some territories became provinces and were ruled directly by a Roman governor, while others were permitted to become client states with a king that was acceptable to the emperor in Rome. One such vassal kingdom was Judea. From the beginning, the Jews chafed under Roman occupation. They resented the arrogance of Roman officials and soldiers, as well as the high taxes that were imposed on all subject peoples. What outraged Judeans most, however, was the fact that the Romans viewed their emperor as a god and expected all peoples within their dominions to worship him as such. This, of course, was abhorrent to the monotheistic Jews.

Rome was not the first great power to colonize the lands of the eastern

3. Genocide in the Middle East through the Ages

Mediterranean. In the wake of Alexander the Great's conquests, Greeks established colonies throughout the Middle East. Even though the legendary general died in 323 BC at age 32, and his empire soon fractured, the Greek settlements he helped to establish flourished. Relations between Greeks and Jews in Judea were often contentious, and occasionally led to acts of violence. Rome first made its presence known in the Middle East with the arrival of General Pompey in 63 BC. In 37 BC Rome accepted Herod the Great as a client king. When Herod died in AD 6, Judea was officially designated a province of the empire. The native population of Jews now felt they had two alien peoples living among them, Greeks and Romans.

The initial spark that led to the First Roman–Jewish War occurred in AD 66, when Greeks in the predominantly Roman city of Caesarea sacrificed birds on the steps of a synagogue. This reckless act led to demonstrations and some vandalism on the part of the Jews of the city. The Roman administration demanded that the Jews pay for the damage. When the money was not forthcoming, the authorities simply seized it from the Temple treasury in Jerusalem. The thought that the Romans would be so bold infuriated the Jewish population, and protests erupted throughout the province. Protests soon grew into anti-taxation riots.[1] In Jerusalem, Roman citizens and soldiers were assaulted. As the violence increased the Roman garrison, outnumbered and isolated, withdrew from the city.

As word of an impending revolt spread, a Roman legion, Legio XII Fulminata, was dispatched from Syria to crush the uprising. The legion, along with its auxiliary troops, was ambushed by Jewish rebels at the Beth-Horon Pass. Due to the narrowness of the pass the Romans could not form their traditional battle lines and were slaughtered. More than six thousand soldiers were killed, captured, or went missing, and the legion's standard was lost. To Romans the loss of a legion's standard was incredibly humiliating. It was not only a symbol of a military unit's prowess but was believed to be imbued with mystical powers. The victory encouraged Jews from towns and villages throughout Judea to rise in rebellion. The Emperor Nero dispatched the able and experienced general Vespasian with four legions to quell the rebellion that quickly spread to the Galilee.[2]

Vespasian appointed his son Titus second in command as they attacked major Jewish strongholds throughout Judea. The most fanatical rebels, known as Zealots, were part of a nationalist movement that had developed some years earlier. The term is a reference to those who are zealous in the service of God. The Zealots' primary goal was to drive the Romans out by force of arms, thereby liberating their homeland.

ISIS and the Yazidis

A common military tactic of the Roman army was to lay siege to fortresses and walled cities that could not be reduced by storm. One such town was Yodfat (also known as Jotapata). The rebel commander was one Yosef ben Matityahu. Following a siege of 47 days the defenders had no choice but to surrender. Thousands were executed or enslaved. Ben Matityahu was captured and taken before Vespasian. During their meeting, the defeated commander predicted that the Roman general would one day become emperor. Spared the traditional fate of a captured foe, ben Matityahu was instead made a slave. Hoping to find a way out of slavery he began to offer military advice to his captors, was soon freed, and became a Roman citizen. Taking the name Flavius Josephus, he is known to history as the primary chronicler of this war.

In Jerusalem, divisions among Jews soon appeared. Moderate Jews clashed with the Zealots over control of the city as well as how best to deal with the Romans. The Zealots believed in fighting to the death and taking the rest of the city's population with them if necessary. This schism would have tragic consequences for the ordinary people during the Roman siege that was to come. As devoted to their cause as the Zealots were, an even more fanatical group emerged from their organization, the Sicarii. The name is Latin for "dagger men," as they carried the small weapons hidden in their clothing. The goal of the Sicarii was to assassinate public officials and cause such fear among the elite that they would be unable to effectively govern the province. Their modus operandi was to arrive at large public events within the crowd, stab Romans and their supporters to death, then quickly escape by disappearing into a sea of people.

The Roman military campaign was briefly interrupted in AD 68 when the Roman Senate, fearful of Emperor Nero's increasingly erratic behavior, declared him an "enemy of the people." Knowing his end was near, the emperor committed suicide. Generals from around the empire laid claim to the throne. Vespasian was no exception; when he departed for the capital, he left his son Titus to finish the war. That year saw three emperors briefly reign, with Vespasian emerging as the fourth and final claimant.

Titus proved to be every bit as clever and brutal as his father in dealing with the rebels. After months of bitter fighting, the Romans surrounded Jerusalem. His army laid siege to the city for two years, bringing its inhabitants to the brink of starvation. When Titus's soldiers caught foraging parties sent out to gather food from the surrounding countryside, he ordered that the captured men be crucified near the city walls in plain view for all to see.[3] While Roman assaults breached two of the city's three

3. Genocide in the Middle East through the Ages

walls within the first few weeks, fierce Jewish resistance prevented the attackers from entering the city.

During the long months of the siege, starvation led to the deaths of thousands. This calamity can only partially be blamed on Titus, as the Zealots, fanatically devoted to their cause, burned food supplies in a desperate attempt to force the people of the city to fight to the end. Josephus first published *The Wars of the Jews; Or, The History of the Destruction of Jerusalem* in AD 75. In it he vividly described the suffering of the inhabitants: "So all hope of escaping was now cut off from the Jews.... Then did the famine widen its progress and devoured the people by whole houses and families; the upper rooms were filled with women and children that were dying by famine, and the lanes of the city were full of the dead bodies of the aged; the children also and the young men wandered about the market-places like shadows, all swelled with the famine, and fell down dead."[4]

The Roman commander also employed psychological warfare in order to sew dissension among the Jews and persuade them to surrender. According to Josephus, the Romans, unlike the people trapped in Jerusalem, had ample supplies of food: "These Romans had great plenty of corn and other necessities out of Syria and out of the neighboring provinces, many of whom would stand near the wall of the city and show the people what great quantities of provisions they had, and so make the enemy more sensible of their famine."[5]

In the summer of AD 70 General Titus's army finally destroyed the third and thickest wall and subsequently took the city. Thousands were slaughtered, and tens of thousands captured, sold into slavery and dispersed throughout the empire. Titus understood there was a profit to be made by enslaving defeated enemies of the state, Josephus recorded: "Caesar gave orders that they should kill none but those that were in arms, and opposed them, but should take the rest alive ... together with those whom they had orders to slay, they slew the aged and infirm; but for those that were in their flourishing age, and who might be useful to them, they drove together." He added: "Titus also sent a great number into the provinces, as a present to them, that they might be destroyed upon the theatres, by the sword, and by the wild beasts; but those that were under seventeen years of age were sold for slaves."[6]

Approximately twelve thousand Jewish slaves were shipped to Rome and added to the massive workforce involved in the building of the Colosseum. Valuables looted from the Temple at the conclusion of the campaign helped fund its construction. This colossal structure, which was begun in

ISIS and the Yazidis

AD 72 under Emperor Vespasian, was completed eight years later by his son and successor, Titus. The human tragedy of massacre and enslavement was compounded by the attempted destruction of the Jewish culture in Judea.

The Temple, which lay at the very heart of Judaism, was devastated and desecrated, its massive menorah taken as a trophy. Still standing today, the Arch of Titus in Rome, which was erected at the time, features a carved depiction of this spoil of war being carried in a triumphant victory procession. While nearly all the city's walls were destroyed, Titus ordered that a small section of the Temple complex remain standing. This was to be a warning to future generations that nothing and no one can withstand the power of Rome. Today it is known as the Wailing Wall and is the holiest site in Judaism.

Following the fall of Jerusalem, and with most of the province having been reconquered, the last Zealots retreated to the mountain fortress of Masada near the Dead Sea. One hundred years earlier King Herod had built two palaces for himself on the rock plateau. The king had chosen an excellent defensive position as its cliff face rises thirteen hundred feet on the east side and three hundred feet on the west. Masada not only held a large stockpile of weapons, but it was also stocked with a vast supply of food, including grains that could be stored for years. The royal engineers also created an ingenious system on the small mesa for collecting and storing what little rain fell in the Judean desert. The stronghold was designed as a fallback position should it be needed by a king who had numerous enemies, as Josephus noted:

> Herod thus prepared this fortress on his own account, as a refuge against two kinds of danger, the one for fear of the multitude of the Jews, lest they should depose him ... the other danger was greater ... which arose from Cleopatra, queen of Egypt, who did not conceal her intentions, but spoke often to Antony, and desired him to cut off Herod, and entreated him to bestow the kingdom of Judea upon her. And certainly it is a great wonder that Antony did never comply ... as he was so miserably enslaved to his passion for her.[7]

In the autumn of AD 72, long after Herod's death, the Romans again resorted to their tactic of surrounding and laying siege to a formidable fortress. Lucius Flavius Silva was appointed the new Roman commander. Silva ordered his men, along with thousands of Jewish prisoners, to construct an earthen ramp that would allow them to slowly climb the side of the mountain. By spring of the next year the Romans completed the ramp and, using a huge battering ram, succeeded in breaching the walls erected by the rebels. The last Jewish stronghold was about to fall. Knowing there

3. Genocide in the Middle East through the Ages

was no hope of victory, the Zealots decided they would not be taken as slaves to be paraded through the streets of Rome. The Jews drew lots: the losers killed the winners, then repeated the process until only one man remained to commit suicide. When the Roman troops reached the top of the plateau expecting a battle, they found instead only dead bodies. Of the 960 Zealots, only two women and five children, who had hidden in the caves atop Masada, survived.

Roman military defeats, although rare after the establishment of the empire, did occur. One such calamity took place during the reign of the first emperor Augustus. In AD 9 the Battle of the Teutoburg Forest in Germany shocked the Roman world. The Roman commander in this instance was Publius Quinctilius Varus, an arrogant man known for his cruelty toward captured enemies. His counterpart was Arminius of the Cherusci tribe. As a young boy Arminius had been sent to Rome by his chieftain father as a hostage in order to secure peace with the empire. This was a common practice in the ancient world. Dominant powers often held royal or highborn children of subservient nations in order to ensure their peoples' obedience. Raised as a Roman, Arminius spoke Latin, and was familiar with the Roman tactics of waging war. Upon his return to Germany, he outwardly acted as a military advisor and loyal Roman subject. In secret he formed an alliance between half a dozen German tribes that had traditionally fought one another in order to launch an attack against his former captors.

Arminius led his new warriors in an ambush of three Roman legions when the columns of legionnaires were stretched out for miles as they marched through the Teutoburg Forest. The Germans knew the Romans would be at their weakest during such a march. After a series of assaults the Romans managed to fortify their camp, then attempted to break through the lines of the German tribes the next morning. As Arminius had planned, when the Romans withdrew, they were forced to march along a narrow ravine at the base of a hill in what is today lower Saxony. Again the Roman army was strung out with no room to maneuver or form battle lines. The tribesmen rained arrows and spears down upon the Romans prior to a fierce attack that devastated their columns. Some twenty thousand men were killed or captured. Rather than be taken alive, Varus committed suicide by falling on his sword. Stories soon reached Rome of captured legionnaires being burned alive in wooden cages by the victorious "barbarians."

In the wake of this shattering defeat, the Roman army adjusted and strengthened its position on the Rhine, but never again permanently occupied German territory east of the river. Emperor Augustus was shocked when he was informed of the event. At the time Rome counted 27 legions dispersed throughout the empire, and three had just been annihilated. It was widely whispered that late at night the emperor roamed his palace crying out, "Quinctili Vare, legiones redde!" (Quinctilius Varus, give me back my legions!).

Despite this defeat, the empire continued to expand. A century after the Battle of the Teutoburg Forest, it reached its zenith. By AD 117 Rome controlled virtually the entire Mediterranean coastline. In AD 132 Emperor Hadrian decided to build a thoroughly Roman city on the ruins of Jerusalem; he named it Aelia Capitolina. As part of this plan the emperor decided to erect a temple to Jupiter on the Temple Mount. Once again Judea became a center of anti–Roman resistance. The Second Roman–Jewish War began as a rebellion under the leadership of Simon ben Koseba, who chose the name Bar Kochba, "Son of the Star." Many Jews came to see this charismatic warrior as the Messiah, one who would end Roman rule and establish an independent Judea.

Rome committed six legions from across the empire to the campaign. It was a brutal war in which two legions, Legio XXII Deiotariana and Legio IX Hispana were slaughtered by the rebel army. The Romans, for their part, completely destroyed 50 Jewish strongholds and 985 villages.[8] Since the Jews could not stand toe to toe with the Roman army in open battle, they employed hit-and-run tactics. After emerging to ambush small units or cut supply lines, rebels rapidly retreated to the underground tunnel system they had carved into the soft, chalky Judean hills. The Jews also used caves in the northern Negev Desert as places of refuge for family members and to store provisions. At first the revolt succeeded, having driven out the Romans, Bar Kochba ruled over a sizable area for two and a half years. Coins were even minted with the inscriptions "Year one of the redemption of Israel" and "Year two of the freedom of Israel."

Although the Jews rejoiced in their newfound independence, it was short lived. A furious Emperor Hadrian summoned additional troops from as far away as the Danube frontier. Eventually the Roman force reached some eighty thousand soldiers. The war lasted four years, with enormous casualties on both sides. At the height of the conflict the Jewish fighters actually outnumbered their enemy by two to one.[9] The rebels may have had more troops in the field, but as had occurred in the First Roman–Jewish War, the latter were better armed, trained, and supplied. Although Bar Kochba's men fought tenaciously, the Roman war machine ground down the resistance as one by one they reconquered Jewish towns.

3. Genocide in the Middle East through the Ages

In AD 135 Bar Kochba and his battered and exhausted rebels retreated to their stronghold of Betar, southwest of Jerusalem. Again the Romans employed a siege to weaken and demoralize their enemy. Upon storming and capturing the fortress, the legionnaires slaughtered everyone inside.[10] There is some dispute as to how Bar Kochba met his end; he may have succumbed to disease or died of natural causes before the final battle took place. With the fall of Betar and the death of Simon Bar Kochba, the rebellion collapsed.

Hadrian's vindictive decrees came swiftly. Firstly, the emperor sought to erase Jewish culture and the memory of ancient Israel by renaming Judea Syria Palaestina. In addition, Jews were forbidden to enter Jerusalem except on Tisha B'Av. This was, and still is, an annual day of mourning disasters in Jewish history, especially the demolishing of Solomon's Temple by the Babylonians. Following the first rebellion against Rome, Jews also lamented the destruction of the Second Temple on this occasion.

It is well known that ancient historians were prone to wildly exaggerate the casualty numbers in times of war. This often occurred either because accurate population figures were unknown, or because those tasked with recording the events wished to enhance the military reputation of their ruler. Josephus is no exception: he claimed 1,197,000 people died in Jerusalem alone during the first rebellion. A more realistic estimate of the number of those who died in the two rebellions combined is approximately 350,000.[11]

The Romans' genocidal policies are clearly evident not only in their renaming of the land, but by the fact that in order to avoid the threat of future revolts, Hadrian expelled the majority of the people from their homeland. This was the beginning of the Jewish diaspora. Henceforth Jews, dispersed and powerless, were compelled to settle in small enclaves from North Africa to Europe. In the years to come their position would place them at the mercy of both Christian and Muslim majorities who were not always charitable in their treatment of minority populations. The ways in which Jews worshipped was also impacted by this catastrophe. With the fall of the Second Temple, which had been the focal point of the religion, synagogues became houses of worship for the faithful and rabbis replaced high priests as spiritual leaders.

Over the next two millennia Jews were victimized in both Muslim and Christian lands. Especially in Europe, Jewish communities were scapegoated for all of society's ills. In the Middle Ages, Jewish communities were often shunned by the larger societies and were subjected to widespread discrimination and periodic massacres. These attacks were often instigated by the Catholic Church in Western Europe and the Russian Orthodox Church in the east. In the twentieth century Jews were targeted for extermination by the most homicidal dictator the world has ever seen. Despite centuries of persecution, the Jewish people survived. Over two thousand years after the Romans forced them into exile, Jews returned to the Holy Land in large numbers to create the modern state of Israel in 1948.

The Crusades (AD 1095–1291)

Ever since Islam swept out of Arabia in the mid-seventh century it has been in conflict with Christianity. While today, most people have come to tolerate those of different religions, there are still some Christians and Muslims who regard adherents of the other faith as misguided at best and evil at worst. There have been physical attacks against Christians in Europe by Muslim fanatics, and some in the West have been susceptible to Islamophobia. However, overall relations between Christians and Muslims are harmonious compared to what they were in the twelfth century. At that time religious hysteria in Europe, along with politics and a lust for power, led to the Crusades. During these military expeditions, the idea of genocide was prevalent in the minds of men who sought to control a land that was considered holy by the world's three great monotheistic religions.

In late November 1095 Pope Urban II called for a crusade to recapture the Holy Land from the "infidel" Muslims. In the medieval world, dominated as it was by the Catholic Church, a papal call to arms was tremendously attractive. It was thought that a Christian would automatically gain admittance to heaven by fighting against the enemies of God. While the pope's religious reason for war was straightforward, he also had more subtle political purposes for persuading men to journey to the Middle East. One year earlier the Byzantine Emperor, Alexios I, had appealed to the West for aid in retaking Christian lands. Urban II hoped that aiding the Eastern Orthodox Christians might help mend the schism that had occurred between Latin and Orthodox believers in 1054.

At the time European society was very much a culture of violence. In between wars, thousands of mercenaries roamed the countryside. These were men with no education and few skills who hired themselves out as soldiers, often abused the peasants, and stole from local communities. In addition, among the nobility only the eldest son inherited the family fortune; therefore it was quite acceptable for the second- and third-born

3. Genocide in the Middle East through the Ages

males to make their way in the world through acts of violence. The church had attempted to limit the destructive nature of both groups by initiating the Peace of God (*Pax Ecclesie*), which forbade attacks against church property, the clergy, and Christian pilgrims. Peasants and businessmen were later added to the list of those who were not to be harmed. A second papal pronouncement, the Truce of God (*Treuga Dei*) forbade fighting from Saturday through Monday and on some Christian holidays.[12] Neither proclamation had the desired effect. Pope Urban therefore decided he should insist that these men journey to the Middle East to fight the infidels. This strategy would not only redirect their violent impulses away from European civilians but might also prove beneficial to the church in terms of wealth and power.

Thousands responded to the Pope's call, including peasants who sought to escape their grinding poverty, soldiers, monks, and camp followers. Many sons of the nobility departed in the hope of acquiring land and booty for themselves. These highborn men quickly assumed positions of leadership within the army, regardless of whether or not they were capable or even competent military leaders. Although Muslims referred to all crusaders as "Franks," in fact many nationalities participated. While some did hail from regions of France such as Normandy and Brittany, others came from German or Italian principalities. One drawback of such a multinational army was that there was no unified command structure and men tended to follow their own regional leaders.

Even before arriving in Asia Minor these soldiers of the cross caused dread in towns and villages that lay in their path. Before they could kill infidels in the Holy Land many sought to eliminate the non-believers along their way. Thousands of Jews were massacred in the Rhineland, Mainz, Cologne, and Prague. To the dismay of townspeople and farmers, these armed hosts also commandeered food and supplies from merchants and peasants alike as they moved eastward. These confiscations of vital supplies understandably led to conflicts with local populations. One large crusader contingent that was murdering Jews and seizing provisions across Germany was considered such a threat that the king of Hungary ordered his army to annihilate the band once it crossed into his domain.[13]

A major crusader army of some forty-five hundred cavalry and thirty thousand infantry crossed the Bosporus from Constantinople in 1097. The total size of this force was approximately 150,000 if one includes family members and camp followers.[14] They came in three successive waves and immediately began to retake land in the interior of Anatolia in the name of Christ. When the crusaders arrived in what is today Turkey, the Islamic world, like Christian Europe, was divided. In the north, Muslim lands were governed by the Seljuk Turks of Rum, who were subservient to the Great Seljuk sultan who ruled from Baghdad. The southern regions (Lebanon, Palestine, and Egypt) were the domain of the Cairo-based Fatimid dynasty. The Seljuks and Fatimids viewed each other as rivals, and refused to present a united front in order to repel the invaders. The Fatimids even tried to form an alliance with the Europeans against the Seljuks. This diplomatic strategy was only abandoned when it became clear that the crusading army was marching toward Jerusalem, which was under Fatimid control.

In October 1097, the crusaders laid siege to Antioch in Syria. After many months of stalemate, they were finally able to storm the city with the help of a turncoat Armenian soldier. On the night of June 3, 1098, one Firuz al-Zarrad, an officer in charge of one of the city's watchtowers and possibly a convert to Islam, aided a small crusader force to scale his position. Once on the wall the Christians killed the guards and opened one of the gates to the city. At dawn, the crusader army poured in, and by the end of the day Antioch was in Christian hands. With characteristic brutality large segments of the population were killed on the spot. After the slaughter of the men, the plundering began. In the words of Bohemond of Taranto, the *de facto* crusader commander, "We kept their wives, children and servants, together with their gold, silver and all their possessions."[15]

Since the sultan's forces were busy fighting in Iran, he could not immediately aid the people of Antioch. Eventually he ordered Kur-Bugha, the governor of Mosul, to mount a relief effort. Unfortunately, by the time Kur-Bugha's men arrived, the city had already been sacked. The Muslim army, comprised of Turks and Arabs, surrounded the city; the tables had turned, and the crusaders found themselves under siege. The Europeans quickly decided it would be more practical to meet their enemy in open battle rather than remain encircled and possibly succumb to starvation. On June 28, 1098, the battle began near the city's main gate. Although outnumbered, the crusaders fought tenaciously, knowing that if captured they would be summarily executed (although a knight, if sufficiently high in rank, might be ransomed). At one point in the battle several combatants claimed to see celestial soldiers among the clouds, which they interpreted as divine endorsement of their cause. Fighting with extreme religious fervor, they forced the Muslims to retreat and won the day.

As the crusaders moved south, they exhibited all the classic signs of those committed to a policy of genocide. People, regardless of age or gender, were murdered or sold into slavery, and their personal property stolen.

3. Genocide in the Middle East through the Ages

When the part of the army commanded by Count Raymond of Toulouse took the town of al-Bara, the entire civilian population was butchered. Two months later, in December 1098, when the town of Ma'arat al-Nu'man fell, twenty thousand men, women, and children were massacred. Ibn al-Adim, an Arab historian from Aleppo, wrote: "They killed a great number under torture. They extorted people's treasure. They prevented people from getting water.... Most of the people died of thirst."[16] And an anonymous merchant who witnessed the cruelty of the Christian soldiers stated: "I am from a city which God has condemned to be destroyed. They have killed all its inhabitants, putting old men and children to the sword."[17]

As horrendous as these massacres were, the greatest atrocity of the First Crusade came with the capture of Jerusalem. On June 7, 1099, the Franks reached the city considered holy by Jews, Christians, and Muslims. Held by the Fatimids, it was a thriving metropolis. Once again, the Christian warriors, unable to immediately take the city by force, prepared for a long siege. This war proved devastating not only to the civilian population caught between warring factions, but also to the conquerors themselves. By this point the crusader army, despite its successes, had been diminished through attrition and disease. It had been reduced to only twelve thousand men-at-arms. This included light infantry, archers, thirteen hundred knights, and their entourages (squires, pages, and grooms).

Despite their shrinking numbers the Europeans were determined to take Jerusalem no matter the cost. The Franks constructed two siege towers as well as catapults with which to attack the city's high walls. The defenders placed bails of straw on the walls to absorb the shock of the stones hurled at their defensive positions. When the final assault was launched on July 13, 1099, flaming arrows rained down, setting the straw on fire. The intense heat drove the Muslim soldiers from the ramparts. After two days the crusaders stormed the city and began indiscriminately killing all in their path, whether soldiers or civilians. Panic seized the city as desperate people sought to escape or hide from the frenzied invaders.

The worst massacre occurred near the al-Aqsa Mosque on the Temple Mount. On that spot the crusaders, overwhelmed by religious fervor and bloodlust, murdered thousands of Muslims and Jews. Since the fall of the Roman Empire, Jews had begun to return to Jerusalem, but in the eyes of the Franks they were infidels and deserved no more mercy than did Muslims. Approximately seventy thousand people were butchered when the city was captured.[18] Raymond of Aguilers, a soldier who chronicled the battle of Jerusalem, wrote that at Solomon's Temple his fellow crusaders rode in blood up to the bridles of their horses. While this is clearly hyperbole, the fact that so many innocents were slaughtered shows the state of religious fanaticism that gripped the victorious combatants at that moment. The killing went on for days. When the massacre was over the victors began looting the Muslim holy sites as well as private homes. The Franks claimed 40 large silver candelabras and nearly two hundred smaller gold and silver objects from the Dome of the Rock (the spot from which Muslims believe the Prophet Muhammad ascended to heaven).[19]

Once the pillaging ended the victors set about consolidating the lands they had wrested from the Muslims. Four small Crusader states were established: Edessa, Tripoli, Antioch, and Jerusalem. Some knights who remained in the newly acquired territories formed bands devoted to piety, chastity, and protecting Christian pilgrims traveling through the Holy Land. The Knights Templar and Knights Hospitaller, whose orders were created on Jerusalem's Temple Mount and at the Amalfitan hospital, respectively, became the most famous of these fighting monks.

Although the crusaders had managed to create a foothold in the Middle East, these outposts of Christianity remained in a precarious position vis-à-vis the Muslim world. As the two sides continued to clash over religion and power, Europeans mounted seven additional crusades over the next 150 years. Most had minimal impact on the region, and one, the Children's Crusade, failed even before its members departed Europe. Today it is the Third Crusade that is best remembered since it involved two of history's most famous figures, England's King Richard the Lionheart and the brilliant Muslim general Saladin.

When his Arab army recaptured Jerusalem in 1187, Saladin proved to be a relatively charitable conqueror. Interestingly, one of the most famous military commanders in Arab history was not an Arab, but rather a Kurd. As his forces surrounded Jerusalem, the general offered peace terms that were originally rejected. Since Saladin, unlike the crusaders a century earlier, had no interest in overseeing the wholesale slaughter of civilians, negotiations continued. As the attack began, the Christians, knowing their city was about to fall, asked for quarter. In order to bolster their position, they made it known that, should this request be denied, they would kill every Muslim inhabitant of Jerusalem and destroy their holy sites, including the al-Aqsa Mosque and the Dome of the Rock. The opposing sides finally came to terms. When Christians surrendered the city on October 2, there was no repeat of the catastrophe that had taken place under the crusaders; instead Saladin agreed to allow all those who could pay a ransom for their freedom to leave the city. Although the price was set unusually

3. Genocide in the Middle East through the Ages

low, thousands of the poorest citizens, who could not raise the needed funds, were sold into slavery.[20]

By the time Richard the Lionheart, king of England, reached the Middle East, Jerusalem was firmly back in Muslim hands. Today he is held in esteem by most Britons, mainly for his courage in battle.[21] Richard was not only a ruler determined to confront the enemies of Christendom, but also a man of his era, all too willing to commit atrocities in the name of his religion. Such was the case following his seizure of Acre. After a two-year siege, the city was his in 1191. As he prepared to press on with his campaign, the king ordered that his three thousand Muslim prisoners of war, including women and children, be taken outside the city walls and beheaded. His motives remain unclear; he may have sought to avenge Christians killed by Muslims, or he may have believed it unwise to leave thousands of prisoners in his rear as he moved farther south. Whatever his motives, the massacre at Acre remains a stain on his reputation.

Saladin and King Richard met only once in battle, at Arsuf. Richard ordered a massive cavalry charge that broke the Muslim ranks and won the engagement. Unfortunately for the king, he was unable to exploit his victory as he was forced to return to England to protect his throne from his scheming brother John. The European knights maintained a tenuous presence in the Middle East for another century. When Acre, the last crusader stronghold, fell to the Muslims in 1291, two hundred years of what Muslims viewed as Christian occupation of their lands ended.

The initial success of the crusaders was not due to any superior military tactic or overall strategy. The opposing armies actually fought in much the same manner. The European knights did have one distinct advantage over their foes in that they were trained to fight as infantrymen should they become dismounted. Although many of these men were battle-hardened soldiers, much like ISIS fighters in our own time, it was their ruthlessness and fanatical religious beliefs that enabled them to conquer and hold territory.

History and memory can be powerful forces. The people of the Middle East have been shaped by their unique history. The past has influenced how they see themselves today and how they view others. This can be used in positive ways to bring peoples closer together or can be used as an excuse to incite acts of violence and murder. Tragically, in our own time the leaders of ISIS have used history for just such a sinister purpose. They often referred to coalition forces in Iraq as "modern crusaders." Although the crusades took place nearly a thousand years ago, ISIS propagandists have successfully used this memory to justify acts of terror against the

ISIS and the Yazidis

West as well as to rationalize attacks on minority communities of Christians and Yazidis in the Middle East.

The Armenian Genocide (1915–1922)

In terms of the sheer number of people murdered, the Armenian genocide was the most horrendous event in the history of the Middle East. It is surpassed in scale only by the Holocaust in Europe a quarter of a century later. In 1914 some two million Christian Armenians lived within the Ottoman Empire. Of that number, approximately 1.5 million Armenian men, women, and children were murdered by the Turks between 1915 and 1922.[22] Though most victims were killed in 1915 and 1916, the last massacres occurred in the early 1920s. Historians consider what befell the Armenian people to be the first genocide of the twentieth century. The Armenian genocide and the Holocaust have numerous similarities beyond simple racist government policies directed at minority populations. Superficially, Christian Armenians and European Jews were singled out for persecution because of their religious beliefs; their oppressors' motives, however, went far deeper than simple theological differences. While separated by time and geography, the heads of both nations claimed that these groups were disloyal to the state and that whatever action was taken against them was a military necessity.

During World War I Armenians were viewed by most Turks as a fifth column for Russia, while in Nazi Germany Jews were portrayed as having "stabbed Germany in the back" in that same war. As a result, these minorities became scapegoats for their nations' military failures. The Committee of Union and Progress (CUP), the political party that ruled the Ottoman Empire during World War I, and the Nazis both used the cover of war to slaughter their victims. The two also used wartime edicts to attempt to hide their deeds from the outside world. In both cases governments employed deception in that Armenians and Jewish victims were told they were to be relocated rather than murdered. This was done in order to make the victims more docile and cooperative with their would-be killers. In most cases the lie worked, although there were instances of resistance: most famously, Armenians fought back in the city of Van, and Jews staged an uprising in the Warsaw ghetto in 1943. The ruling bodies in both instances created organizations the main purpose of which was to carry out mass murder. In the case of Nazi Germany the *Einsatzgruppen* (which was composed of SS men) murdered Jews in Eastern Europe, and in

3. Genocide in the Middle East through the Ages

Turkey bands of criminals were brought together, armed, and unleashed in order to annihilate the Armenian population. These killers were placed under the supervision of the Special Organization (SO). Both governments made use of trains as the most efficient method to deport the ethnic groups to concentration camps. Both brought about the deaths of tens of thousands by starvation and exhaustion through long forced death marches, although the Turks employed this strategy at the beginning of the process of genocide, and the Nazis at the end, i.e., the final weeks of World War II.

Eventually most people in the two quite different nations came to believe that these minority members were "polluting" the dominant culture and thereby weakening the state. This idea, spread by political parties in power, as it permeated society, allowed the government to murder people with relatively little opposition or complaints from large segments of the population. In both instances, once the massacres began, the perpetrators employed collaborators to aid in mass murder. The Turks made use of Arab and Kurdish bandits, while the Nazis enlisted groups from among the conquered peoples of Eastern Europe. Those who assisted in the killing did so either out of feelings of racial or religious hatred or with the understanding that they could enrich themselves by taking the victims' possessions in exchange for their service.

Of course there were differences between the two events. Whereas the Turkish leadership sought to appeal to their citizens' sense of Muslim and Ottoman identity, Germans were encouraged to accept the idea that they belonged to the superior race on earth. Western European Jews were much more assimilated in their respective societies than were most Armenians into that of the Ottoman Empire. However, the Jews of Eastern Europe were more akin to the Armenians in that they had always lived apart from the larger society in their own insular communities.

Adolf Hitler referred to the earlier genocide on August 22, 1939, as he prepared to unleash his armies upon Poland. In a meeting with his generals at his private residence, he stated:

> Our strength consists in our speed and in our brutality.... I have issued the command—and I'll have anybody who utters but one word of criticism executed by a firing squad—that our war aim does not consist of reaching certain lines, but in the physical destruction of the enemy. Accordingly, I have placed my deaths-head formations in readiness—for the present only in the East—with orders to them to send to death mercilessly ... men, women, and children of Polish derivation and language. Only thus shall we gain the living space which we need. Who, after all, speaks today of the annihilation of the Armenians?[23]

ISIS and the Yazidis

Armenia has had a tumultuous history. Its people have lived in eastern Anatolia and the south Caucasus region for centuries. In antiquity an ancient Armenian kingdom existed between 321 BC and AD 428. The population accepted Christianity in the fourth century. When Islam arrived in the region, religious tensions increased dramatically between Muslims and the Armenian community. In the fifteenth century the Ottoman Turks expanded their conquests to include western Armenia. Within the expanding empire Armenians were granted a small degree of autonomy. Muslims viewed them as sharp businessmen and traders. While their skills in commerce were respected, most Muslims continued to regard them with suspicion as they were considered "infidels." By the early nineteenth century, the eastern lands of Armenia had been annexed by the Russian Empire. Hoping for better treatment under the tsars, Armenians began moving east beginning in the 1820s. Though the Russians were fellow Christians, relations between Armenians and the Russian Orthodox Church were not always harmonious. Tensions also surfaced in terms of secular acculturation when the last two Russian tsars, Alexander III and Nicholas II, instituted intensive Russification policies aimed at all minorities within their empire.

At about the same time, the Ottoman sultan, Abdul Hamid II, began to embrace the idea of extreme nationalism and Pan-Islamism. He believed that both his empire and Islam in general were under assault by the ideas, culture, and especially the religion of the West. As a result the sultan lashed out at his Christian subjects. In 1894, using the flimsy excuse that Armenians in the town of Sasun had refused to pay their taxes, he ordered his military to slaughter some two hundred thousand Armenians.[24] It was a chilling precursor of what was to come during World War I.

In August 1914 two blocs of European nations went to war with each other. The Triple Entente, better known later in the war as the Allies, was composed of Great Britain, France, and Russia. Opposing them were Germany, Austria-Hungary, and Bulgaria, labeled the Central Powers. It was this second alliance that the Ottoman Empire joined in late October 1914. Even though these were Christian nations, Ottoman officials thought such an alliance would be of great benefit to the state. By siding with the enemies of Russia it was hoped that a decisive victory could be achieved over an old adversary. Interestingly, at the same time the Ottomans declared war on the Allies, a call to jihad, or holy war against non–Muslims, was issued throughout the empire. This dictate inflamed passions and allowed many to claim that killing Christian Armenians was a righteous, religiously sanctioned duty.

3. Genocide in the Middle East through the Ages

The Ottoman strategy was to move north into the Caucasus, and advance south to seize the Suez Canal (which the army was ultimately unable to accomplish). Unfortunately, the Russians struck first and invaded eastern Anatolia in November 1914, taking the town of Sarıkamış. An Ottoman counteroffensive failed to dislodge the tsar's forces. A humiliated Turkish leadership sought a scapegoat to explain their military failure. The minister of defense and military commander of the Ottoman Army at Sarıkamış, İsmail Enver, immediately blamed the Armenians. Better known as Enver Pasha, he, along with the minister of the interior, Mehmed Talaat, referred to as Talaat Pasha, were the two men most responsible for the Armenian genocide.[25] While Sultan Mohammad V ruled the empire in name, the real power was in the hands of Enver and Talaat. With the British-ANZAC (Australia and New Zealand Army Corps) attack across the Dardanelles at Gallipoli in April 1915 a siege mentality developed within government circles.[26] The two ministers cleverly played on their peoples' fears of a disloyal internal element that might aid a foreign enemy, either the British to the west and south or the Russians to the east. In the coming months they would use this suspicion and the cover of war to commit mass murder.

In order to maintain the appearance of legality, the government passed the Temporary Law of Deportation in May 1915. At this point officials hoped to avoid openly announcing their plans for genocide, so the word "Armenians" was intentionally omitted, but military commanders knew all too well to whom the law was to be applied. According to this statute, any segment of the population could be deported "on suspicion of espionage, treason [or] military necessity."[27] This was followed in September by the Temporary Law of Expropriation and Confiscation. Ostensibly this law was designed to register, safeguard, and hold in trust property until those deported returned. In reality it was simply a way for the Turkish government to steal the holdings of those they meant to murder.

While the term "deportation" was used, it was merely a euphemism for killing. Beginning in 1915 the Armenian communities of eastern Anatolia were targeted by the state. Those who were not executed on the spot were forced on long death marches over hundreds of miles to makeshift concentration camps in the Syrian desert. The few who survived these hellish treks, with little food or water, were subsequently left to die of starvation and/or exposure in camps such as Deir ez-Zor in eastern Syria. Each column of deportees had a small number of soldiers who were referred to as an "escort." Rather than care for the Armenians, these guards robbed and abused the people as they walked toward Syria. They were not alone in

ISIS and the Yazidis

this type of behavior as the provincial police, or gendarmes, also took an active part in this eviction process. The police were responsible for forcing victims from their homes in towns and villages, as they helped themselves to any valuable household items they desired.

Any Turkish official who opposed the deportation orders coming from Constantinople not only put his career in jeopardy, but in many cases his life as well. The provincial governors in Ankara and Aleppo were dismissed from their posts for refusing to implement the policy against the Armenians, and two other governors were reportedly murdered for their noncompliance.[28] Ordinary Muslims also risked their lives should they offer help to the deportees. General Mahmud Kâmil, commander of the Ottoman Third Army then stationed in eastern Anatolia, issued an order stating in no uncertain terms that "any Muslim who protects an Armenian will be hanged in front of his house, which will also be burned down. If the culprit is an official, he will be dismissed, and court marshalled."[29]

Many mid-level officials agreed to carry out the mass killings because they genuinely believed in the actions of the state, wished to rise politically,

The arrest of Armenian men in Mezre. This photograph was published in the diary of Danish missionary Maria Jacobsen, who witnessed the deportations. Attached to the photograph was written "Armenian men are escorted out of the city to be killed, 1915" (provided by the Armenian Genocide Museum-Institute, Armenia).

3. Genocide in the Middle East through the Ages

hoped to line their own pockets with the sale of seized valuables, or a combination of all three. Two such men were Kemal Bey, the lieutenant governor of Yozgat province, and Nail Bey, the CUP secretary for the province of Trabzon. Kemal Bey had the blood of thousands of people on his hands. In one instance he demonstrated to Turkish villagers the most effective way of cutting a person's throat. A true believer, while viewing the murder of women and children he was "observed smoking a water-pipe amidst the moans, groans, and shrieks of the people in mortal agony."[30] Nail Bey refused to spare even Armenian children and insisted they either be deported or murdered on the spot. During these ongoing actions the CUP's representative indulged in his own depravity; he selected 10 beautiful Armenian girls and "kept them in a house for his own pleasure, and the amusement of his friends."[31]

Since most Turkish soldiers were deployed to the front lines, the CUP created the Special Organization, or SO (*Teşkilat-ı Mahsusa*) to supervise the deportations. The SO organized groups of convicted criminals, most having recently been released from prison, for the sole purpose of massacring Armenian civilians. As payment for their work these men were allowed to take anything of value (especially gold jewelry) possessed by the Armenians. These convict bands, or *chetes*, numbered between thirty and forty thousand, and were commanded by junior officers of the Turkish army. It was thought that these lieutenants and captains would ensure the ruthless killings would be accomplished efficiently. The government's cynical ulterior motive for using criminals to carry out such a policy was that it could subsequently deny any responsibility for committing mass murder.

The process was the same for each town that was to be emptied. Once the *chetes* surrounded a community, the first order of business was to disarm the population. This strategy was almost identical to that used by ISIS against the Yazidis a century later. Without weapons the Armenians had no way to resist and could be easily controlled. People were told that although they were being deported, no harm would come to them if they cooperated. Armenian men in the Ottoman army were also forced to surrender their weapons and transferred to labor battalions, where most were ultimately worked to death. As Turkish soldiers expelled Armenians from their homes and placed them in caravans to be moved south, men were separated from the women and children. The men were then marched some distance away and executed. Without men to protect them, the women and children were at the mercy of the Turkish military and their henchmen. This, of course, was the same tactic ISIS fighters used against the Yazidis years later.

ISIS and the Yazidis

A German commander in Eastern Anatolia, one Colonel Stange, described the *chetes* as *Gesindel* (scum or trash) who "in the area of Tercan killed without exception all the Armenians of the convoy coming from Erzurum with the assistance of the military escort."[32]

Twenty-six years before the Holocaust in Europe, tens of thousands of Armenians were loaded onto railway cattle cars to be transported to their deaths. The terrified people, given no food or water, were packed 90 to a car that ordinarily held six horses. The trains rolled to the city of Konia, where the Armenians were forced to continue toward Syria on foot. In November 1915, Anna Harlowe Birge, an American traveling from Smyrna (Izmir) to Constantinople (Istanbul) wrote:

> At every station where we stopped, we came side by side with one of these trains. It was made up of cattle-trucks, and the faces of little children were looking out from behind the tiny barred windows of each truck. The side doors were wide open, and one could plainly see old men and old women, young mothers with tiny babies, men, women, and children, all huddled together like so many sheep or pigs—human beings treated worse than cattle are treated.[33]

As one might expect, the survival rate on such brutal journeys was extremely low. Along these death marches Armenians died of exhaustion, starvation, and dehydration. In one instance a column of eighteen thousand people left eastern Anatolia, bound for Aleppo, Syria. After a 17-day forced march only 150 women and children remained alive.[34] In addition to the physical hardships, fear, and uncertainty the deportees experienced during the forced marches, young women were also vulnerable to sexual assault. Almost every night the military guards raped many of their captives. It was also quite common for the soldiers to sell the most attractive women as slaves to marauding bands of Arab or Kurdish bandits.

Throughout the war the authoritarian Turkish regime publicly downplayed the numbers of Armenians who were being killed. Privately Enver and Taalat received constant reports updating them on the growing numbers of their victims. Taalat, as minister of the interior, directly controlled the gendarmes and coordinated the deportations. He hoped to conceal the state's murderous actions from the international press as long as possible, but, as with other mass killings in history, the news leaked out to the world. At first it was only rumors and hearsay, but this was soon followed by firsthand accounts of survivors. Foreign diplomats, stationed as they were throughout the Ottoman Empire, became aware of the massacres and reported the news to their respective governments.

Members of the American diplomatic corps constantly sent dispatches to the State Department in Washington, D.C., informing their

3. Genocide in the Middle East through the Ages

government of the Turkish actions. They were also determined to do what they could for the Armenian victims. This was especially true of the top American diplomat in the country, Ambassador Henry Morgenthau. While his son, Henry Morgenthau Jr., would become well known to Americans as Franklin D. Roosevelt's secretary of the treasury, it was the elder Morgenthau who had the daunting task of trying to persuade Taalat and Enver to end the slaughter of their fellow countrymen. As his nation's highest-ranking representative, Morgenthau met on a regular basis with both ministers. He described Taalat as a powerfully built man with an "ogre like face" and little formal education, but deemed him clever nevertheless. While he liked to laugh and enjoyed a good story, Taalat was, above all else, a man of relentless drive and determination. The minister once told Morgenthau that he did not expect to die peacefully in his bed. It was an astute prediction.

The ambassador's opinion of Enver was quite different. He found the minister of war to be a military man at heart, which is understandable since he had made a career in the army. His manners were refined; he was audacious and quite arrogant. Morgenthau wrote that, upon arriving at Enver's home one evening, he noticed a large picture of Napoleon on the wall. Another of Frederick the Great hung a few feet away, and in between them sat Enver. He had been military attaché in Berlin and was completely enamored with Prussian militarism. A highly intelligent man, he sought closer relations with Germany in order to get technical and material assistance (e.g., German companies provided the expertise to build the Baghdad railway). The diplomat was amused that even though Enver never achieved

Enver Pasha on a postcard (provided by the Armenian Genocide Museum-Institute, Armenia).

any major victories in battle, he still thought of himself as a great military leader.

In 1915 the United States had limited influence with the Turks. Commercial ties were minimal, the Standard Oil Company had only recently begun to make its presence known in the region, and America's only imports from the Ottoman Empire were relatively small amounts of tobacco, figs, and rugs. According to Morgenthau, most Turks viewed America as a nation of idealists. Writing two years before the United States entered the war, Morgenthau believed that, in diplomatic terms, America's neutrality worked to his advantage in dealing with the two ministers. Since Taalat believed the United States had no territorial designs on the empire, he felt free to discuss Turkish policies with the ambassador including those aimed at the Armenians.

As the Armenian population in Anatolia was being systematically deported, the government placed economic pressure upon all Christians. Interestingly this policy did not apply to Jews, as Morgenthau noted:

> An official boycott was established against all Christians, not only in Asia Minor but in Constantinople, but this boycott did not discriminate against the Jews, who have always been more popular with the Turks than have the Christians. The officials particularly requested Jewish merchants to put signs over their doors indicating their nationality [religion] and trade—such signs as "Abraham the Jew, tailor" and "Isaac the Jew, shoemaker," and the like. I looked upon this boycott as illustrating the topsy-turvy national organization of Turkey, for here we had a nation engaging in a commercial boycott against its own subjects.[35]

As the killings in the east continued, Morgenthau frequently received telegrams from U.S. consuls stationed throughout the empire informing him of the atrocities being committed against Armenians. Leslie A. Davis in Harput and Jesse B. Jackson in Aleppo kept their superior updated and did what they could to aid the victims. Both men saw firsthand the results of genocide. On one occasion a local Turk confided to Davis that he had seen thousands of dead bodies around Lake Goeljuk. The consul, wanting to see the evidence for himself, rode on horseback with the man for several hours. The scene they came across was truly horrific: hundreds of bodies—almost all women and children—were strewn over the ground decomposing. Davis later spoke to a survivor who described how she and the entire population of her village had been taken to this site and killed. The gendarmes had left her for dead among the corpses. Davis gave her enough money to escape to Russian Armenia.[36]

When Davis was informed that deportations in the Harput area were

3. Genocide in the Middle East through the Ages

to begin, he and six others, mostly foreign missionaries, arranged to see the *vali* (governor) to protest the decision. The *vali* informed the group that he was powerless to cancel the order since it had originated in Constantinople. As in other parts of Turkey, Armenian men were separated from the women and children. Davis described a massacre that occurred on Wednesday, July 7, 1915. He reported:

> On Monday, many men were arrested both at Harput and Mezreh and put in prison. At daybreak Tuesday morning they were taken out and made to march towards an almost uninhabited mountain. There were about eight hundred in all and they were tied together in groups of fourteen each. All their money and most of their clothing had been taken from them. On Wednesday morning they were taken to a valley a few hours' distant ... the gendarmes began shooting them until they had killed nearly all of them. Some who had not been killed by bullets were then disposed of with knives and bayonets.... No charge of any kind had ever been made against any of these men. They were simply arrested and killed as part of the general plan to dispose of the Armenian race.[37]

Davis knew he had to act. He made it known that he would offer sanctuary in the consulate to any Armenian who could claim the slightest connection to the United States. Any link, no matter how tenuous, e.g., a distant relative living in America, would be enough for him to justify his actions to the Turkish authorities. Dozens of desperate people hurried into the U.S. outpost. Every day, as soldiers patroled the streets outside the walled consulate, Davis went to the market to buy bread for his new guests. As more people moved in and space became scarce, many began to sleep outside in the consulate's garden. In total he saved 80 people by giving them refuge in the American compound.

U.S. Consul Jesse Jackson also sent Morgenthau updates on the events occurring in and around Aleppo. On August 15, 1915, he sent word that virtually the entire Armenian populations in the provinces of "Van, Erzeroum, Bitlis, Diarbekir, Mamouret ul-Aziz, Angora and Sivas have already been practically exterminated, and even conservative estimates already place the death toll well over 500,000."[38] As the Armenians moved through the city under guard, Jackson was able to gather firsthand accounts from the traumatized survivors. He was shocked by the stories of starvation, and that groups of Arab brigands had been allowed to raid the defenseless columns in order to rape, rob, and abduct thousands of women. He wrote:

> One of the most terrible sights ever seen in Aleppo was the arrival early in August, 1915 of some 5,000 terribly emaciated, dirty, ragged and sick women and children, 3,000 in one day and 2,000 the following day. These people

ISIS and the Yazidis

were the only survivors of the thrifty and well to do Armenian population of the province of Sivas, where the Armenian population had once been over 300,000.[39]

Like Leslie Davis in Harput, Jackson sought to aid the victims of what today we would call "ethnic cleansing." Twice a week he visited the temporary encampments created by the Turks that ran along the railroad tracks on the southwest side of Aleppo. In these squalid camps he distributed food and money to the Armenians. Although the authorities had issued strict orders forbidding anyone from assisting the deportees, Jackson simply ignored the edicts. Moreover, prisoners who escaped and arrived at the consulate were protected by Jackson and his staff. He recorded that every day Turkish officials came to the diplomatic outpost looking for Armenians. At night, the Americans quietly led the refugees out to the consulate and placed them with either sympathetic residents of Aleppo or trustworthy Bedouin Arabs camped near the city.

By autumn 1915, word of the Armenian genocide was beginning to reach the outside world. In addition to foreign diplomats, travelers and missionaries also sent word to their home countries detailing the immense scale of the tragedy. The press in Europe and the United States began to take note. In the last few months of the year, the *New York Times* alone ran 145 stories about the massacres.[40] In response to these articles, and the urgent pleas from Ambassador Morgenthau, American philanthropists created and funded the American Committee for Armenian and Syrian Relief, which later became Near East Relief. This organization, just one of many aid societies founded during World War I, raised over $100 million to assist the survivors of the genocide. As soon as he was informed of efforts at home to collect funds, Consul Jackson immediately requested $150,000 a month, which he would use to save the lives of the women and children moving through Aleppo. By early winter 1915 the consular staff had indeed begun to spend the money to feed and clothe the destitute and starving Armenians.

In the United States the question of whether to intervene militarily on behalf of the Armenians was a bone of contention between the sitting president and one of his predecessors. While Woodrow Wilson and Theodore Roosevelt agreed on some domestic reform issues (even though Wilson was a Democrat and Roosevelt a Republican), they vehemently disagreed on foreign policy and disliked each other intensely on a personal level. Wilson felt the former Rough Rider was a bombastic narcissist, while Roosevelt considered Wilson a weak-willed, indecisive idealist. Ex-president Roosevelt, an ardent internationalist (and imperialist), opposed Wilson's

3. Genocide in the Middle East through the Ages

isolationism and felt passionately that the United States should go to war in order to stop the Armenian genocide. Roosevelt declared that what was taking place on Ottoman territory was "the greatest crime of the war." While Wilson sympathized with the Armenians' plight, he rejected the idea of military action that might, as a consequence, draw the United States into the wider European war. Politically, this strategy paid off, as he was re-elected in November 1916 with the slogan "he kept us out of war."

Theodore Roosevelt had nothing but contempt for Wilson's statements on neutrality, which he labeled "weasel words." Always one to speak his mind, he further stated that the president acted cowardly in not declaring war on Germany following the sinking of the British ocean liner *Lusitania* in May 1915. That incident, which shocked the nation, resulted in the deaths of 1,198 civilians, including 125 Americans. Another two years would pass before the United States entered the war on the side of the Allies. Ultimately Woodrow Wilson felt he had no choice but to go to war once Germany resumed its strategy of unrestricted submarine warfare and the public was made aware of the Zimmermann Note.[41]

In the second year of the Great War, the Ottoman Empire's most important partner was Germany. Had the kaiser's government applied serious diplomatic pressure, many thousands of Armenian lives could have been saved. Unfortunately, most German members of the foreign service had no desire to do anything that might show their ally in a negative light. Even as he was informed of multiple massacres of Armenians, the German ambassador, Hans Freiherr von Wangenheim, opposed the publication of such incidents in Europe. He believed reports of these events could be used by the press in Allied nations to damage the reputation of the Ottoman government in the eyes of the world. When Henry Morgenthau appealed to him to intervene with the Turks on behalf of the Armenians, he was utterly rebuffed. Morgenthau said of the German: "He was a man who was devoid of sympathy or human pity, and I turned from him in disgust."[42]

A short time after this encounter Wangenheim suffered a stroke and died. His successor, Paul Wolff Metternich, proved to be more willing to call out the Turkish leadership for its actions. When Germany's new representative met with Taalat, the minister of the interior repeated the standard—and by then well-rehearsed—statement that the deportations were a necessity of war. He was also told that since these people could not be trusted to be loyal to the state, action against them was inevitable. In addition to the Turks, Wolff Metternich was also stifled by his own government. When he suggested to officials in Berlin that the German press be

ISIS and the Yazidis

allowed to publish stories of Turkish atrocities, the German chancellor, Theobald von Bethmann Hollweg, dismissed the idea: "Our only aim is to keep Turkey on our side until the end of the war, no matter as a result Armenians perish or not."[43]

Unlike his chancellor, one German soldier was committed to telling the world of the tragedy that was unfolding within the Ottoman Empire. Armin T. Wegner, a second lieutenant and medic stationed in Syria, was an eyewitness to the death marches. He had joined the army in 1914 at the outbreak of World War I and had been awarded the Iron Cross for courage under fire in rendering aid to wounded soldiers in Poland. The next year he was transferred to the Middle East, where he chronicled the horrific events he observed. In violation of standing orders, he took hundreds of photographs and had many of them spirited out of the country with soldiers returning to Germany. In addition, he wrote letters home describing what he witnessed in the sprawling camps around Deir ez-Zor. These hellish places were erected in the Syrian desert in which the arriving Armenians, exhausted and emaciated, were expected to die. Of the forty-five thousand people who survived the marches to reach Deir ez-Zor, only 40 remained alive at the end of the war.[44] Following the war, Wegner published his collected letters under the title *Der Weg ohne Heimkehr* (The Road of No Return).

Writing after a visit to the camps around the northeastern Syrian city of Ras al-Ayn, he observed:

> ...hunger, death, disease, desperation on all sides. You would smell the odor of feces and decay. From a tent came the laments of a dying woman. A mother identifying the dark violet badges on my uniform as those of the Sanitary Corps, came towards me with outstretched hands. Taking me for a doctor, she clung onto me with all her might, I who had neither medicine nor bandages, for it was forbidden to help her. But all this is nothing compared to the swarms of orphans which increases daily. At the sides of the camp, a row of holes in the ground covered with rags, had been prepared for them. Girls and boys of all ages were sitting in these holes, heads together, abandoned and reduced to animals, starved, without food or bread, deprived of the most basic human aid, packed tightly one against the other trembling from the night cold, holding pieces of still smoldering wood to try to get warm.[45]

Wegner took copious notes on what he saw. He even carried letters written by Armenian deportees begging for help to Constantinople, where he delivered them to Ambassador Morgenthau. Unfortunately, a letter sent to his mother was intercepted, and Turkish authorities demanded his removal from the area. He was ordered back to Germany. Even as he

3. Genocide in the Middle East through the Ages

departed, he continued to show considerable fortitude. At great personal risk he smuggled negatives of photographs he had taken out of the country by hiding them in his belt. The young medic always believed, however, that it was the regime that was responsible for the genocide, not the Turkish people as a whole.

In the years that followed Wegner became an outspoken pacifist, an author, and a critic of totalitarian governments (including that of the Soviet Union). This principled man continued to oppose the persecution of minorities. In 1933 he wrote an open letter to Adolf Hitler in which he criticized Nazi policies toward Jews. In September of that year he was arrested by the Gestapo, tortured, and sent to the concentration camp at Oranienburg. Over the next year he was transferred to several other camps. Upon his release he fled to Italy, never to return to his homeland. In 1967 Wegner was named one of the Righteous Among the Nations by Yad Vashem in Israel. A year later he was invited to Soviet Armenia and honored for his efforts on behalf of the Armenian people.

Unquestionably the Armenians bore the brunt of the government's murderous policies designed to bring about Pan-Ottomanization and the strengthening of the Islamic faith. However, other minorities suffered persecution during the war years. Hundreds of thousands of Greeks were either killed or expelled because they adhered to the Greek Orthodox faith. Since most Greeks lived in western Anatolia, it was relatively simple for the authorities to send these Christians, including families who had lived along the coast for generations, across the Aegean Sea to the Greek islands or to mainland Greece. Assyrians, or Syrian Christians, were also viewed with suspicion. Assyrians claim descent from some of the first Christians, and even today are found in modern Syria and northern Iraq. At first, they were subjected to discriminatory practices on the part of local Ottoman administrators hoping to gain favor with their superiors in Constantinople. Although no official deportation orders were ever issued, they nevertheless suffered tens of thousands of casualties inflicted by Arab tribesmen in the name of Islam. These Muslim fanatics were never held accountable for their actions.

The Yazidis, as so often happened in their history, were also targeted as an unwanted minority. The Yazidi population of eastern Anatolia had lived in peace with the Armenians for centuries, but they too suffered at the hands of Ottoman troops. In the Erzurum region seventy-five hundred Yazidis were massacred, and in the Kars region approximately five thousand were murdered. Yazidis were forced to abandon their homes as news of the attacks spread. Many found refuge with their religious brethren in

ISIS and the Yazidis

the vicinity of Mount Sinjar in Iraq, while others moved east into the Russian Empire. Some 15,500 fled to the Russian provinces of Armenia and Georgia.[46]

Since the killings and deportations came upon the Armenian community so rapidly in the spring and summer of 1915, many people had no time to escape. Those who were able to stay one step ahead of the gendarmes and the SO sought refuge wherever they could. A few thousand Armenians fled southeast to Sinjar, the traditional Yazidi homeland. Unlike Yazidis farther north, the inhabitants of Sinjar had their own tribal militias that could be called upon to defend their people.[47] Near the mountain, which became the scene of the rescue of fifty thousand Yazidis almost a century later, lived the Yazidi tribal leader Hemoye Shero. Shero and his people identified with the persecuted Christians and provided the Armenians with food and shelter. Once the pursuing Ottomans arrived, military officers dispatched a messenger with a letter demanding that if Shero did not surrender the refugees, Yazidis would suffer the consequences.

In reply to this threat, the elderly chieftain defiantly tore up the letter declaring that he would not abandon the Christians who were now under his protection. He reportedly declared that defending these people was a matter of honor and that he and his sons were prepared to die, if necessary, in order to uphold this principle. Surprisingly, the Yazidis were able to force the Ottomans back, and a military stalemate ensued (of course Yazidi efforts to resist were aided by the fact that the Turks were busy fighting the allies on other fronts). Shero not only cared for the people who had reached Sinjar on their own, but also led raids on the deportation caravans in nearby Syria. In this way he rescued numerous Armenian women and children, returning with them to his homeland.[48] Most of the Christian families that arrived in Sinjar in 1915 were still living peacefully in the area when ISIS attacked in 2014.

In the capital, Ambassador Morgenthau became increasingly frustrated in his dealings with the two most important ministers. Whenever he brought up the topic of the Armenians, Taalat stated that measures had to be taken against them since they were in constant communication with, and spying for, the Russians. In one meeting the minister asked the ambassador, "Why are you so interested in the Armenians anyway? You are a Jew; these people are Christians.... Why can't you let us do with these Christians as we please?" Morgenthau indignantly responded, "You don't seem to realize that I am not here as a Jew, but as American Ambassador. My country contains something more than 97,000,000 Christians and something less than 3,000,000 Jews. So at least in my ambassadorial

3. Genocide in the Middle East through the Ages

capacity, I am 97% Christian. But after all, that is not the point. I do not appeal to you in the name of any race or any religion, but merely as a human being."[49] As the two officials ended their meeting the ambassador remarked that Americans would not forget these massacres. Taalat remained unmoved, and Morgenthau noted that trying to change his mind was like talking to a stone wall.

On another occasion Taalat made what Morgenthau remembered as the most astonishing request he had ever heard. The minister had been informed that many Armenians had taken out life insurance policies with two American companies. He nonchalantly asked the ambassador, "I wish you would get the American life insurance companies to send us a complete list of their Armenian policy holders. They are practically all dead now and have left no heirs to collect the money. It of course all escheats to the state. The government is the beneficiary now. Will you do so?" At that point Morgenthau lost his temper, angrily shouted "You will get no such list from me,"[50] and stormed out of the room. The American recalled that, privately, Taalat was immensely proud of what his government was doing

U.S. Ambassador Henry Morgenthau, March 2, 1920 (provided by the Armenian Genocide Museum-Institute, Armenia).

to the Armenians, once boasting to close friends: "I have accomplished more toward solving the Armenian problem in three months than Abdul Hamid accomplished in thirty years!"[51]

The U.S. ambassador's opinion of Taalat never changed; he considered the Turk to be both bloodthirsty and brutish. Enver, however, was a different sort of man altogether. Morgenthau viewed him as a much more astute politician with a somewhat disarming personality. Nevertheless, when it came to the subject of the Armenians, he was as determined as Taalat to be rid of them. Of the two men, Morgenthau believed he had a better working relationship with the minister of war. One day a message arrived at the U.S. embassy from the consul in Smyrna (today known as Izmir). It informed the ambassador that seven Armenian men had been convicted on trumped-up charges and sentenced to be hanged. The governor general of Smyrna, who believed the men were innocent, wired the capital pointing out that under Ottoman law the men had the right to appeal for clemency to the sultan. The reply to the governor general showed Morgenthau what the government thought of Armenian rights. The wire read: "Technically you are right; hang them first and send the petition for pardon afterward."

Talaat Pasha on a postcard (provided by the Armenian Genocide Museum-Institute, Armenia).

An incensed Morgenthau decided to act:

> I visited Enver in the interest of these men on Bairam, which is the greatest Mohammedan [Muslim] religious festival, it is the day that succeeds Ramadan, their month of fasting. Bairam has one feature in common with

3. Genocide in the Middle East through the Ages

Christmas, for on that day it is customary ... to exchange small presents, usually sweets.... I said to Enver: "Today is Bairam and you haven't sent me any present yet." Enver laughed. "What do you want? Shall I send you a box of candies?" "Oh no," I answered, "I am not so cheap as that. I want the pardon of the seven Armenians whom the court-marshal has condemned at Smyrna." The proposition apparently struck Enver as very amusing. "That's a funny way of asking for a pardon," he said. "However, since you put it that way, I can't refuse." He immediately sent for his aid and telegraphed to Smyrna, setting the men free.[52]

The end of World War I found the Ottoman Empire on the verge of collapse. Enver and Taalat, still popular with most Turks, managed to elude the victorious Allies by escaping aboard a German submarine in late 1918. As the scale of the genocide was revealed to the world, the Turks sought to prove to the British and French that their courts could bring those responsible to justice. By April 1919, some 107 men had been arrested and were held in Turkish jails on charges of war crimes.[53] In July, Enver and Taalat were convicted *in absentia* of crimes against the Armenian people and sentenced to death, while a handful of officials were convicted and executed, including Kemal Bey. At his funeral hundreds demonstrated and referred to him as an innocent victim. Many other participants were charged only with "disturbing national security" and received light sentences. In the following weeks, a wave of nationalism swept the country and Turkish courts began releasing dozens of men accused of involvement in the mass killings. This action led the Allies to question Turkish resolve and to take matters into their own hands.

Over the next year and a half the British arrested 117 accused war criminals and held them on the islands of Mudros and Malta. Meanwhile, in August 1920, Turkish officials signed the Treaty of Sèvres, which created zones of allied occupation and began the process of dismembering the empire. France established a mandate over Syria and Lebanon while Great Britain did the same in Iraq and Palestine. Unfortunately, the British commitment to punishing the accused murderers in their custody faltered. Frustrated in their dealings with the Turks over the issue and hoping to put the war and its messy aftermath behind them, the British released their prisoners in 1921.

In the immediate aftermath of World War II the Allied powers held the Nazis responsible for their crimes. This was, of course, just and set a precedent that is still respected today. Decades earlier the international community had no appetite for such a reckoning. Following World War I there were no international war crimes tribunals to mete out justice to those responsible for killing innocent people in the name of national and religious unity in Turkey.

Enver and Taalat, the two men most responsible for the deaths of more than one million people, managed to avoid the gallows. Each man, however, died violently soon after the war. Taalat's prediction that he would not pass away peacefully came true on March 15, 1921. On that date he was assassinated in Berlin by Soghomon Tehlirian, an Armenian survivor of the genocide. After a short two-day trial, Tehlirian was found "not guilty by reason of temporary insanity." Enver was killed in battle a year later while fighting the Red Army in the Soviet Republic of Tajikistan.

In 1923 Mustafa Kemal (later known as Atatürk), a former general and victor of the Battle of Gallipoli, emerged as Turkish head of state.[54] The new leader formally abolished the Ottoman Empire and proclaimed the modern state of Turkey. Atatürk, to his great credit, transformed Turkey into a secular, democratic state that included women's suffrage and equal rights for all under the law. Unfortunately, he had no interest in holding lengthy trials of those accused of genocide. Some of these murderers were put to death, however, but not for their involvement in the killing of Armenians. Objecting to the new form the state had taken, several individuals plotted to assassinate Atatürk. In the summer of 1926 two sets of trials were held in which 11 men were charged and convicted of conspiracy to kill the Turkish leader and seize control of the government. Seven of those executed, including Nail Bey, had also been involved in the planning and implementation of the murder of more than one million people.

4

Yazidi Stories of Survival and the War Against ISIS

The following interviews took place in the winter of 2019. In each case ISIS permanently disrupted the lives of ordinary people, instilled terror and inflicted pain upon them simply because they were Yazidis. These individuals have, however, shown remarkable resilience in the face of an enemy that sought to symbolically destroy their culture and physically annihilate their people.

Faisal I.

At age 32 Faisal has suffered more than most and yet has maintained a positive outlook on life and his future. Faisal was born with a facial deformity. To this day he must endure expensive treatments for this painful condition. In addition to dealing with his medical issue, he also survived two catastrophic events in Iraq perpetrated by Islamic extremists, the car bombings in 2007 that leveled his hometown and the ISIS attack in 2014.

In the early evening of August 14, 2007, as Faisal worked serving customers at a café in the town of Qahtaniyah (Til Ezer), coordinated car bombs were detonated and the town was engulfed by the colossal explosions. The building was instantly turned to rubble, and Faisal found himself dazed and covered in debris. As he heard the screams of children and the cries for help from adults, he slowly moved out from the rubble. He stated: "Right in front of me I watched my friend and neighbor in the shop burning, and I was unable to help him or provide first aid. My friend died from his burns. Lying near me were dozens of bodies and body parts thrown everywhere. Those are moments and hours I will never forget. I was lucky I survived." More than one thousand people were killed or wounded. Fortunately at the time of the blast Faisal's family was not in their home, and although the house was destroyed, his parents and

ISIS and the Yazidis

siblings were unharmed. Faisal recovered, secured a job as a day laborer working construction, and eventually married and had two sons. Despite his limited income, he was happy until the ISIS attack on August 3, 2014, altered his life forever.

Faisal and his family awoke before dawn to the sound of gunfire in the distance. He was shocked to discover that the soldiers of the Peshmerga had withdrawn without having fired a shot to defend the town. Although he owned a car, it could not accommodate his entire extended family. Packed into the small vehicle, several of his relatives fled, as did thousands of others, toward Mount Sinjar. Faisal decided to walk toward the mountain accompanied by twenty relatives, fourteen men and six women. As they approached the mountain, they were attacked by six ISIS fighters. Faisal was shot in the shoulder; his cousin, who was standing nearby, was wounded in the leg; and his nephew Sardar was killed. As Faisal sat on the ground in intense pain, the terrorists forced three men and six women toward their vehicles at gunpoint. The captives' hands were tied, and, as the women were pushed into their cars, the ISIS militants ordered one of their company, a twelve-year-old boy, to execute the three men. The child soldier complied, shooting each of the hostages in the head twice.

Faisal and his comrades walked several miles to a village near the mountain. They quietly entered the large home of the village leader and, to their surprise, found scores of prisoners being held in the house including the six women who had been savagely taken from their group. As there were only a few ISIS fighters guarding the villagers, there was a chance to escape. With the help of the village leader, the group, including the six women, was able to escape to the mountain. Once on Mount Sinjar, Faisal, along with thousands of others, suffered from the intense heat and lack of food and water. When asked about the American aid effort, he responded: "On Mount Sinjar people knew it was the United States that was dropping food and water to help them. People were saying America is coming to help us. Whenever people saw planes in the sky, they assumed they were American. People said if America won't help us no one will." Faisal heard explosions in the distance and assumed they were bombs that were being dropped by U.S. warplanes on ISIS positions.

He also expressed his gratitude toward the YPG that broke through to the Yazidis on the mountain. He stressed the fact that it was the Syrian Kurds, rather than the Syrian or Iraqi governments, who helped the desperate Yazidis along the evacuation route by providing security and provisions.

Faisal was fortunate in that his brother had worked as a translator for the U.S. military. As a result, on October 21, 2015, he and his family were permitted to immigrate to the United States. He reflected: "Before 2014 relations between Yazidis and their Arab neighbors were good, people visited each other's houses. Once ISIS came, many Arabs joined them and killed Yazidis they knew. Arabs who lived nearby even helped to identify those who were Yazidis to foreign ISIS fighters. Why were they so brutal? Because they were religious fanatics."[1]

Ahmed M.

Ahmed is a tall man with an easygoing, pleasant personality. He hails from the town of Hanisor near Sinjar, and though he misses Iraq, he lamented that even prior to the events of 2014 there was widespread religious prejudice within Iraqi society. He stated: "For example Yazidis and Christians were not allowed to become judges or pilots in the air force." Before the ISIS attack forced him from his home, he had worked as a translator for the U.S. military. Fearing Arab reprisals for taking such a job, he only informed fellow Yazidis that he worked with the Americans. From 2008 to 2016 he taught English as a second language. He posed the question that Yazidis have asked since 2014: "Why did ISIS attack us [when] we did nothing to them?" The answer, of course, is that religious extremists thrive on hate and must have scapegoats on whom to focus their anger.

Ahmed pointed out that in Iraq identity papers include a person's religion, so ISIS fanatics had no problem identifying Yazidis, Christians, and Shia Muslims. Even if people were captured with no papers, they could often be categorized based on their clothing or first names. In addition to Yazidis, thousands of Christians and Shias fled to Kurdistan following the ISIS invasion. He stated that while Christian and Shia women were also robbed and terrorized, they were not enslaved. Today there are some three thousand Yazidi women and children still missing, and every month one or two almost miraculously return from captivity.

Ahmed is still incredibly disappointed that the Peshmerga did not stand and fight ISIS after vowing to protect the Yazidi people. By the time Mosul fell in June everyone knew what ISIS was and that their next target would be Sinjar. The information had spread rapidly on social media, especially Facebook, and on television. Once the Kurdish militia departed, the Yazidis were left to defend themselves. Ahmed explained that their resistance was not organized and therefore could not be especially effective. "Some Yazidis had AK-47s and pistols for defense. Some men had been in the army or Peshmerga and had kept their weapons. The Iraqi army was too far to the south to help stop the ISIS attacks." Once Yazidi men were taken prisoner, they were given a choice to convert or die. When speaking of the militants' idea of converting Yazidis, he said, "ISIS members believed if you force a person to convert you get more of a reward from God than if you just kill someone. But the convert does not matter, he or she can then be killed."

Ahmed was lucky in that he was forewarned and had time to escape before the terrorists arrived. He and his family raced north into Kurdistan. Like others who fled, Ahmed had little time to gather any possessions. He stated: "Friends from the south called and told me to run. I took just some money in my pocket, some water and the clothes on my back. We lived in Zakho camp, which was run by the UN and the Kurdistan Regional Government. We were six people in a small tent, 25,000 in the camp, and it is still there today." While Ahmed avoided being trapped on Mount Sinjar, his uncle and his family were forced to remain there for 10 days. Referring to the American action to free Yazidis on the mountain, Ahmed commented: "President Obama did a great job by using airstrikes against ISIS." Other family members also had to face the terrorist army. He related: "My aunt's family tried to reach the mountain but were stopped by ISIS fighters. My aunt's son, my cousin, was killed, and my other uncle was taken away—also probably killed. My aunt's three daughters were kidnapped. They did not return for a year; the three girls were ransomed at different times. My aunt paid a total of $26,000." After the Americans withdrew in 2011, Ahmed feared for his life; in 2016 he was able to immigrate to the United States.[2]

Omar R.

This distinguished looking, older gentleman, who bears a strong resemblance to the actor Sam Elliott, arrived in the United States in 1998. Long before the rise of ISIS, Yazidis faced discrimination in Iraq. Omar came to the United States in order to escape the abusive treatment meted out to Yazidis by Saddam Hussein's regime. He stated: "Life under Saddam Hussein was very harsh. There were no freedoms, no freedom of religion or speech, people could only make positive remarks about Saddam." The dictator officially renamed Yazidi towns from their original Kurdish names to new Arabic designations. The government changed Yazidis' ethnic group from Kurdish to Arab (although Yazidi continued to be listed as the religion on identity papers).

In schools Arabic rather than Kurdish was spoken and taught until Saddam was driven from power. In addition, the officials who were sent from Baghdad to oversee these changes were notoriously corrupt. Most attempted to enrich themselves at the expense of the local communities. Saddam even considered dispersing the Yazidi people, which would have denied them access to their sacred sites and degraded their religious identity. Omar explained: "The regime even created a plan in 1975 to relocate Yazidis from their historic homeland in the north to the south of Iraq; fortunately, it was abandoned as the government turned its attention to fighting the Iran-Iraq war in 1980."[3]

Mesur H.

Mesur came from Hanisor, the same town as Ahmed M., and, like his friend, he too escaped with his family as the militants approached. They stayed one step ahead of the terrorists: "My family and I fled to Zakho near Duhok [Kurdistan] in a small car. We lived in an incomplete building, then moved to a refugee camp. Life in the camp was hard: there was no electricity for 24 hours at a time, not enough water, and no regular meals. The UN and local Kurdish groups did what they could in the beginning, but they were overwhelmed." In 2016 Mesur was able to immigrate to the United States, but due to the catastrophic events of the summer of 2014 his family was scattered and living in several countries. He elaborated: "The most difficult part of this experience has been family separation. My mother, father, two sisters and two brothers are still in Iraqi Kurdistan. I have a sister and brother that went to Germany and myself, my wife, and children are here in the U.S." Mesur is especially grateful to Germany for accepting Yazidi refugees. Tens of thousands made the difficult journey to Europe to find a safe country in which to live. He stated: "Many people paid smugglers to guide them from Greece to countries farther north, fortunately after they arrived in Germany they were allowed to apply for political asylum."[4]

Falah R.

Falah came from Khana Sor near Sinjar City. He had been a translator for the U.S. Army for a year; his brother Faisir had worked in that same capacity for five years. In 2008 Islamic extremists detonated a car bomb.

ISIS and the Yazidis

The tremendous explosion killed Faisir and injured three American soldiers. Falah's brother, who was doing his part to make Iraq a safer place, was only 26 years old when he died. Falah pointed out, as have so many of his religious brethren, that when ISIS attacked Sinjar the local Arabs, who until then had been good neighbors to the Yazidi, suddenly turned on them and collaborated with the terrorists. He could not say what caused such a change in attitude. Perhaps it was fear of the well-armed force of religious fanatics, a newly found greed for Yazidi land and valuables they might acquire, or both. Falah and his family quickly moved north and found safety in Kurdistan. He said: "I did hear that the U.S. was dropping food and water to the people on the mountain. The attitude was no one will help us except the Americans. The image of the U.S.A. for minority groups in the Middle East is that it will help us." Falah thought for a moment and commented: "I also heard that ISIS members north of the mountain were afraid the U.S. military would come to help the Yazidis on the mountain, so they withdrew to the south. They were afraid of American air power. As a Yazidi I thank the U.S. for helping at that time." He proceeded to relate how friends stranded on the mountain sent him photos via cell phone that he forwarded to the United Nations High Commissioner for Refugees (UNHCR), hoping it would act immediately. He is incredibly grateful to the YPG for fighting ISIS on the ground: "The YPG attacked ISIS and helped the people get off the mountain. The Peshmerga helped too, but I would say it was 60% YPG and 40% Peshmerga." Falah found his way to the United States in 2016 along with his mother, sister, and brother.[5]

Amel H.

Amel is an intelligent, attractive young woman in her early twenties. She speaks English fluently with no hint of an accent even though she has only been in the United States a few years. As she told her story of narrowly escaping the terrorists, pain and sadness were etched on her face. She began: "I was 17 years old when ISIS came to my town of Khana Sor near Sinjar City. My parents were up all night frightened about what might happen." Like so many others, she and her family left with only the clothes they were wearing. Amel's extended family consisted of her mother, father, three brothers, two sisters, five cousins, an aunt, and her family. Packed tightly into several cars, they drove toward Kurdistan. Although they decided to bypass Mount Sinjar, the family passed thousands who were moving in that direction, many in vehicles and some on foot.

4. Yazidi Stories of Survival and the War Against ISIS

Tears began to fill her eyes as Amel described the traumatic moments their convoy was attacked. From a distance ISIS fighters began firing semi-automatic weapons at their cars; her cousin was shot, but, fortunately, he survived. There was a great sense of relief once they reached Kurdistan. She stated: "We went to Zakho. I do not hate all Muslims; some are good people and helped Yazidis in Zakho. They gave food and shelter to my family and many others." Amel echoed what others have said about good relations between the Yazidis and their neighbors, but she was shocked that so many Arabs sided with ISIS: "It felt like you were being killed by your own family. The Arabs could have run away like the Yazidis, and we saw some that did."

As more Yazidis arrived in the Duhok area, authorities began placing them temporarily in schools and other public buildings. Over the next few months people were transferred to hastily erected refugee camps. Life in the camps was challenging. Amel noted: "Since there were eight in my [immediate] family we got two tents. There was no electricity and no water in the tents. We had a gas stove but there was not much gas available. My dad was a teacher but there were no jobs in the camp. Aid organizations gave each family $100 a month which was not much." To make matters worse, corruption was rampant among the Peshmerga soldiers who guarded the camp. Amel elaborated: "Sometimes people would send money and clothes into the camp; the Peshmerga would steal it. They would take new clothes and replace them with old used clothes. The guards got rich, some even bought new cars for themselves."

Amel continues to have the utmost respect and admiration for the YPG. She remembered: "The Peshmerga said we will fight ISIS to the last drop of blood, and then they ran away. The YPG did all the fighting and saved the people on the mountain. They also saved many Yazidi women who had been kidnapped." The family spent two years in the refugee camp. Since Amel's father had worked as a translator for the U.S. Army years earlier, the immediate family was allowed to immigrate to the United States. The assumption was that a translator—or anyone who aided the American effort in Iraq—was at greater risk of retaliation by Islamic extremists than other Iraqis. Although Amel has settled into American life well, she is saddened by the fact that her family is not living together. She lamented: "My family is separated: my older brother and his family are still in Iraq, some family members are in Germany and some in France. My uncle spoke out against President Barzani [of Kurdistan] and criticized the Peshmerga for running away from ISIS, so he had to go to Germany, or he would have been put in jail. I still love Iraq, but would not go back. I would not feel safe there. I wish my whole family could come to this country." Amel knows the value of education. When asked what she intends to do with her life, she responded: "I am studying pre-med. I saw many sick children in the camp, and I would like to become a pediatrician. I want to work with an organization such as Doctors Without Borders and help people that are in similar situations to that which I went through."[6]

Shahab B.

Shahab is a friendly, wise, affable man. He comes from the town of Borek north of Sinjar City. Prior to 2014 Borek was a peaceful town of some twenty thousand people located five miles north of Mount Sinjar and 10 miles from the Syrian border. Shahab taught biology and English. He and his wife, Hanaa, had welcomed a baby daughter only one month before the ISIS onslaught. He first heard about ISIS from television reports and friends in the Iraqi military. Shahab, like Amel, reiterated the fact that Yazidis enjoyed good relations with their Arab neighbors prior to the arrival of ISIS. His teachers were Muslims and treated all their students equally. Once the terrorist army was on the move, however, everything changed. He related: "Many people joined ISIS because they were powerful. The Arabs shared information with ISIS fighters on how best to attack Yazidi villages and towns. Our own neighbors did this."

To this day Shahab is still outraged that the twelve thousand Peshmerga soldiers withdrew from their positions, leaving the Yazidis to face ISIS alone. He, like so many others, believes that Masoud Barzani, the president of Kurdistan at the time, made this decision in order to save his troops. When discussing the brutal ISIS attack of August 3, he said, "For us everything was gone in a minute. Today there are still about two hundred thousand Yazidis in 21 refugee camps in Kurdistan." He also expressed sympathy for others who had to flee the onslaught: "There were Christian villages nearby. In the 1890s when Christian Armenians were being massacred in Turkey some escaped to Sinjar and established towns here. They also had to run to escape ISIS."

Shahab slowly reeled off a list of atrocities committed against his people in the days after the initial ISIS victory: "They took women; many were given to ISIS fighters, and some were ransomed back to their families for up to $10,000. They took young boys to train them to be terrorists; they stole everything from Yazidi homes and then blew up the houses. When they occupied Sinjar City, they demanded to see people's I.D. cards. Yazidi

4. Yazidi Stories of Survival and the War Against ISIS

men were killed immediately." He pointed out that Shias in the city without identification could, and sometimes did, claim to be Sunnis in order to save their own lives. Although there were no Shia villages in the vicinity, members of this Islamic sect began to arrive in Sinjar City following Mosul's capture. Knowing the Shia were on the run from ISIS, in a sign of goodwill some Yazidis offered food and shelter to these Muslim refugees.

Shahab and his wife awoke at 2:00 a.m. on August 3 to what they assumed was a fire near the Syrian border; it turned out to be ISIS shellfire. Events moved rapidly that morning. At 6:00 a.m. panic-stricken people began to leave their homes and drive toward Kurdistan. Since his family had no car, he, his wife, baby daughter, uncle, and cousin walked south toward Mount Sinjar. People had received cell phone calls from friends informing them of ISIS massacres and were understandably frightened. He stated: "We heard that in the village of Herdad on the north side of the mountain all the men had been killed and the women taken away. In Arab towns north of Mount Sinjar Muslims who opposed ISIS fled to Kurdistan; those who remained joined the terrorists. In the Muslim village of Grezirka, for example, the people who stayed actually assisted ISIS fighters as they murdered Yazidis in the neighboring village of Duhola." Shahab described the situation on Mount Sinjar as extremely chaotic. The mountain teemed with tens of thousands of bewildered people unsure of what to do next. In addition, the refugees suffered from a variety of maladies including sun exposure, cuts, scrapes, and stings from scorpions.

On the second day from a high vantage point Shahab viewed a chilling sight. Using binoculars he saw seven cars flying the black flags of ISIS. On the fourth day, running low on food and water, Shahab had no choice but to descend the mountain. He skillfully managed to avoid ISIS fighters and entered the village of Ossiva. He returned to the mountain with all the supplies he could carry. Fortunately, he was familiar with Mount Sinjar. He stated: "I was 31 years old at the time and had hiked on the mountain many times. I shared water with those that needed it most. A clearly exhausted woman with a baby at her breast begged me for water. I also gave water to a man along the way that had not eaten in days." About the armed struggle against ISIS, Shahab said: "We knew the YPG was fighting ISIS to the west. On the sixth day I saw war planes attack an ISIS convoy, and from a distance I saw an explosion. But I did not know at the time if they were American planes attacking the terrorists." He continued: "Hanaa and I knew that if we did not get out, our baby daughter would die. We walked for 10 hours looking for a safe corridor. There were 50 other people also trying to escape." After a long trek they eventually found their way to Kurdistan. Having arrived in a relatively safe area, Shahab continued his career as an educator. He stated with pride: "In 2016 I opened an elementary school in Kurdistan. I was the principal, and seven hundred Yazidi students attended the school. A year later I got a call that my U.S. visa had been approved and my family and I came to America."[7]

"What do you like best about living in the United States?" was a question asked separately to each person. The answers were almost identical. The Yazidis responded with statements such as "the freedoms that citizens enjoy here" and "the freedom and security that exists here." Too often Americans and Europeans take for granted the liberties that are the fundamental components of Western democracy. It is well to remember that millions of people around the world are denied such rights. In his 1941 State of the Union address President Franklin D. Roosevelt articulated four freedoms that he believed people everywhere had a right to enjoy: freedom of speech, freedom of worship, freedom from want, and freedom from fear. The last ideal on the president's list was expressed most eloquently by Amel H. when she stated that she had felt afraid in Iraq since she was seven years old, but when she arrived in the United States, she felt a sense of safety she had never known before.

The Coalition's Counterattack Against ISIS

In a few cases, Yazidi men fought ISIS militants as best they could. Since their first priority was to protect their families, standing their ground was clearly not the best strategy to accomplish this goal. One must keep in mind that not all Yazidi men possessed weapons or had military training at the time of the attack. Pitted as they were against well-armed religious fanatics, the choice to flee was the right decision in order to save the lives of those they loved. Nonetheless, a few chose to stand and fight. Men in the village of Tal Qasab did what they could to resist the terrorists.

Mohsen Elias told Amnesty International that after the Peshmerga departed in the early morning of August 3 the Yazidis tried to defend themselves. He recounted: "Me and many other men from the village took our weapons—most of us had Kalashnikovs for the protection of our families—and clashed with IS [ISIS] militants. At about 7 or 8 a.m. we ran out of ammunition and ran toward the mountain. We stopped at the village of Qiniyeh, near the foot of the mountain. We were about 90 men and youths, and with us were more than one hundred women and children from our

4. Yazidi Stories of Survival and the War Against ISIS

families."[8] Knowing they would be executed if ISIS fighters found them armed, the men buried their weapons, which were useless anyway since they had exhausted their supply of ammunition. As some 20 ISIS vehicles closed in, they prepared for the worst. Mohsen continued:

> They split us into two groups, men and boys of 12 and older in one group and women and younger children in another group. They started to load the women and children into their vehicles and made us [men and boys] walk to the nearby wadi [a dry creek bed]. The youngest of the group was my brother Nusrat, 12 years old. We were made to squat by the edge of the wadi.... They told us to convert to Islam and we refused.
>
> One grabbed me by my shirt from behind and pulled me up and tried to shoot me but his weapon did not fire. My brother Nusrat was scared and crying. They opened fire from behind us. I fell into the wadi and was not injured.... Nusrat was right next to me and was killed. My father, Elias, and my four brothers, Faysal, Ma'amun, Sa'id, and Sofian were all killed. Most of the other men and boys were also killed. After the ISIS men left, I waited then ran away to the mountain. I only know four others who survived.[9]

Unlike the Yazidi civilians, the international forces of the coalition that were being assembled had the wherewithal and training to effectively confront the terrorist army. On the ground, however, it was a different story. Many Iraqi soldiers lacked the motivation and unit cohesion necessary to defeat this new enemy. Although the Peshmerga had reorganized and counterattacked, the Iraqi army had to address several internal issues before it could become an effective fighting force.

The first American special operations soldiers were deployed by CENTCOM to Iraq on June 22, less than two weeks after ISIS had captured the city of Mosul. What they found at the upper echelons was a disorganized and disheartened Iraqi military. Upon his arrival in Baghdad, U.S. Major General Dana Pittard described his first encounter with the Iraqi generals charged with the defense of their nation. He was not encouraged by what he found. He stated:

> I met with the prominent members of the senior Iraqi military leadership. They seemed to be lacking in confidence. Most of the Iraqi generals could not even look me in the eye. Worse, Iraqi senior military leadership was focused mostly on tactical engagements and responding to constant inquiries from Prime Minister Maliki's office rather than strategic or operational aspects they should have been concentrating on.
>
> ISIS seemed unstoppable to them. Only one Iraqi general seemed to have confidence.... General Kenani commanded the elite U.S. Special Forces-trained Counter Terrorism Service (CTS). The CTS was one of the few Iraqi Security Forces units that did not retreat from ISIS—they stood and

ISIS and the Yazidis

fought.... Kenani quietly looked me in the eye and said, "With your help, we are going to beat Daesh! [ISIS]"[10]

The fact that most Iraqi troops were dispirited was understandable since soon after the fall of Mosul, ISIS also took the cities of Tikrit, Ramadi, Samarra, and Fallujah. New military equipment had to be supplied and morale had to be rebuilt. It had already been decided for political reasons that the United States would not reengage in Iraq with a massive military effort on the ground but would instead use a "light footprint strategy" to confront this new threat. Accordingly, the mission of the relatively few American troops deployed was to accompany, advise, and assist Iraqi and Kurdish security forces as they went into action against the jihadis. This policy would also show the Iraqi public that its government was capable of defending its territorial sovereignty and ensuring the safety of its citizens. To that end, in early 2015 some thirteen hundred paratroopers of the 82nd Airborne Division were deployed to train and equip five Iraqi army brigades to spearhead the counterattack against ISIS.

The light footprint strategy consisted of several components, each designed to weaken the enemy. It included attacking ISIS command centers and other high value targets in Iraq and Syria, supporting Iraqi army operations with close air support, and disrupting ISIS's financial networks to reduce the organization's cash income.[11]

At the height of its power ISIS controlled approximately one hundred thousand square kilometers (sixty-two thousand square miles) of territory in Syria and Iraq. The members of the international coalition were determined to reclaim it and liberate those who lived under its draconian rule. The air campaign not only played a vital role in recapturing land but also bought time for the Iraqi army to train and prepare for battle. Between autumn 2014 and winter 2016 coalition forces launched some seventeen thousand airstrikes against 31,900 ISIS targets. These well-coordinated attacks resulted in the deaths of approximately twenty-three thousand ISIS militants.[12]

Although it was a slow and bloody process, eventually the Iraqi cities occupied by ISIS were retaken. Ramadi was liberated in March 2016, Fallujah three months later, and Mosul was back in Iraqi hands by July 2017. This monumental effort called for ground forces to coordinate their efforts, which was not always easy given the mutual suspicion and often hostility that existed between the Iraqi army and the Peshmerga. While Shia militias also aided in the struggle, they had their own agenda and were not fully trusted by the coalition's military leadership. When describing the

4. Yazidi Stories of Survival and the War Against ISIS

various groups opposing ISIS, General Pittard colorfully stated: "Working with the anti–ISIS coalition was like herding cats—wildly cunning feral cats that clawed each other even as they fought a mutual enemy. A contentious coalition of Iraqi Security Forces, Kurdish Peshmerga, Shia militias, Syrian Kurds, Iraqi Sunni tribes, and even Syrian Army troops. On top of that, other anti–ISIS forces included our foes Iran and Russia."[13]

As for retaking the preeminent Yazidi city of Sinjar, it proved to be a difficult, drawn-out task. It was a challenging operation since ISIS fighters had been fortifying their positions in the year and a half since they had captured the city. The coalition's first step was to launch airstrikes against terrorist positions in and around the city in preparation for a ground assault. The raids began in late 2014 but were not as effective as coalition leaders had hoped since ISIS members had constructed a series of underground tunnels that connected houses within Sinjar. In April 2016, the U.S. Army released a Threat Action Report that detailed the campaign to liberate Sinjar. With regard to the subterranean passageways it stated: "These tunnels provided protection for fighters and served as a means of subterranean command and control. The sandbagged tunnels, about the height of a person, contained ammunition, prescription drugs, blankets, electric wires leading to fans and lights, and other supplies. In total, there were at least 30–40 tunnels."[14]

The coalition's offensive to liberate Sinjar began at dawn on November 5, 2015, with airstrikes that targeted ISIS positions in the city. The Kurdish ground forces, after having launched several rocket barrages, moved south into the city's outskirts. Kurdish military units included the PKK, YPG, Peshmerga, and the YBS Yazidi militia. Progress was slow, as urban warfare often favors the defenders. The fighting was particularly fierce since many of the fanatical defenders proved willing to fight to the death. In addition, ISIS tactics included the use of snipers, roadside IEDs (improvised explosive devices), and suicide bombers, all of which hampered the Kurdish advance. ISIS snipers had a particular advantage since they had occupied the city for months and were well aware of the routes the Kurds would have to take upon entering the city. Expecting an attack, they emerged from their underground tunnels to positions that had been prepared in advance. As fighting in the city continued Peshmerga and PKK units advanced from the east and west, respectively, to cut off the ISIS supply route along highway 47 between Raqqa and Mosul.

On November 13, the last ISIS fighters were killed or captured, and the Kurdish forces declared victory. Even though the battle was over, the city was for the most part uninhabitable since approximately 80 percent

ISIS and the Yazidis

of its infrastructure had been destroyed or severely damaged.¹⁵ Even after ISIS fighters had been driven from the city, their presence was still felt. Scores of booby traps, laid by ISIS, remained scattered throughout Sinjar and would take several months to clear. Understandably people who had been forced to flee were eager to return home, but since the military situation was still fluid, it was too dangerous for Yazidi civilians to move back to their beloved city. Tragically, following the recapture of Sinjar, Kurdish soldiers began discovering mass graves. At least 29 such sites were found containing the bodies of Yazidi men who had refused to convert to Islam.

Shockingly, one mass grave on the edge of the city was found to contain the remains of 78 women between the ages of 40 and 80. According to a witness who later escaped, the terrorists only wanted to enslave younger women and teenagers. The others were shot to death.¹⁶ This was further evidence of the callous inhumanity of ISIS rule during the 15 months the group held sway over the city and its people. Such grim discoveries made Kurds even more determined to expel the invaders from Iraq. As the various Kurdish armies contributed to the fight, the coalition of nations that comprised Operation Inherent Resolve continued to make slow but steady progress against the Islamic State.

Retaking Sinjar and cutting ISIS supply lines to the east was the first step in isolating and eventually driving the terrorists out of Iraq's second largest city, Mosul. The battle for Mosul was a long, drawn-out affair that eventually took nine months to complete. The operation, code-named "We are coming, Nineveh," began with a series of coalition airstrikes in early October 2017. This essential first phase was conducted by British, French, Dutch, Australian, and American combat aircraft. On October 16 Iraqi army units attacked from the south while the Peshmerga advanced from the east clearing ISIS fighters from villages near the city. Although there were a few thousand Turkish troops in the area they played no major role in the upcoming battle. Iraqi Prime Minister Haider al-Abadi made his position abundantly clear to Turkish leader Recep Tayyip Erdoğan. While he appreciated Turkish participation in the coalition, their assistance in combat operations within Iraq would not be necessary. Iraqi government officials feared that once ISIS fighters had been cleared from the area the Turks might attack Kurdish units or even the Iraqi army. Al-Abadi knew he must deal with the Turks in order to defeat their common enemy; yet he resented the presence of even a small contingent of their soldiers on Iraqi soil.

On November 1, the Iraqi military began to move into the city. The

4. Yazidi Stories of Survival and the War Against ISIS

battle pitted some one hundred thousand Iraqi troops against approximately ten thousand ISIS extremists and saw some of the fiercest urban fighting since World War II. As in Sinjar City, ISIS militants had prepared elaborate defenses and in a despicable tactic also used civilians as human shields.

By late January 2017, the eastern half of the city was controlled by Iraqi troops. In mid–February, after consolidating its position, the Iraqi force launched an offensive to take western Mosul. Heavy fighting continued for months; victory was not achieved until July 20, 2017. In addition to combat casualties, tens of thousands of civilians were killed, wounded, or driven from their homes. These unfortunates had no alternative but to become refugees in order to escape the ongoing battle. It was a costly triumph, but tactical victories such as this helped restore Iraqi soldiers' sense of pride in themselves and confidence in their commanders.

Like Sinjar, much of the city, including the 850-year-old Great Mosque of al-Nuri (the location from which Abu Bakr al-Baghdadi had proclaimed his caliphate three years earlier) was in ruins. ISIS spokesmen claimed the landmark had been destroyed by U.S. airstrikes, but, according to Iraqi military officers, it was ISIS militants who had detonated explosives within the mosque in order to prevent its recapture. Fortunately, the world has not lost this important cultural monument forever. In 2018 the government of the United Arab Emirates (UAE) pledged $50 million to reconstruct the mosque. It is a joint project between that Persian Gulf nation, the Iraqi ministry of culture, and UNESCO (United Nations Educational, Scientific and Cultural Organization). The project is expected to be completed by 2023.

Weapons of a Brutal War

As the battle for Mosul intensified the coalition's air component was essential in achieving victory. From the first strikes on ISIS targets near Erbil and Mount Sinjar the United States and its allies had effectively relied upon aircraft to inflict massive losses on the militants. In June 2017 alone, 4,448 bombs were dropped on terrorist positions.[17] Under the extremely difficult conditions of urban warfare around Mosul pilots did their best to avoid civilian casualties. The U.S. Air Force released a statement: "Despite the dense urban terrain, trapped civilians and barbaric ISIS tactics using civilians as human shields, air planners and aircrews went to incredible lengths to minimize harm to civilians, to include ensuring that every

ISIS and the Yazidis

munition delivered was precision-guided and coordinated closely with Coalition advisors and ISF [Iraqi Security Forces]."[18]

While most bombs and missiles were used in support of ground forces, the coalition also targeted car bomb factories and ISIS controlled oil production facilities. The destruction of wellheads, refineries, and storage sites severely limited the terrorists' capability to produce and sell oil, which led to a dramatic drop in revenue for the organization. The aircraft used in such raids were among the most advanced in the world, including fighters, bombers, and drones. While ISIS had no air force, it did possess Russian-made anti-aircraft shoulder-fired missiles, which were easily acquired on the international arms market. Coalition pilots had to be on constant guard against these deadly weapons. A decade earlier Chechen separatists had used them with lethal effect as they shot down several Russian helicopters in the early 2000s.

The British relied upon Eurofighter Typhoons and Tornado GR4 fighter jets armed with 2,000-pound Paveway laser-guided bombs, Storm Shadow cruise missiles, and 27-millimeter cannons. In August 2014, shortly after the United States bombed ISIS positions at the base of Mount Sinjar and the Yazidis had been evacuated, the British deployed Tornados to RAF base Akrotiri on the island of Cyprus. A reconnaissance mission was flown on September 29, and the following day two Tornados conducted the first British airstrikes against ISIS targets. Over the next few years these aircraft flew hundreds of missions from Akrotiri against ISIS positions in Syria and northwest Iraq. The French contribution to the international coalition was to attack targets using their Mirage fighters based in Jordan and the United Arab Emirates. In mid–February 2015 France deployed the aircraft carrier *Charles de Gaulle* to the Persian Gulf. This vessel carried a complement of nearly 40 fixed-wing fighters and helicopters. These included the Dassault Rafale fighter and the E-2c Hawkeye airborne early warning aircraft. In November of that year the carrier received orders to proceed to the eastern Mediterranean off the coast of Syria. This placed the ship and her war planes in a better position from which to reach ISIS occupied territory.

The U.S. Navy's arsenal included impressive fighter aircraft such as the F/A-18 Hornet and Super Hornet. The F/A-18 (C) is a one-man fighter, while the (D) version is manned by a pilot and a weapons systems officer. This fighter first saw combat in 1986 when it was used against Libyan air defenses. That year President Ronald Reagan authorized Operation El Dorado Canyon in retaliation for the bombing of a disco in West Berlin frequented by off-duty American soldiers. The flagrant attack had been

4. Yazidi Stories of Survival and the War Against ISIS

masterminded by Muammar Gaddafi's intelligence agents. The resulting explosion killed two U.S. servicemen and wounded 229 people. The F/A-18 Hornets and the slightly larger more advanced F/A-18 Super Hornets were armed with 500-pound bombs, 300-pound missiles, and 20-millimeter cannons.[19] For operations in Iraq the aircraft often carried AGM-65 E/F Maverick air-to-ground missiles or Paveway laser-guided bombs. The cruising speed of these formidable warplanes was up to 820 miles per hour, and the combat range extended to 1,250 miles. At times they were joined by EA-6B Prowlers. With a crew of four, this electronic warfare aircraft was capable of intercepting and jamming enemy radio frequencies. Once these signals were detected the fighter was able to destroy ISIS positions by launching its complement of AGM-88 HARM missiles.

U.S. Air Force pilots flew the iconic F-15 Eagle and F-16 Fighting Falcon (commonly referred to as "vipers" by pilots and crews). In the war against ISIS, F-15s first saw action on September 23, 2014, when a flight attacked an ISIS training compound and command and control facility. Even though the F-16 has been in service since 1978, this legendary fighter has constantly been modified and today carries a wide range of missiles and bombs. These include a 20-millimeter cannon and AIM-120 Advanced Medium-Range Air-to-Air Missiles (AMRAAM). The F-22A Raptor, equipped with stealth technology, was also deployed. The major advantage enjoyed by this aircraft is that it is extremely difficult for an enemy to detect and/or track it by radar.

Obviously, heavy bombers could not be used in operations involving urban warfare in which large numbers of non-combatants would be placed at risk. Civilians were often subject to danger either because they could not escape ISIS-occupied cities or were being held as human shields by the militants. However, bombers such as the B-1B Lancer were used to strike stationary targets as well as ISIS convoys in open country. The B-1 can launch long-range cruise missiles, hold up to 84 bombs, and stay aloft for up to 10 hours without refueling. When the B-1s were sent stateside for upgrades to their avionics, their role was assumed by the legendary B-52 Stratofortress. Six of the seemingly ageless bombers were deployed to Al Udeid Air Base in Qatar from 2016 to 2018 to support Operation Inherent Resolve. By February 2017, the strategic bombers had carried out 729 sorties against ISIS targets.[20] The multitudes of U.S. aircraft were kept aloft by a fleet of KC-135 Stratotankers also based at Al Udeid. The crews of these workhorses usually flew missions lasting seven hours as they transferred an average of fifty thousand gallons of aviation fuel to a variety of combat aircraft.

ISIS and the Yazidis

Remotely piloted aircraft (RPA) such as the MQ-1 Predator and the MQ-9 Reaper were also extensively used against the militants. The use of these military assets, commonly known as "drones," has steadily increasingly over the past two decades. As they are unmanned, there is no risk of a pilot losing his or her life in combat should the drone be destroyed by enemy groundfire. The men and women who operate these satellite-linked machines are often located in control centers hundreds or even thousands of miles away from the battlefront. Prior to launching an operation against al-Baghdadi's followers, drones were often used to carry out high altitude reconnaissance flights over enemy targets. The information gathered was then relayed to Kurdish and Iraqi ground forces. In addition to surveillance, the Predator could also, when fitted with two Hellfire missiles, provide close air support to friendly troops. The larger, more powerful Reaper accomplished the same task but was designed to fly twice the range of the Predator and could carry a payload of thirty-eight hundred pounds, including both bombs and missiles.

On the ground the combatants arrayed against ISIS carried arms similar to those possessed by the terrorists. Both sides were armed with AK-47 assault rifles. In the first years of the conflict ISIS fighters often captured large stockpiles of arms from Iraqi and Syrian soldiers and police. Weapons such as RPGs and .50-caliber Browning heavy machine guns could also be easily purchased on the black market. Militants used the latter to great effect by mounting them in the beds of pickup trucks.

As vital as weapons are, an army's fighting spirit is equally important. An American soldier deployed early in the war remembered: "ISIS was a brutal enemy, and inhumane to the core. They needed to be obliterated beyond all trace. But the terrorist army seemed fearless. Even as we hit them with airstrikes again and again, they quite literally fought to the last man." He added: "ISIS was nothing if not zealous and aggressive.... Of course we'd later learn a contributing factor was that they gave their fighters opiates and cocaine before battles and threatened punishment or torture for failure or cowardice. Religious extremism coupled with mind-altering drugs and fear of torture was certainly a way to create a seemingly indomitable force."[21] This fanaticism coupled with vast quantities of arms made ISIS a terrifying foe. In June 2014 when five Iraqi army divisions broke and ran before the ISIS onslaught, the extremists captured heavy weapons that would soon be turned against coalition troops. Included in the tally were 52 155-millimeter M198 Howitzers with a range of 20 miles and fifteen hundred U.S.-made Humvees.[22] In the first few months of the war al-Baghdadi's men added twenty-five hundred armored vehicles and some two hundred tanks to their force. In Syria they were equally successful, taking an additional one hundred tanks (mostly Russian T-55s), self-propelled artillery, and 70 Soviet-made tracked infantry fighting vehicles.[23]

Many Western military experts predicted that ISIS did not have people with the technical skills needed to operate, maintain, and repair such high-tech weapons of war. ISIS leaders, however, were well aware of their limitations. To that end they made a concerted effort to recruit foreign fighters and Iraqi and Syrian Army defectors who were mechanics or electrical engineers or had been assigned to tank crews. Most of these technicians were sent to a central repair facility in Wilayat al-Raqqa. More than 150 armored vehicles were repaired and/or upgraded at this location between July 2014 and its fall to Syrian Army troops in June 2017.[24]

Since the 1930s most conventional armies have created large, armored units in order to maximize the effectiveness of armored forces in battle. ISIS, however, tended to disperse its armor and use it as support for infantry, which was more reminiscent of the military tactics used in World War I. The failure to concentrate tanks and armored vehicles reduced their effectiveness and made them more susceptible to coalition attacks. Through attrition in battle, losses to allied airstrikes, and mechanical breakdowns the number of tanks in working order began to decline. As ISIS eventually lost ground the terrorists employed another tactic that further depleted their dwindling number of armored vehicles. ISIS fighters began to convert these weapons into armored vehicle-borne improvised explosive devises (AVBIEDs) and launch them on suicide missions toward Kurdish or Iraqi army lines. On some occasions they reached coalition troops and the resulting explosions were catastrophic; on others they were stopped by anti-tank weapons. In both cases, of course, the vehicle itself was lost. By 2017 ISIS's armored vehicles were completely destroyed and played no further role in the war.

The Murder of Western Hostages

While terrorist acts have been all too common around the world for years, the number of such incidents grew dramatically with the founding of the Islamic State. As ISIS lost territory to coalition forces its leaders launched attacks in Europe to show the world that it was still a powerful entity and could lash out at its enemies worldwide. ISIS militants themselves were responsible for some of these deadly assaults, while others were

ISIS and the Yazidis

carried out by people who were inspired by, and pledged loyalty to, the terrorist group. Today, through the internet, millions of people around the globe have easy access to websites and chat rooms that are filled with positive and altruistic ideas and information. Unfortunately the same is true of racist, xenophobic, and hate-filled material such as that disseminated by ISIS. It did not take long for those militants adept at using technology to spread their malicious philosophy online in order to win over new adherents.

The first major ISIS attack against a European nation occurred on November 13, 2015, in Paris, France. Islamic extremists armed with AK-47s and suicide vests launched coordinated assaults on six different locations around the city. By the time police regained control of the situation 130 people were dead and hundreds injured. ISIS claimed the massacre was in response to French participation in the international coalition. Rather than withdraw from the war, within days France increased its bombing raids against the caliphate. It began with a large force of 12 French aircraft that struck an ISIS command and control center, a weapons depot, and a training camp in Raqqa. Sadly, the air raids did nothing to dissuade ISIS members and sympathizers, who continued to indiscriminately kill civilians.

Extremists inspired by ISIS have also struck in North America. On October 20, 2014, in Montréal, Québec, a man hit two soldiers with his car, killing one. Less than a week later, in the Canadian capital, Ottawa, another terrorist killed a soldier standing guard at the National War Memorial. The perpetrator then attempted to attack Parliament Hill, where he was shot to death by police. The following year in the United States a married couple from San Bernardino, California, shot 14 people to death before they too were killed by police. In June 2016, a man who pledged his loyalty to ISIS murdered 49 people and wounded 53 at the Pulse nightclub in Orlando, Florida. Between January 2015 and March 2016 alone, 84 ISIS-coordinated or inspired attacks occurred worldwide, costing the lives of more than one thousand people.[25] By 2021 the number of violent ISIS assaults had nearly doubled, resulting in death or injury to thousands of innocent people.

Those Americans and Europeans within reach of al-Baghdadi's fighters in the Middle East were also in peril. People who had gone to Syria either as journalists to cover the ongoing civil war or as international aid workers seeking to help refugees were targeted. Regardless of their motivations for being in the country, the militants viewed them as interlopers, pawns to be kidnapped, used for political propaganda, and ultimately

4. Yazidi Stories of Survival and the War Against ISIS

murdered. They were seen as foreigners, Christians, symbols of the West who had no rights under their brand of Sharia law. Although some of the hostages were ransomed back to their home countries, most were forced to endure months or even years of captivity only to be murdered in a most gruesome way. The terrorists sought to shock the world and so chose decapitation as the manner of execution. In many cases a video was shot of the event and then posted online.

Americans abducted in Syria included journalists James Foley, who was reporting on the civil war when he was kidnapped in November 2012, and Steven Sotloff, taken near Aleppo in August of the next year. Other hostages were international humanitarian aid workers helping to ease the suffering of civilians caught in the civil war. Peter Kassig, a former U.S. Army Ranger, had served in Iraq in 2007. Following his discharge from the Army he devoted his time to humanitarian efforts in Syria and Lebanon. Kassig was taken captive while travelling to Deir ez-Zor, Syria to deliver supplies of food and medicine. Kayla Mueller was captured in August 2013 after leaving a Doctors Without Borders hospital in Aleppo. ISIS also held two British subjects, David Haines and Alan Hemming, both of whom had been kidnapped in 2013.

Some countries paid enormous ransoms for the safe return of their citizens, however the United States and Great Britain refused to discuss the matter with ISIS representatives. It was the policy of both governments not to negotiate with terrorist organizations. The logic behind this position, although frustrating and heartbreaking to the families of those kidnapped, was sound. To acquiesce to such demands would not only provide funds, which ISIS could devote to its war effort, but would also encourage the group to abduct more innocent people.

The FBI and MI5 (British intelligence) conducted multiple interviews with the few hostages who had been ransomed in order to glean from them any information that might aid in the recovery of their citizens. The tactic yielded valuable information. The two agencies learned that numerous hostages were being held at an abandoned oil refinery near Raqqa. This news was passed along to the U.S. military, and a raid to rescue the prisoners was planned. The mission was carried out on July 4, 2014, by some two-dozen Delta Force soldiers and Navy Seals in four Black Hawk helicopters. Sadly, when the special operations soldiers arrived, they found the facility empty. They discovered evidence that the hostages had been held there recently including writings on a cell wall and some hair that was thought to be that of Kayla Mueller.[26] It is believed that the captives had been moved only 24 to 48 hours earlier. While on the ground a firefight

ISIS and the Yazidis

erupted in which between five and eight ISIS fighters were killed. One American was wounded.

In early August 2014, in addition to having occupied the city of Mosul, ISIS terrorists were also in possession of Mosul Dam. Situated on the Tigris River, it is the largest and most important structure of its kind in Iraq. American, Iraqi, and Kurdish leaders feared that the extremists might cut off the power generated by the dam to the surrounding communities. An even worse scenario saw them destroying the dam, which would have had devastating consequences for the people downstream. The release of such a huge torrent of water would surely have killed thousands. After some reservations, the Iraqi army and Peshmerga agreed to work together in a joint effort to retake the complex. After several days of fighting, on August 17, the offensive succeeded, and the dam was reclaimed.

Two days later, in retaliation for this defeat, and to divert the world's attention, the religious fanatics beheaded James Foley. A video of the horrendous murder was made and posted online. This was the beginning of a pattern in which a hostage was murdered whenever ISIS suffered a military defeat.[27] In early September 2014, Steven Sotloff was killed in the same grisly manner following the Iraqi army's retaking of Amerli. Later that month David Haines was also murdered after coalition forces recaptured Haditha.

Like the Western hostages, any coalition soldiers unfortunate enough to fall into the hands of ISIS could expect no mercy. In mid-November, the terrorists beheaded Peter Kassig. While the camera cut away before the actual beheading, the video, which was subsequently posted online, showed the terrorists cutting the throats of more than a dozen captured Syrian soldiers. Perhaps the grisliest murder was that of Jordanian pilot Muath al-Kasasbeh. The F-16 pilot was captured on December 24, 2014, when his aircraft crashed near Raqqa. In exchange for his release ISIS demanded the Jordanian government turn over Sajida al-Rishawi, a woman convicted of possessing explosives and planning a terrorist act. Al-Rishawi had been involved in the 2005 Amman bombings in which Islamic extremists targeted three hotels popular among Western visitors. The resulting explosions killed 60 people and injured more than 150. Al-Rishawi's suicide vest failed to detonate, and she was put on trial, convicted, and sentenced to death. Negotiations broke down, however, and an ISIS video released on February 3, 2015, showed the pilot being burned to death while locked in a metal cage. It is believed he had been immolated a month earlier. A furious King Abdullah of Jordan ordered al-Rishawi to be

4. Yazidi Stories of Survival and the War Against ISIS

immediately hanged, and a new round of airstrikes launched. The attack lasted three days and killed dozens of militants.

The treatment of Kayla Mueller by her captors was especially disturbing. The humanitarian aid worker from Arizona was tortured and raped multiple times over the course of a year and a half. According to two Yazidi girls who were imprisoned in a house with Mueller, Abu Bakr al-Baghdadi gave the young woman the choice of either becoming his fourth wife or being beheaded.[28] Although she chose the former, the forced marriage did nothing to alter her status as a captive. The other women prisoners sympathized with her plight and viewed her as an older sister. They were especially impressed by her courage and compassionate nature. The caliph was not above "sharing" her with one of his top lieutenants, Abu Sayyaf (his nom de guerre). Sayyaf was the ISIS emir for energy and antiquities. A female hostage named Amshe, herself forced to marry an ISIS commander, later reported that the men found Mueller especially desirable because of her fair skin and the fact that she was an American.[29] On February 6, 2015, ISIS released a statement stating that a female American captive had been killed in a Jordanian airstrike on Raqqa. The U.S. government rejected the claim. While the circumstances of her death remain unclear, Amshe, who survived her ordeal, stated her "husband" once proudly told her that Mueller had in fact been executed. Her body has not been found.

Three months after Kayla Mueller's murder, on the night of May 15, 2015, U.S. Army Delta Force soldiers mounted a cross-border raid on Abu Sayyaf's compound in Deir ez-Zor, Syria. The objective of the mission was to capture the ISIS leader and his wife. Umm Sayyaf (her nom de guerre) and her husband not only possessed information concerning ISIS operations, but were directly involved in the seizure and detention of hostages. The operation was partially successful. Abu Sayyaf refused to surrender and was killed, but his wife was captured, and a young Yazidi woman held as a slave by the couple was rescued.

General Joseph Votel commanded the Joint Special Operations Command (JSOC) from 2011 to 2014 and United States Central Command (CENTCOM) from 2016 to 2019. When asked about Western and Yazidi hostages held by ISIS, he responded, "We always paid attention to the hostage situation, but our principal goal was to defeat ISIS by taking away its territory. Our overall strategy was the same in Syria and Iraq, we fought to take away their terrain and physically destroy the Caliphate. To stop the atrocities ISIS was perpetuating we had to work with our allies in both countries."[30] In a wide-ranging interview the 40-year U.S. Army veteran expressed his views on waging war against ISIS:

ISIS and the Yazidis

We worked quite well with the Iraqi Army. After we left the country in 2011 their army deteriorated; it had become politicized. Three years later, in 2014, it had to be rebuilt, retrained, and rearmed. Many of our officers still had good personal relationships with Iraqi officers from before, so that also helped. We were there to help security forces retake their country. As for the Shia militias, there were no direct communications with the Shias. We were both fighting ISIS so we had to coexist in the same environment, but it was problematic because of our history with them in Iraq. The roles of our coalition partners were vital in achieving victory. They provided logistical support and reconnaissance flights; some provided close air support like France and Britain. The British sent advisors to train ground troops, and some countries provided funding. President Obama was also quite involved in the war. As we formed the plan, he wanted to know all about the timing and phases of the operation. He was engaged in what we were doing on the ground, and he understood the strategy quite well.[31]

As the ground war moved from Iraq into Syria General Votel commented that the battle to retake Mosul had clearly been a turning point in the struggle to weaken the Islamic State. He noted: "After the city was taken it became evident to the world that ISIS would be defeated in Iraq. In Syria, the battle of Kobanî was critical. We provided support to the YPG, but they won that battle."[32] The northern city of Kobanî, with its Kurdish majority, along with its surrounding environs was liberated in April 2015. The grueling battle lasted several months. Although the American military aided the effort in October 2014 by dropping weapons, ammunition, and medical supplies from C-130s to the Kurds, it was their ground forces that drove the terrorists out of Kobanî. Sadly, the city they entered lay in ruins as almost 70 percent of the metropolitan area had been destroyed.

In the battle for Kobanî, as in many other military engagements with ISIS, the women of the YPJ distinguished themselves. They clearly demonstrated, by their words and deeds, that they would not be intimidated by the Islamic fanatics. One senior commander speaking to her subordinate referenced the ordeals captured Yazidi women were experiencing at the hands of ISIS fighters. In a heartfelt comment she stated, "They would do the same to us. You must take revenge for the Yazidis and for all the women they have brutalized. Daesh [ISIS] thinks that you are useless, that you are nothing, that you have no value at all. Show them what you are capable of. Prove yourself in this battle. And remember that this fight is not just for you. It would be better to die with dignity here, today, than to become their slave."[33] The militants often attempted to intimidate the soldiers of the YPJ by tuning in to their radio channels and speaking directly to them. In one instance a jihadi threatened, "We are coming for you, and

4. Yazidi Stories of Survival and the War Against ISIS

we are going to take you as our slaves. We are going to rape each one of you and then we are going to kill you. Your families will see it all." A woman combatant brazenly responded in Arabic: "You talk about killing us. We are going to come and kill you first."[34]

In the months ahead the coalition faced new military and diplomatic challenges. Militarily, although ISIS had suffered defeats on the battlefield, it was still a potent enemy. Politically, the leaders of the alliance were forced to contend with a myriad of competing interests in Syria as that country was still embroiled in a bloody civil war. In addition to the Islamic State, which had carved out its own territory within that fractured nation, the alliance had to deal with both extremist and moderate Arab militias. Naturally, some of these local armies were more cooperative than others. The Kurdish YPG, with its proven fighting ability, was relied upon more than ever. Since the coalition's goal was to destroy ISIS rather than bring about regime change, it was decided that members would not directly engage the Syrian Army. That armed force, while trying to suppress a popular rebellion and keep a brutal dictator in power, also viewed ISIS as a serious threat and occasionally engaged the militants in skirmishes throughout the country. External forces were also at work as foreign powers sought to increase their influence within a divided Syria. Iran, Turkey, and Russia, although each favored the demise of ISIS, complicated the situation even further as they made their presence known by either aiding or opposing the dictatorship of Bashir al-Assad.

5

Fighting the Islamic State in the Chaos of Syria

As the roughly six thousand Yazidi women and children, so violently abducted in mid-2014, languished in ISIS captivity, coalition forces remained focused on destroying their oppressors. This task, however, was made all the more difficult by the rebellion that had sprung up in Syria even before the Islamic State had been established. It had begun in response to years of repression by Bashir al-Assad. The Syrian dictator assumed control of the state upon the death of his father Hafez al-Assad in 2000. Following in the footsteps of the elder al-Assad, his son tolerated no opposition to his rule.

The average Syrian who demonstrated in the streets in 2011 was inspired to a large degree by similar protests then sweeping North Africa and a handful of countries in the Middle East. The movement soon became known as the Arab Spring. Between 2010 and 2012 people held enormous rallies in Tunisia, Libya, Egypt, Yemen, and Bahrain. Their goals were laudable. The men and women who marched hoped to end authoritarian regimes that had long ruled their respective countries. These repressive governments were responsible for establishing kleptocracies, stifling free and fair elections, and perpetrating massive human rights violations. In place of these regimes average citizens sought to establish representative democracies. To no one's surprise the strongmen in power responded with all the state mechanisms of repression, and eventually the Arab Spring ground to a halt. Although no true democracies were created, the movement is credited with ousting several dictators from power. Among these were Zine el Abidine Ben Ali in Tunisia, Muammar Gaddafi in Libya, Egypt's Hosni Mubarak, and Ali Abdullah Saleh in Yemen.

In Damascus, Bashar al-Assad kept a close eye on developments abroad. While people were aware of and took heart from events occurring in other countries, the spark that ignited rebellion in Syria was the arrest of 15 schoolboys in the city of Daraa. They were detained for the crime

5. Fighting the Islamic State in the Chaos of Syria

of writing pro-democracy slogans on the walls of their school. Protests sprang up in the capital and rapidly spread throughout the country. As the momentum for change grew, chants and slogans aimed at al-Assad were heard: among the most popular was "it's your turn, doctor" (the title "doctor" referred to al-Assad's degree in ophthalmology).

In response to the unrest, Bashar al-Assad labeled all those who opposed him as either terrorists or agents of the United States, Saudi Arabia, or Israel. Demonstrators were met by a tremendous show of force on the part of riot police, the Army, and *shabiha* (militias loyal to the al-Assad government). Protesters who were arrested were quickly taken away to prison. The *Mukhābarāt* (the security service charged with quelling internal dissent) was especially active and feared by the population. According to Human Rights Watch, once in prison men and women were subjected to brutal interrogations. The methods used by the secret police to elicit confessions included electrocutions, acid burns, beatings, whippings, mock executions, and rape.[1]

As in Iraq, Syrian society is composed of both Sunnis and Shias. Sunnis are in the majority in Syria, however. They make up some 75 percent of the population, as opposed to the Shias who comprise just 13 percent. Bashar al-Assad and his clan belong to an offshoot of Shia Islam; they are Alawites. The Alawites, although a minority, have been in control of the government since the 1970s. Alawites and the majority of the country's Shias supported the regime either due to political patronage, or because they feared losing power to the Sunnis. Supporters of the regime, not to be outdone by the opposition, coined their own slogans; one of the most chilling was "Assad, or we burn the country."

The most fanatical and brutal of al-Assad's allies were the *Shabiha*. These gangs of thugs and petty criminals were paid by the government to fight on its behalf, and when atrocities were committed, naturally no one was punished. In 2012 a member of one of these militias proudly stated: "We love Assad because the government gave us all the power—if I wanted to take something, kill a person, or rape a girl I could."[2] On May 25, 2012, the *Shabiha* committed one of the worst crimes of the civil war in the town of Taldou in the Houla region of Homs. In order to disperse a crowd of demonstrators the army bombarded Taldou with tank shells and mortars for two hours. The paramilitaries then moved into the town along with the regular troops. They proceeded to go from house to house shooting or slitting the throats of 108 people, including 34 women and 49 children.[3] More than three hundred people were wounded in the vicious attacks. Although the government's position was that the civilians had been killed by fighters loyal to al-Qaeda, witnesses who spoke to human rights groups and Western reporters refuted that claim. One opposition activist interviewed by the BBC stated: "The *Shabiha* militias attacked the houses. They had no mercy. We took pictures of children under 10 years [old] their hands tied and shot at close range."[4] A subsequent UN investigation laid the blame for the massacre squarely at the feet of the al-Assad regime. In some cases atrocities such as this had the desired effect of terrifying people into inaction; in others they spurred thousands to join anti-government militias, both moderate and jihadist. By the autumn of 2015 the national government controlled only about one-third of the country.

The first military force to emerge from the protests to oppose al-Assad was the Free Syrian Army (FSA). Composed of former army officers and soldiers who had defected, its strategy was to conduct guerrilla warfare in the countryside and attack targets in the major cities, especially Damascus. While Turkey supplied its units with money and arms, the United States provided only non-lethal aid, fearing that heavy weapons could fall into the hands of jihadist groups. Although the FSA made some headway in the first few years of the rebellion, internal rivalries and a decentralized command structure hindered its military efforts to topple the regime.

As the Syrian government struggled to quell the uprising, its war effort was given a tremendous boost in September 2015 when the Russians intervened to support their ally. Once al-Assad requested Russian participation, Vladimir Putin was quick to agree. In the ongoing rivalry with the United States, Putin seized upon this opportunity not only to establish a presence in the Middle East but to reinforce the idea that his country was still a global power. Until Russia's invasion of the Ukraine on February 24, 2022, this deployment of military units was the largest of its kind since the fall of the Soviet Union. The Russians based their air force at Khmeimim Air Base southeast of the city of Latakia, and their naval personnel at the deep-water port of Tartus on the Mediterranean. In all some four thousand Russians arrived in Syria along with fighter jets, bombers, and attack helicopters. Fawaz Gerges, a professor of International Relations at the London School of Economics and Political Science, noted, "Mr. Putin's decision to intervene in Syria and shore up Mr. Assad with new fighter jets, military advisors and advanced weapons stopped the bleeding of the Syrian Army and allowed it to shift from defense to offense."[5]

American pilots flying sorties against the Islamic State were instructed to give a wide berth to their Russian counterparts. The U.S. military was careful not to provoke an incident that could escalate tensions between the two powers to a dangerous level. In theory, since Putin

5. Fighting the Islamic State in the Chaos of Syria

had pledged to help destroy the Islamic State (even though Russia was not part of the international coalition), Russian servicemen were there to help defeat ISIS. In reality, since their true purpose was to prop up Assad's government, they, like the Syrian regulars, primarily attacked moderate opposition forces rather than Islamic State targets. Unfortunately, the rules of engagement for the Russian Air Force were far less stringent than those adhered to by coalition pilots; as a result civilian casualties quickly mounted. As an experienced American JTAC (joint terminal attack controller) observed: "Russia demonstrated incredible recklessness and brutality against the Syrian populace with their airstrikes. We knew Russia did not possess the advanced targeting systems or experience comparable to the U.S. to carry out the kind of precision strikes we routinely accomplish. Even so, their air campaign reeked of cruelty, targeting incompetence, and an utter disregard for humanity."[6]

In 2015 the international news organization Reuters reported that almost 80 percent of targets attacked by Russian aircraft were located in areas outside of the Islamic State.[7] While some strikes were aimed at al-Qaeda affiliated militias, the majority were launched against anti-Assad groups, including those supported by the United States. Rather than directing their firepower at ISIS, most Russian sorties were flown in support of government offensives in the provinces of Idlib and Homs. The Syrian Observatory for Human Rights, a UK-based monitoring group, announced that, in just the first three weeks of October 2015, Russia's bombing campaign had killed 370 people, 123 of whom were civilians.[8]

The powerful documentary *For Sama* dramatically illustrates the fear and trauma the average citizen experienced during the civil war in Syria. Produced and narrated by Waad al Kateab, the young woman recounts her experiences living through the siege and shelling of the rebel-held city of Aleppo. Kateab, a journalist, and her husband, Hamza, one of the few remaining doctors in the city, must decide whether to abandon their home and leave the country for the sake of their baby daughter, Sama. As a doctor, Hamza feels he must stay and do what he can to aid wounded civilians, all the while knowing his first responsibility is to protect his family. Especially noteworthy are the deliberate attacks mounted by regime and Russian aircraft upon non-military targets, particularly hospitals and medical facilities in the rebel-held neighborhoods of Aleppo. The film was nominated for an Academy Award in 2020 in the Best Documentary Feature category.

As efforts to defeat the rebels escalated, government forces increasingly began to use internationally banned chemical weapons. In 2016

ISIS and the Yazidis

al-Assad's troops unleashed chlorine gas on sections of Aleppo, and the next year sarin gas was used against the town of Khan Sheikhoun in Idlib province. Some 87 civilians were killed in the attack. While the Syrian government had been the greatest violator of human rights in the war, there is plenty of blame to go around. The various anti–Assad Islamist militias also murdered noncombatants as they staked out territory for themselves. Between February and April 2018 groups such as Jaysh al-Islam (Army of Islam) and Faylaq al-Rahman (al-Rahman legion) killed or injured hundreds of civilians in random attacks in Damascus. In Idlib, the al-Qaeda linked Hay'at Tahrir al-Sham (Organization for the Liberation of the Levant) murdered journalists and political opponents and prevented the distribution of desperately needed humanitarian aid to the civilian population within its territory.[9]

With Russian assistance the dictator al-Assad seems poised to reassert his control over the entire country, but at a staggering cost to the nation. Human rights groups have estimated the death toll from this conflict at over five hundred thousand. According to the United Nations High Commissioner for Refugees (UNHCR), approximately 6.6 million people have been internally displaced, and some 5.6 million have been forced to leave Syria.[10] The majority of those who have emigrated have sought refuge in the neighboring countries of Turkey, Jordan, and Lebanon. Some have traveled farther, seeking safe haven in Europe. In a desperate attempt to escape the turmoil of the Middle East, many Syrians have made Germany their destination. This nation in particular has been especially appealing because of its liberal asylum laws and booming economy. The German government has been accommodating and to date has allowed more than half a million Syrians to resettle within its borders.

Since the early days of the uprising there has been an international aspect to this conflict. It has pitted Iran, Bashar al-Assad's closest ally, against other countries in the region whose leaders sought a political change in Damascus. Over the years Iran has not only supported the dictator financially but has also pressured its proxy, the Lebanon-based Shia militia Hezbollah (Party of God), to send fighters across the border to aid him militarily. Saudi Arabia, Iran's archrival, has also had a hand in this war. One of the Saudi government's major foreign policy goals has long been to offset Iranian influence in the Middle East. To that end it has funded several militias that oppose al-Assad. Saudi Arabia at the same time is a member of the U.S.-led coalition and has contributed to the fight against ISIS. The smaller Gulf states, as Sunni majority countries, have also attempted to blunt Iranian influence. Kuwait, Qatar, Oman, Bahrain,

5. Fighting the Islamic State in the Chaos of Syria

and the United Arab Emirates have followed the Saudi lead and supplied money and weapons to opposition groups within Syria.

Turkey has also played a pivotal role in the chaos consuming its southern neighbor. Since 2011 Turkey has called for the ouster of al-Assad and has supplied money and weapons to opposition groups. As a member of NATO and an ally of the United States the country has also been called upon to participate in the war against ISIS. In a serious miscalculation, when ISIS first emerged onto the scene, government officials in Ankara felt the jihadis could serve their interests by weakening the Syrian regime. As a result Turkey was accused of allowing thousands of foreign fighters to cross its southern frontier to join ISIS. The Turks neither closed the border nor increased the number of their troops at crossing points in order to confront the Islamists.[11] By 2015, as the true nature of the Islamic State was revealed, Turkey joined the coalition, began to arrest potential ISIS recruits, and allowed American war planes to attack ISIS positions from its air base at Incirlik.

Over the past few years, the American partnership with the YPG has strained U.S.-Turkish relations. The same Syrian Kurdish militia that rescued the Yazidis on Mount Sinjar in 2014 proved to be the most formidable ground force to confront the Islamic State. Turkey, however, considered the YPG a terrorist organization because of its close ties to the Kurdistan Workers Party (PKK). While the Turkish state wanted ISIS destroyed, of equal importance was a change in leadership in Syria. Some three million Syrian refugees have crossed into Turkey in order to escape the war, and Recep Tayyip Erdoğan made it clear his government favored repatriating them as soon as possible. Naturally, this was not possible as long as the civil war continued, and al-Assad remained in power.

When asked what the most difficult part of his job as CENTCOM commander was, General Votel replied, "It would be northern Syria: The Turks and the YPG hated each other. The Turks at times were helpful, but more often they were obstructionist. I always considered them an impediment to victory."[12] Beginning with the liberation of the city of Kobanî in early 2015 the YPG made substantial territorial gains against the Islamic State. The Kurdish militia became the heart of the Syrian Democratic Forces (SDF). This alliance of moderate Sunni Arab militias and Kurds was funded by the United States, which also embedded Green Berets as military advisors with its various units.

As the war against the Islamic State moved into Syria, the YPG was, for the United States, the logical armed force with which to form a partnership. Not only were its Kurdish members highly motivated to fight ISIS

ISIS and the Yazidis

Smoke rising over the Syrian city of Kobanî after an airstrike, October 18, 2014 (Kai Pfaffenbach / Reuters Pictures).

on the ground while the Americans provided air cover, but this arrangement also fit the U.S. government's policy of maintaining a "light footprint" in Syria. Although both the Americans and the Kurds would like to have seen the end of the Assad regime, the Kurdish militia's main focus was on defeating the Islamic State, which they viewed as the greater threat. With military success, however, came political ambitions. The YPG is the military arm of the Democratic Union Party (PYD). In the chaos of northern Syria this political party began to take the place once held by the Syrian government. It now governs the Kurdish majority region known as Rojava. Like Iraqi Kurdistan, to the delight of Syrian Kurds, Rojava has gained a measure of autonomy in recent years.

Life in the Islamic State

At the height of its power and territorial expansion, between eight and ten million people lived within the borders of the self-proclaimed caliphate. Most were enthusiastic supporters of al-Baghdadi's government, although there were those who had lived in these areas for generations and were just trying to survive. People recognized that their options were limited. In Syria they had to either accept ISIS and its radical interpretation of Islam or the brutality of Bashar al-Assad. In Iraq, many Sunnis chose to side with the Islamists in order to be free of the sectarianism and corruption that was endemic within the Iraqi government.

5. Fighting the Islamic State in the Chaos of Syria

Men joined ISIS, as one might expect, for a variety of reasons. The "true believers" flocked to al-Baghdadi's army because of their deep-seated belief in his extreme interpretation of Islam. Many young men were drawn in by ISIS recruiting videos posted online. These slick productions, complete with music, glamorized both battle and the idea of martyrdom. Some men were willing to become martyrs in a holy war against not only those they considered infidels, but also fellow Muslims (e.g., Shias). Other men were more pragmatic: in areas where jobs were scarce, ISIS offered employment and a steady paycheck. There were those who found it thrilling to join an organization that was rapidly becoming a new regional power; others, fearing that power, felt it was better to go along rather than oppose the new state. Then there were the opportunists. These individuals worked to move up in the ranks of the bureaucracy of the nascent state or hoped to acquire wealth (and women) through conquest. ISIS fighters included people born Muslim as well as European converts, the latter determined to prove their devotion to their chosen religion.

Beginning in 2014, several thousand foreign fighters from around the world made their way to Syria in order to enlist in the army of the Islamic State. More Muslim extremists arrived from Russia than any other nation, totaling almost thirty-five hundred (many came from the predominately Muslim republic of Chechnya). Saudi Arabia, Jordan, and Tunisia each saw more than twenty-five hundred of their citizens move to the caliphate in order to start new lives. Some two thousand people left France and more than eight hundred traveled from Great Britain for the same purpose.[13] While the overwhelming majority of foreign arrivals were men, there were also a few cases of women who either followed their husbands to the Islamic State or came looking for men to marry and hoping to live life according to the strict interpretation of Islam espoused by al-Baghdadi.

Within the borders of the new entity, which was not recognized by the international community, sharia law was observed and rigorously enforced. The ancient Islamic code governed every aspect of an individual's life. For example, men were expected to grow beards; the rationale behind this dictate was the belief that since man was made in the image of God, by shaving, one was altering the Almighty's creation. All shops and places of business had to close during prayer services. ISIS even created a special police force, the *Hisbah*, charged with ensuring that people complied with the myriad of new statutes.

These enforcers of "public morality" roamed the streets searching for anyone violating ISIS's draconian laws. They demanded drivers listen only to the official ISIS radio station, checked cell phones of people at random for text messages critical of the movement, and set up checkpoints at which they could more easily control the public. Anyone deemed untrustworthy for having a suspicious past (e.g., former police officers, Syrian soldiers who had switched sides, or human rights workers) was forced to carry a "repentance card" that had to be presented on demand. The list of acts considered "un-Islamic" was long, and the penalties for committing such offenses were severe and included public floggings and executions. Smoking was forbidden. The punishment for drinking alcohol or slandering the Islamic State was 80 lashes. The death penalty was imposed upon people who renounced Islam or were caught spying for enemies of the caliphate.[14]

Homosexuality was deemed a capital offense. The prescribed form of execution for such a "crime" was for the offender to be thrown from a tall building and, in the unlikely event he survived the fall, to then be stoned to death. Scores of gay men were killed in this way in areas under ISIS control. The extremists posted numerous videos online that showed these executions in excruciating detail. Men accused of homosexuality were tortured by the jihadis until they revealed the names of friends and acquaintances, who were then also arrested. The death penalty for gays was by no means unique to ISIS; it also exists in both Saudi Arabia and Iran. In addition, the Taliban also used capital punishment against gay men when that group ruled Afghanistan from 1996 to 2001. The most tolerant Arab country in the Middle East for homosexual men and women continues to be Lebanon. While same-sex relationships are illegal in that nation, the statute is rarely enforced.

ISIS's treatment of women can only be described as incredibly repressive. The Islamic State forbade women from wearing makeup or perfume and required all females to dress "modestly." To that end a woman in public could dress only in a full-length black abaya (cloak) with a niqāb (veil), thereby ensuring she was covered head to toe. The logic behind this policy was that a woman should not reveal her figure, which might attract the attention of men. The al-Khansaa Brigade, an all-female organization, was created by ISIS to monitor the behavior and actions of women. This semi-official police force had the power to detain and flog any woman found outside the home unaccompanied by a male relative or in violation of the dress code.[15] As with all women, the Yazidi captives were forced to adhere to this mandatory style of dress in public, e.g., when transferred from one holding facility to another or when traded between fighters. In private homes, however, many who were later freed reported that they were

5. Fighting the Islamic State in the Chaos of Syria

forced by the militants to wear skimpy Western clothing that revealed the shapes of their bodies.

Women found guilty of adultery were stoned to death. ISIS philosophy demanded that women be subservient to their husbands in all aspects of life. A woman was expected to be married by age 17, and her main purpose was to have children, serve her husband, and maintain the home. If circumstances forced a woman to work outside the home, she should not be employed for more than three days a week, so as not to cause a major disruption to the domestic life of the family.

According to a manifesto posted online by the media section of the al-Khansaa Brigade, girls should only be educated to the age of 15, and the curriculum should focus mainly on religious studies. Any form of higher education for women was clearly out of the question. The document left no room for doubt as to the main role of women in society. It explicitly stated: "The purpose of her existence is the Divine duty of motherhood."[16]

Much like a crime syndicate, ISIS made vast amounts of money through a variety of methods, including kidnapping, looting (including the theft of funds from Iraqi banks following the capture of a city), and the illegal sale of artifacts taken from archaeological sites. As a self-proclaimed state it also collected money through taxes and fees paid by businesses, and the lucrative sale of oil on the black market. This last source of income began to shrink as coalition forces steadily regained control of the oil fields in northern Iraq and Syria. The revenue stream generated by taxes paid by businesses also declined following the ejection of ISIS from conquered cities such as Mosul. Overall, ISIS's income fell dramatically after 2014. That year saw $1.9 billion flow into the coffers of the caliphate; by 2016 that figure had plummeted to $870 million.[17]

The sale of ancient artifacts on the international black market was also very lucrative. Next to the murder and enslavement of people, the destruction of centuries-old treasures was the worst crime perpetrated by ISIS. Shortly after the terrorists captured Mosul in 2014 the world was horrified by the sight of jihadis rampaging through the Mosul Museum smashing statues and reliefs with sledgehammers. The vandals, convinced they were doing God's work, triumphantly destroyed anything from cultures that pre-dated Islam or objects they considered anti–Islamic. The museum was the second largest in the country after the Iraq Museum in Baghdad and was home to works of art dating back millennia. Fortunately, art experts agree that about half the artifacts lost were copies, with the originals housed in Baghdad at the Iraq Museum. The city's libraries were also targeted. Rare manuscripts were stolen and soon

ISIS and the Yazidis

appeared for sale on the black market. Having no further use for these seats of knowledge, the militants obliterated the buildings. The library at Mosul University was burned to the ground and the main public library blown up.

Twenty miles south of Mosul lie the ruins of Nimrud, the ancient capital of Assyria. This site also drew the attention of ISIS militants and their ideology of intolerance. Beginning in the 1840s British archaeologists began excavating the buried city. Over the years many of its colossal stone sculptures were spirited away to museums such as the Metropolitan Museum of Art in New York City and the British Museum in London. The latter is also home to two awe-inspiring carved gypsum winged bull statues found at Khorsabad, north of Mosul. Dating from 710 BC, they were acquired by the museum in 1850. Today, as in the past, there are those who believe these relics should never have been taken by the British from the Middle East. That controversy aside, at least having been relocated to Europe they were saved from destruction at the hands of these religious fanatics. Both Nimrud and Khorsabad were looted and destroyed by ISIS adherents who used bulldozers to thoroughly complete the job.

The hostility of ISIS toward artwork and artifacts that did not fit neatly into its narrative of history has drawn comparison to other groups past and present. The Nazis classified paintings and sculptures they found objectionable and unsuited to their worldview as "degenerate art." They proceeded to either destroy or quietly sell thousands of such works of art on the international market in order to raise money for the state. Muslim fundamentalists such as the Taliban have held similar views. In 2001 the world was outraged when the Afghan group blew up two enormous sculptures of Buddha that had been carved into the cliffside in the Bamiyan Valley seventeen hundred years ago.

One of the most important archaeological sites in the Middle East was Palmyra. Designated a World Heritage Site by UNESCO, it held Roman era buildings and columns that were constructed over two thousand years ago. The city itself dates to the second millennium BC. For centuries tourists had traveled to this part of Syria specifically to view its famous ruins. It did not go unnoticed by ISIS. The militants captured the area in May 2015 and soon set about destroying irreplaceable structures and artifacts. In June, the jihadis blew up the tomb of Mohammad bin Ali, a descendant of Muhammad's cousin Ali and considered to have been a saint by the Shia. Two months later explosives were again used to destroy temples dedicated to the Canaanite sky god Baalshamin, as well as that of the fertility deity Baal. The fanatics not only continued to destroy historic relics but were also not above murdering those who studied and cared for them. The respected archaeologist Khaled al-Asaad, a man who had spent 40 years of his life excavating artifacts from the site, was captured, tortured, and eventually killed for protecting the artifacts. Just before ISIS fighters arrived, the elderly academic, true to his calling, had supervised the removal of ancient treasures from Palmyra's museum. The octogenarian was tortured for a month in order to force him to reveal the location of the valuable objects. Unable to break his will, the terrorists beheaded the scholar with a large sword in a public square.[18] In a final barbaric act, al-Asaad's body was subsequently hung from a Roman column in Palmyra with a placard attached declaring him an "apostate" and "the director of idolatry."

Yazidis Enduring Slavery in the Islamic State

For as long as the Islamic State existed, Yazidi women were bought, sold, and traded as if they were so many sheep or cattle. Some were sold for a ridiculously cheap price. Psychologically this act was meant to humiliate the woman. In some instances in order to further degrade the captive, she might be given away, sending the message that she was worth nothing as a human being.[19] In addition to the feeling of superiority such a transaction provided the male "owner," there was another purpose for keeping a woman captive. The sharing of a Yazidi slave for sexual purposes between ISIS fighters became a bonding experience for the men in which militants cemented their comradeship.

While women tried to cope with the terrifying ordeal of being kidnapped, sexually abused, and faced with an uncertain future, their children, having had their worlds turned upside down, were no less traumatized. Having already been torn away from their homes, families, and daily lives, girls, as they grew older, faced the prospect of separation from their mothers, rape, and being sold as slaves. Boys, upon reaching their eighth birthday, were forced to become child soldiers and expected to give their lives for the caliphate. There were several steps in this process. Firstly, the young boys were stripped of their Yazidi identity as they were made to convert to Islam, given new Arab names, and instructed to speak only Arabic. Yazidi boys were placed alongside Arab Sunni youths who were also being trained to be ISIS soldiers. Housed together in groups of 10 to 12 they were indoctrinated in the radicals' philosophy and forced to learn and recite verses from the Quran. Their daily activities centered around

ISIS and the Yazidis

military drills such as learning to use AK-47s, hand grenades, and RPGs. They were also compelled to watch ISIS propaganda videos that glorified jihad and suicide bombings against non-believers.[20]

The ISIS instructors employed a reward and punishment system with their young pupils. Those who learned quickly and performed their tasks well were given small sums of money with which they were allowed to buy personal items in Raqqa. Boys who failed to memorize their Quranic verses or performed poorly handling their weapons were physically beaten. Not only did the young recruits suffer the emotionally crippling effect of having no communications with their families, but ISIS instructors also made every effort to erase the boys' memories of their former religion and culture. Over months and in some cases years, the boys were relentlessly indoctrinated in ISIS beliefs and taught to view Yazidis as inferior and to regard them as a threat to Islam. Following their basic training, the youths were distributed across ISIS held territory to fulfill jobs as military necessity dictated. As with other recruits, some became frontline fighters while others were assigned to guard supply lines or compounds in rear areas.

The idea of a state enslaving and converting children of a minority religion and having them serve that entity was not unknown in history. The Ottoman Empire subjected its Christian subjects to such treatment for hundreds of years. The Janissary corps was composed of Christian boys taken mainly from the Balkans, forcibly converted to Islam and made to serve the sultan as his personal bodyguard. Although they were technically considered slaves and as such not allowed to marry, they did receive a salary and a pension upon retirement. For centuries Janissaries were renowned for their discipline, superior fighting capabilities, and above all their fanatical devotion to the sultan. Eventually, however, the Janissary corps came to be seen as antiquated. In 1826 Sultan Mahmud II announced his decision to form a new army modeled on European lines. This prompted the Janissaries, who feared losing their prestige and position in society, to revolt. In what became known as the Auspicious Incident, the rebellion was quickly crushed, thousands of rebels were executed, and the Sultan abolished the Janissary corps.

As the war progressed and the Islamic State's territory continued to shrink, occasionally a boy found his way back to the Yazidi community. This usually occurred as the result of his capture on the battlefield. It was standard procedure for both the YPG and Peshmerga to interrogate ISIS prisoners soon after they had been taken. If it was determined that the child soldier was no longer a threat and wished to be reunited with his family, he was sent to Kurdistan. After returning to Iraq the next step was to locate any extended family members who had survived the ISIS onslaught. Most relatives, of course, were living in refugee camps. Even with the love and support of their families, these youths faced a difficult adjustment period in order to be reintegrated into Yazidi society. In some cases boys who had been with ISIS for years had to relearn the Kurdish language as they had forgotten their mother tongue and by then spoke only Arabic. These children, who had been forced into adulthood overnight, suffered psychological damage that would haunt them for years. Those who had survived to return to Iraq had to wait many agonizing months to be reunited with their mothers and sisters; others, tragically, would never see them again.

Yazidi Women Return to Their People

Only about half of all the women and children who were so violently kidnapped in 2014 have returned to their loved ones in the refugee camps of Kurdistan. Of the six thousand people taken, roughly three thousand have found their way home to Iraq; 2,717 are still missing as of July 2022. Of those unaccounted for, some women were murdered at the hands of the men claiming to be their "owners," while others died from disease or were accidently killed in coalition airstrikes. An unknown number were also forced to accompany ISIS fighters when they fled to other areas of the Middle East as the caliphate collapsed between 2017 and 2019.[21]

As the women struggled to survive their imprisonment, and the war drew nearer, most never gave up hope of regaining their freedom. An abducted Yazidi woman had only three options through which to regain her liberty. She could be rescued, ransomed back to her family, or attempt an escape on her own. None of these pathways was guaranteed, and all involved risks.

Of the three, rescue was the least likely, at least in the first few months following the onslaught of 2014. Women were kept far from the front lines, and it would have been difficult to mount numerous rescue operations as long as the Islamic State retained a powerful fighting force. Moreover, from the beginning the coalition's first priority was to reclaim territory through battlefield victories; hostages remained a secondary concern. Nevertheless, some captives hoped for a miracle.

In her riveting book *The Girl Who Escaped ISIS*, Farida Khalaf relates how, shortly after being taken, in an effort to reassure her

ISIS and the Yazidis

terrified friends, she confidently stated: "Look, the Americans are on our side now, aren't they? Perhaps their army is well on the way to liberate us."[22] The other young women needed hope to help buoy their spirits as they were constantly harassed and degraded by the ISIS guards. The jihadis showed the low regard in which they held all Yazidis by callously referring to Yazidi men as "dogs." One claimed they had the right to kill the men since they were infidels. Another quickly added, "And take their wives. That's why you belong to us now, and we can do what we like with you. You don't have any rights."[23] As the Islamic State shrank and the Syrian Democratic Forces advanced, occasionally Yazidis were freed. In mid-2016 during the SDF offensive to drive the militants out of the Syrian city of Manbij, YPJ soldiers succeeded in rescuing a group of Yazidi girls from their tormentors.[24] After having their sense of humanity restored by the Kurdish women, the girls were sent on to Kurdistan to be reunited with their families.

In some cases a militant would allow his Yazidi *sabaya* to be ransomed back to her family. This occurred either because of greed on the man's part, because he had tired of his captive, or both. The ransom amounts varied from a few hundred dollars to several thousand. Yazidis took up collections from family members and friends. If the amount demanded could not be reached in this way, the family went into debt by borrowing additional funds.[25] Smugglers who ran alcohol and cigarettes into the Islamic State were used as go-betweens to deliver the money. The Arabs who transported these "forbidden" items were already well aware of the dangers involved in crossing into ISIS territory, as it was a capital offence to import such goods into the caliphate. The men were paid handsomely for their efforts as delivering ransom money was no less dangerous than trafficking in illegal items. In some instances the exchange took place as agreed; in others the intermediary arrived at a predetermined point only to be robbed and murdered by the extremists. If all went well, following the exchange, the young woman would be transported back to Iraq by the hired smuggler.

The third and most dangerous option for a Yazidi woman to regain her freedom was to attempt an escape. Depending on the city and neighborhood in which she was being held, she might find sympathetic locals willing to aid her or others who would turn her away or report her to ISIS officials. Sometimes a captive was able to acquire a cell phone and secretly call a relative for help. In such cases a family member would then reach out to a middleman, who might be a Yazidi, a Kurd, or an Arab.

The middleman in turn, using Google Earth, would find the woman's

5. Fighting the Islamic State in the Chaos of Syria

position in order to locate exactly where she was being held. He would instruct the family to give his telephone number to the captured woman so she could call him directly. When the woman called, a plan would be made as to when and how she might slip away from her captor. She would also be given a code word to be used with whoever came to meet her along with a place to rendezvous. The middleman would then hire a smuggler for the dangerous trip to pick up the hostage. Once safely away from her ISIS "owner," the escapee would be sheltered in a safe house for a few days until the inevitable ISIS search for her ended. The final stage of this lengthy process involved driving the woman out of ISIS controlled territory. Usually the trip across the Syrian-Iraqi border went smoothly as the smugglers knew where best to cross. In some instances this last leg involved crossing the Turkish border then on to northern Iraq and a tearful reunion with her family.[26]

In almost all cases a cell phone was the vital piece of equipment needed in order to facilitate a successful escape. The men of ISIS were well aware of this and forbade their *malak yamiin* (spoils of war) from possessing the devices. Those who were caught with phones were severely punished. Nofa, who escaped with her baby son in 2015, had been imprisoned in a house with 20 other young women. She related that the Yazidis had hidden two cell phones in baby formula or buried them outside when they were not being used to call for help. When the jihadis discovered the forbidden items, they were determined to make an example of the two women on whom the phones were found. An act of unbelievable cruelty followed. According to Nofa, who was an eyewitness, "The fighters made us all come outside to watch. Then they tied the women to the back of a pickup truck and dragged them through the street until they were covered in blood."[27] The women survived, but just barely.

Although returning women were overjoyed to be free and with their families again, many expressed anxiety about their futures. In accordance with the tenets of their religion any Yazidi who had sexual contact with a person of another faith was automatically banished. There has never been any distinction made between rape and consensual sex. Throughout the Yazidis' long history, women who had been violated or had fallen in love with a non–Yazidi were forbidden to rejoin the community or number themselves among the faithful.

What the women could not have known, however, was that only two weeks after the catastrophic ISIS attack in 2014 the baba sheikh, Khurto Hajji Ismail, had made an unprecedented decision. The elderly Yazidi supreme spiritual leader, after a lifetime of ensuring that traditional

ISIS and the Yazidis

customs were followed, recognized the uniqueness of the situation and had issued a decree. His religious edict stated that all returning women, especially those who had been raped by ISIS men, were to be welcomed back into the community and were still considered members of the Yazidi faith. Women who were unmarried at the time they were taken were encouraged to marry, and it was made clear to all that the tragedy that had befallen them was in no way their fault. The baba sheikh also devised a purification ceremony at Lalish for women and girls returning to the fold. The ritual was performed in a holy fountain inside the caves of the Lalish valley and could be repeated as often as a woman wished.[28] This new baptism was meant to renew the soul and restore a sense of peace to the individual. Well aware of the terror their abducted family members had been through, the vast majority of Yazidi men also welcomed this ritual cleansing and viewed it as a way to regain a sense of normalcy to lives that had been so viciously upended.

Accepting the children of Yazidi mothers and Muslim fathers proved to be much more problematic for the tight-knit community. Some jihadis provided contraception to the women they had kidnapped, while others did not. As a result hundreds of young women became pregnant and gave birth to babies fathered by Muslims. The Yazidis refused to allow such children to return with their mothers. While this position seemed heartless and harsh, it did serve a purpose. In traditional conservative societies, such as that of the Yazidis, such policies have helped to insulate the group from the outside world. For millennia it has been the case that, for a child to be considered a Yazidi, both parents must be of the faith.

Under Iraqi law, since the fathers of these boys and girls were Muslim, they too were considered to be of that religion. Islam is a patrilineal religion (unlike Judaism, which is matrilineal). According to Islamic tradition, should a Muslim man marry a non–Muslim woman, the children born of such a marriage are automatically considered to be of the same faith as their father. In addition, should the father pass away, the mother must continue to raise the children as Muslims.

After territory in northeastern Syria was liberated from ISIS, the mothers of these children had to choose between crossing the border to rejoin their people or remaining with their children. For some the decision was easy, for others agonizing. Doctor Nemam Ghafouri, the founder of Joint Help for Kurdistan, a relief agency that aided Yazidis, knew all too well the situation in which these young women found themselves. She thoughtfully stated: "There are women who have been through so much during their captivity that every time they look at the baby, they will remember all the torture, all the horrible things they have gone through, and they don't want to keep these babies." She continued: "But for others, the only thing they carry is the love of a mother for a child."[29]

Undoubtedly, more than one mother questioned how she could afford to raise a child, or children, with no money and no financial or emotional support from family. In the end, while some young mothers chose to remain with their children, most made the heartbreaking decision to leave their babies and/or toddlers in Syria. An orphanage run by Syrian Kurds assumed the responsibility of placing the children with local Kurdish families. Mahmoud Rasho, a Yazidi Syrian, made clear that these boys and girls would be placed in loving homes: "The family we are giving them to must be a good family. Their thinking must not be radical Islamic. They must be secular and open-minded."[30]

The physical injuries these women suffered at the hands of their abductors mended relatively quickly, but it will take years for their psychological scars to heal. Having had their lives shattered and male relatives murdered, the healing process will be long and slow. Many have reported having nightmares and trouble sleeping; others suffer from severe depression and thoughts of suicide. One organization that has helped hundreds of Yazidis work through the trauma of capture and enslavement is the German-Kurdish aid organization Wadi. In 2015 the group opened a center for women in Dohuk. Teams were sent into the IDP camps to refer women in need to their facility, where they could receive medical treatment and psychological counseling. Recently freed women were encouraged to join small, all-female therapy groups. During the sessions, women were urged to share their stories, free of judgment, with others who had been through similar experiences. In order to help returnees readjust to normal life the center also offered legal assistance, as well as agricultural and vocational courses.

In a magnanimous gesture the German government created a program whereby these women and their families were granted asylum in Germany and provided extensive psychological treatment. Non-governmental organizations working within the refugee camps spread the word, and more than one thousand women and children accepted the offer. Twenty shelters were established across Germany in which an individual or family could reside. The locations of these residences were not disclosed to the public in order to protect the Yazidis' privacy. Although the new guests found the culture, lifestyle, and food of Europe much different from what they had known in Iraq, the psychological counseling was beneficial. It proved to be a valuable and necessary step in the healing process. After several months, some families chose to remain in Germany, while others decided to return to the Middle East.

The Defeat of the Islamic State

By May 2017, the Syrian Democratic Forces had fought to within a few miles of ISIS's de facto capital of Raqqa. The YPG and YPJ, which numbered sixty thousand fighters, comprised the bulk of the army, while the Arab and Assyrian Christian militias added another twenty thousand soldiers, which would be needed for the coming fight.[31] They were augmented by some five hundred U.S. special operations personnel (U.S. Army Special Forces, Navy SEALS, and Marine Raiders) serving as military advisors. Opposing this force were approximately four thousand militants. SDF commanders knew it would be a difficult and costly battle as the jihadis held formidable defensive positions in and around the city, and many were prepared to fight to the death. As with other urban battles, it was assumed that civilian casualties would be high. Prior to the rebellion against the al-Assad regime the population of Raqqa had exceeded two hundred thousand, but by the time of the operation to reclaim it from ISIS only half that number still resided in the city.

In the days leading up to the Raqqa operation, even though the global coalition was still occupied with winning the battle of Mosul, it had the resources to supply the SDF with heavy weapons, including mortars and RPGs. These arms would be needed in order to counter the inevitable ISIS suicide car bombs. YPG leaders were convinced that, as ISIS's territory continued to shrink and the jihadis became more desperate, they would again resort to this deadly battlefield tactic. As in earlier campaigns this offensive began with airstrikes carried out by the U.S. Air Force. Ground troops attacked the city at dawn on June 6, 2017. The SDF advanced on the city from the north, east, and west. What followed were weeks of heavy street fighting as ISIS fanatics defended their positions and YPG soldiers maneuvered through streets filled with snipers and booby-trapped buildings.

By June 24, the YPG and its allies had completely surrounded Raqqa as squads of militants continued to launch fierce counterattacks. Even before the battle began, the ISIS leadership, in a particularly despicable move aimed at bolstering the spirit of its fighters, offered a bounty of 20 golden dinars ($4,000) to any fighter who killed an American soldier or a foreign (non–Syrian) member of the SDF.[32]

At the end of July the SDF controlled 50 percent of the city. As the

5. Fighting the Islamic State in the Chaos of Syria

campaign intensified, civilians as well as ISIS militants suffered from a lack of food, water, and medicine. Under such hardships it is understandable that tens of thousands of noncombatants sought to escape Raqqa. Many attempted to avoid the crossfire and American bombs in order to reach SDF-held areas. Such undertakings were extremely dangerous not only because they took place in the midst of battle, but also because ISIS fighters tended to use civilians as human shields. Those who did cross the front lines, although safe, were nevertheless wary of how they would be received by the Kurdish YPG as many of the now homeless civilians had been supporters of ISIS.

By the middle of August the Syrian Democratic Forces had taken most of the old city. This area included the vital neighborhood of al-Thaknah, home to ISIS's government buildings. Several prominent public squares were also located nearby; these sites had been the locations for public punishments and bloody executions. Increased airstrikes in September allowed the YPG to capture additional sections of the city, and by October the ISIS defenders were exhausted and ready to negotiate a peace deal. On October 15, in order to end further bloodshed, the SDF allowed more than three hundred jihadis to leave the city in a convoy that also included some three thousand of their family members and supporters. To no one's surprise, the terrorists also forced some four hundred civilians into accompanying them as human shields.[33] A few dozen ISIS fanatics refused to leave and continued to fight to the death. Over the next few days the last pockets of opposition were eliminated, and on October 20, 2017, the SDF declared victory in Raqqa. After three long years the Islamic State of Iraq and Syria could no longer claim it had an empire or capital city. Raqqa was in ruins. The devastation that ISIS had wrought in so many places, including Sinjar, had now been visited upon its preeminent city. The United Nations estimated that some ten thousand buildings had been destroyed or severely damaged and that 80 percent of the city was uninhabitable. More than a year later evidence of ISIS's bloodthirsty reign was once again revealed to the world. On the outskirts of the former capital a mass grave was discovered that held the remains of an estimated thirty-five hundred people. At the time, eight other mass graves had already been found near Raqqa. Some of the remains at these sites were thought to be of people who died in the battle for the city. The majority, however, are now believed to have been people executed by ISIS for a variety of crimes against the state.

Although the Islamists had lost their capital, the war continued for another year as pockets of ISIS fighters were ferreted out by the SDF. More territory in northern Syria fell to the coalition until what remained of the

ISIS and the Yazidis

caliphate had, by early 2019, shrunk to just a few square miles around the town of Al-Baghuz Fawqani. The empire that, at its height in 2014, held sway over one third of Syria and nearly 40 percent of Iraq was on the verge of total collapse. The last redoubt lay some 150 miles southeast of Raqqa on the Euphrates River along the Iraqi border. By February 2019, the SDF had surrounded the town of some ten thousand people. As the battle began General Votel estimated that there could be as many as twelve hundred fighters and that the SDF and supporting coalition forces should be prepared for a difficult military engagement. The CENTCOM commander warned: "It's a relatively confined space, it's heavily urbanized, it's laden with a lot of explosive hazards, improvised explosive devices, for example.... They have had the opportunity to prepare this for a while, and there is a presence of civilians in the area—family members of ISIS and then others that reside in the area, so I think this poses a significant concern for us."[34] The general was correct. It took six weeks of heavy fighting to capture the town and destroy the last vestiges of ISIS's power.

In late February, an SDF spokesman announced that the force had once again come across a mass grave. This site was identical to those found earlier in cities that had the misfortune of experiencing ISIS rule. The site

Two U.S. Navy F/A-18 Hornets over Iraq (U.S. Air Force photograph taken by Staff Sergeant Corey Hook).

5. Fighting the Islamic State in the Chaos of Syria

contained the remains of dozens of men and women who, for whatever reason, had run afoul of the militants and paid with their lives. The shocking discovery was made even more horrendous by the fact that many of the bodies were without heads, clear evidence that the victims had been decapitated before their ignominious burial.

As Kurdish military units drew near Baghuz, Abu Bakr al-Baghdadi quietly slipped out of town. On January 7, together with a few dozen loyal fighters, the ISIS leader departed even before the battle began. Once safely away, al-Baghdadi issued instructions that ISIS families should evacuate the area. Even as his empire crumbled, his animosity and contempt for Yazidis was evident. While the wives and children of his supporters were encouraged to leave, Yazidi captives were not to be released. His men were directed to continue to hold Yazidi women, many locked in underground cells. Not all ISIS adherents followed this dictate. As thousands streamed out of the town to turn themselves over to the SDF (including some jihadis posing as civilians in order to save themselves), dozens were accompanied by their enslaved Yazidis. Makeshift camps were hastily created to hold these noncombatants, and members of the YPG soon began circulating through the facilities, questioning people and checking them for arms. Kurdish fighters identified and freed 40 Yazidi women and children, who were subsequently returned to Iraq.[35]

Fierce clashes continued into mid-March. ISIS fighters prolonged the battle for Baghuz by using an elaborate tunnel system they had constructed under the town to move unseen and rapidly emerge to ambush SDF troops. Eventually, however, the superior numbers of the YPG, YPJ, and Arab militias, along with their sheer determination, proved decisive. The fighting ability of these ground troops, in conjunction with the constant coalition airstrikes, drove the last of the jihadis into a small pocket along the banks of the Euphrates. On March 23, 2019, the SDF declared victory, and al-Baghdadi's caliphate as a physical entity was destroyed.

6

A Complicated Part of the World

As the United States and its allies fought to defeat ISIS, the al-Assad regime slowly and methodically regained territory and crushed the rebellion. By December 2016, after a four-year siege, Aleppo, Syria's most populous city and a major rebel stronghold, fell to the dictator's forces. At that point most of the country, with the exception of the last rebel bastions in Idlib province, was once again controlled by the central government. Today the movement toward democracy in Syria has all but collapsed.

One American Ally Attacks Another in Syria

The long-standing tension between the Kurds of the YPG and Turkey erupted in violence in late 2019. On October 9, the Turkish military launched a cross-border assault against the Syrian Kurds. This move was facilitated by President Donald Trump's ill-conceived decision to order the withdrawal of the small number of U.S. troops along the Syrian-Turkish border. Three days earlier the Americans, who had been advising and assisting the SDF in the fight against ISIS, were ordered to pull back, thus giving the Turks a "green light" to begin their attack. Turkish President Recep Tayyip Erdoğan, along with the vast majority of his countrymen, considered the YPG a terrorist organization because of its close ties to the Kurdistan Workers Party (PKK). Most Turks viewed the PKK as posing a direct threat to their country. Erdoğan's motives for striking into Syria included dealing a crippling blow to the YPG militarily and creating a buffer zone along the Turkish border.

Turkey must be given credit for having taken in millions of Syrian refugees during the first years of the rebellion. By 2016, however, the political landscape had changed. The Turkish economy slowed, and public opinion shifted against the arrival of additional Arab immigrants. In addition

6. A Complicated Part of the World

to dealing with the YPG, Erdoğan justified the move south by stating his desire to resettle some of the 3.6 million Syrian refugees in Turkey in this newly designated area. The Turkish president was also concerned that on a purely fiscal level, the Syrians who had fled the civil war were becoming a burden on the Turkish state. For its part, the YPG insisted that it took no orders from the PKK and, unlike that organization, did not support the idea of an independent Kurdish state created from Turkish lands.

Within two days of what the Turks dubbed "Operation Peace Spring," more than one hundred thousand people had abandoned their homes and were forced to move south to avoid the fighting. Eventually that figure exceeded three hundred thousand. As YPG soldiers engaged the Turkish army, there were fears that men who had been guarding camps in which some twelve thousand captured ISIS fighters were held would also be sent to the border. Fewer guards meant greater chances for ISIS prisoners to escape and potentially reorganize themselves into a fighting force. Fortunately, there were no mass escape attempts, although there were reports that a small number of ISIS militants slipped out of the holding camps amid the turmoil.

Since the start of Syria's civil war the Turkish military had been involved in several skirmishes along the 600-mile border. At times it clashed with ISIS; at others it fought the Syrian Army or the Kurds. While the government in Ankara was no ally of al-Assad, the instability within Syria threatened to allow the Kurds, and by extension the YPG, more influence in the north. Thus the Turks were ever wary of the growing power of the Kurdish militia. In February 2016, for instance, the Turkish army shelled YPG positions for two days around the city of Aleppo.

For years, the fact that U.S. troops operated in the area as advisors to the SDF forces fighting ISIS prevented major Turkish military operations directed against the YPG. As a fellow member of NATO, Turkey had to act judiciously. It goes without saying that, had American soldiers been accidently killed while serving alongside Kurdish fighters, it would have been disastrous for U.S.-Turkish relations. In August 2019, the U.S. government attempted to reduce tensions between the two American allies. Acting as a mediator, it pressured the YPG to withdraw from a handful of positions along the border so that Turkey could establish a roughly three-mile-deep buffer zone within Syria. For a short time the area was jointly patrolled by U.S. and Turkish troops. Unfortunately, President Erdoğan was not satisfied with the arrangement. He sought a much larger neutral zone, one that would extend some 20 miles deep and three hundred miles long.

In late 2018 President Trump, after a telephone conversation with his

ISIS and the Yazidis

Turkish counterpart, seriously considered withdrawing U.S. soldiers from northern Syria. According to his former national security advisor, John Bolton, Trump thought such a move would serve a domestic purpose in that it would aid in his reelection campaign. Bolton voiced his objection, stating that ISIS remained a threat in the region and that Iran's influence within Syria would undoubtedly increase. He predicted that, should U.S. troops leave, the Kurds would be forced to ally with Bashar al-Assad, and by extension Iran, since they viewed Turkey as their greatest threat.[1] Several international figures also objected to the proposed pullout, including the Israeli ambassador to the United States and French President Emmanuel Macron, who warned Trump that the Turks would attack the Kurds and compromise with ISIS. Erdoğan continued to try to influence Trump, in one instance stating that he loved the Kurds and they loved him but that the PKK and YPG were terrorists and did not represent the Kurdish people. Bolton concluded that Trump was falling for Erdoğan's propaganda.[2] The U.S. president reiterated to Bolton in January 2019: "My base [political supporters] wants to get out [of Syria]."[3] This combination of domestic concerns and Erdoğan's pressure for American withdrawal would cause Trump to make a decision nearly a year later that would have a devastating impact upon the Syrian Kurds and U.S. credibility.

On October 6, 2019, after another conversation with the Turkish president, Trump, disregarding advice from experts in the Pentagon and State Department, ordered American troops out of Syria. Three days later the Turkish army crossed the border. It was obvious that the YPG could not contend with the power of the Turkish state. Within days the Kurdish fighters had to abandon their positions and move south along with tens of thousands of panic-stricken civilians. Included among those forced to flee were some of the five thousand Syrian Yazidis. More than five hundred people had to abandon their homes in eight of 15 Yazidi villages in northern Syria. Every Yazidi community in the area lost electricity when the local power station was hit by a mortar, and several people in the village of Tal Khatoun were injured by sniper fire. Civilians from three Christian towns nearby also had to evacuate and move quickly in order to reach safely in areas still controlled by the YPG.[4]

In addition to the Turkish military, the YPG and local inhabitants had to deal with the actions of pro–Turkish Arab militias. Members of these armed groups were fiercely anti-Kurdish, and many were eager to assist the Turks in driving out the Kurds. Human rights groups accused members of these militias of mistreating, and in some cases executing, captured YPG and YPJ soldiers. Kurdish civilians were also shown little

6. A Complicated Part of the World

mercy. The locals were terrorized, their homes looted and burned, and their lands and businesses stolen.

The decision made in the Oval Office on October 6 demonstrated Trump's admiration for dictators around the world. He already had a long track record of flattering and lavishing praise upon strongmen including Russia's Vladimir Putin, Saudi Arabia's Mohammed bin Salman, and Egypt's Abdel Fattah el-Sisi. Recep Tayyip Erdoğan was no exception. The American president admitted that he liked such rulers in a series of interviews with famed journalist Bob Woodward. As opposed to his sometimes-frosty relationships with the leaders of Western democracies, he boasted of these autocrats: "The tougher and meaner they are, the better I get along with them."[5] Trump seemed oblivious to the outrageous acts perpetrated by such men. It is no secret that these dictators (despite the fact that many cloak themselves with the title of president) have violated human rights, murdered political opponents, and jailed journalists. A Turkish joke illustrates the point: "A prisoner goes to the prison library and asks for a certain book. 'We don't have the book,' says the librarian. 'But we do have the author.'"[6]

Later that same day the White House issued a short statement on the removal of U.S. troops from Syria. Incredibly, it contained no mention of the YPG whose destruction was what motivated the Turkish attack. It also failed to note that the Kurds had been a vital ally in the war against ISIS for the previous five years. The press release merely stated, "Turkey will soon be moving forward with its long-planned operation into Northern Syria. The United States Armed Forces will not support or be involved in the operation, and United States forces, having defeated the ISIS territorial 'Caliphate,' will no longer be in the immediate area."[7] Although the Syrian Democratic Forces had been aware of the movement of Turkish troops near the border, the SDF was unprepared for the sudden onslaught. The feeling of abandonment by the United States was palpable. A bewildered SDF spokesman stated: "There were assurances from the United States of America that it would not allow any Turkish military operations against the region." He continued: "The (U.S.) statement was a surprise, and we can say that it is a stab in the back for the SDF."[8]

In the United States, the president was roundly criticized for his decision. From across the political spectrum politicians and pundits expressed views that this move would undermine U.S. credibility as a dependable ally. In Congress, the House of Representatives passed House Joint Resolution 77, which expressed that body's opposition to the president's order by a vote of 354 to 60. The media and the American public also weighed in against the president. Trump, stunned by the criticism, began to pressure the Turks in order to bring about a ceasefire. On October 14, he issued a statement in which he made known his intention to issue an executive order that would impose sanctions on individual Turkish officials and "any persons contributing to Turkey's destabilizing actions in northeast Syria." Also included was the president's desire to increase the tariff on Turkish steel to 50 percent. In addition, it declared: "The United States will also immediately stop negotiations, being led by the Department of Commerce, with respect to a $100 billion trade deal with Turkey."[9] Three days later Vice President Mike Pence and Secretary of State Mike Pompeo arrived in Ankara to negotiate a ceasefire agreement.

Several European nations also acted against Erdoğan's government. The European Union announced that it, along with Canada, would suspend the sale of weapons to Turkey. While this move did not rise to the level of a permanent embargo, it was designed to send a message to the Turkish president that his aggression in Syria would not be tolerated. Diplomatic relations between the Erdoğan government and those of Western European countries were already strained over the issue of immigration. The Turks had agreed not to allow the millions of Syrian refugees who had crossed into their country to escape the civil war to move on to Europe *en masse*.

This immigration debate divided people across Europe. Some welcomed immigrants and refugees and saw it as their duty to aid people in need. Others, however, were reluctant to allow multitudes of low-income refugees from Africa and the Middle East into their countries. There were those who cited economic concerns, noting that the newcomers could become a burden on their economies. Many members of conservative political parties objected on racial and/or religious grounds, fearing that waves of immigrants could bring about a change in the ethnic makeup of their homelands. Erdoğan, too, saw the value of using the refugees for political purposes. Occasionally, in bellicose speeches designed to demonstrate his power, he threatened to open the floodgates and overwhelm the European continent with Syrian refugees.

The ceasefire the vice president and secretary of state negotiated did not please either side, but it did end the fighting. Having also contacted the YPG, the two men announced at a press conference in the Turkish capital on October 17 that a five-day truce was to take effect immediately. During this ceasefire, the YPG agreed to withdraw from Turkey's new "buffer zone." In exchange, the Turkish government agreed to take no military action against the predominantly Kurdish border city of Kobanî.

6. A Complicated Part of the World

The same day the ceasefire agreement was reached in Ankara, six thousand miles away in Dallas, Texas, Trump held a campaign rally. In an effort to win political points with the crowd, he referenced the Turkish attack and his handling of the crisis. While conveniently omitting his own role in bringing about this disaster, he callously remarked: "Like two kids in a lot, you've got to let them fight and then you pull them apart."[10] Meanwhile, outside the venue, hundreds of protestors, many of them Kurdish-Americans, assembled carrying signs denouncing both the Turkish aggression and the president. One banner read "We want Turkey out of NATO," another "Trump betrayed the Kurds."

Despite the president's attempt at spin control, the damage to American prestige had been done. John Bolton, who had left his position as national security advisor one month earlier, commented: "The result of Trump's decision was a complete debacle for U.S. policy and for our credibility worldwide."[11] General Joseph Votel expressed the sentiments of many military professionals when he remarked: "Trump's decision to withdraw U.S. troops from the border was disastrous. That move undermined our partner the YPG. We gave up our influence to find a political solution in that part of the world."[12]

Seeing an opportunity, Russia quickly stepped in to fill the void left by the Americans. On October 22, Vladimir Putin and Recep Tayyip Erdoğan reached a deal that extended the ceasefire and allowed for joint patrols by Russian and Turkish troops within the newly created "buffer zone." There was no timetable set for a Russian withdrawal. Russia's newfound prominence became even more pronounced two months later, as the Kremlin's soldiers appeared in Raqqa. Two years after the city had fallen to YPG troops supported by coalition forces, Russians rather than Americans walked the streets of the former capital of the caliphate. There was no sign of the Kurds who had actually done the fighting and had seen many of their comrades killed or wounded in the struggle to defeat ISIS.

As the result of Turkey having achieved its goal, the Kurdish military units were forced to seek an accommodation with the al-Assad regime. This new de facto alliance had clear benefits for both sides. The Syrian government was reassured that the Kurdish region of Rojava would remain within Syria proper, thus bolstering the dictator's power. For the Kurds it served as a check against any future Turkish territorial ambitions. The Trump administration, in a final effort to save face, announced that it would keep a few hundred U.S. soldiers in eastern Syria. A small force remained to secure the Conoco oil field and was stationed at the Green Village base. General Mark Milley, chairman of the Joint Chiefs of Staff,

ISIS and the Yazidis

pointed out that this was necessary in order to avoid the re-emergence of ISIS in the region. While the SDF welcomed the continued presence of American troops, it is worth remembering that it was they who did the bulk of the fighting and lost some ten thousand men and women in the war to destroy ISIS.

Syria for all intents and purposes is still a fractured nation. It is currently divided into four sections. The government exercises control over most of the country, with the Kurds retaining their semi-autonomous status in the northeast. To the northwest, Idlib province remains in the hands of Hay'at Tahrir al-Sham, a jihadi group that once had ties to al-Qaeda. Over the years the living conditions in this part of Syria have grown steadily worse as people have arrived by the thousands since 2011 fleeing the fighting in other parts of the country. The situation became even more desperate when a government offensive, supported by the Russians, drove more than one million people into Idlib and its surrounding communities in 2020. The fourth section consists of the Turkish "safe zone" along the northern border with Turkey. President Erdoğan has remained committed to the idea of repatriating approximately two million of the more than three million Syrians who were taken in by the Turkish state. In the two months after its creation, 371,000 people voluntarily chose to move into the strip of land between the towns of Ras al-Ayn and Tell Abyad.[13] More than one hundred thousand additional people, mostly Arabs, who had fled south also returned to their hometowns and villages once the fighting ended. Most Syrian refugees in Turkey, however, remain extremely reluctant to return to their homeland, fearing retaliation by the al-Assad government. Instead, they hope to remain in Turkey or move to Europe, where they can live safer more economically secure lives.

Although the Turkish government was generous in allowing millions of displaced Syrians into the country after 2011, it was less accommodating when dealing with Yazidis. In their desperate attempt to escape the ruthless ISIS invasion in 2014, thousands of Yazidis sought shelter across the border in Turkey. The Muslim Turks shared many of the same preconceptions about the religious minority as did their Arab coreligionists. Erdoğan used hateful rhetoric against them and accused Yazidis of not believing in God.[14] This discrimination was clearly evidenced by the fact that those Yazidis who crossed the border were neither welcomed nor cared for by the national government. It was the Kurdish municipalities in the southeast that took on the responsibilities of aiding those who had lost everything to ISIS. Cities and towns in eastern Anatolia erected camps for the arriving Yazidis. When these facilities reached their capacity, the newcomers

6. A Complicated Part of the World

moved into the homes of locals. Some twenty-five hundred were taken in by the people of Silopi, fifteen hundred in Cizre, and thirty-five hundred lived in and around the Kurdish city of Batman. NGOs and local governments, rather than national ministries, aided the people in the camps. The Turkish government did not allow the new arrivals access to the public healthcare system. Local officials, however, did what they could to help, including issuing vouchers to Yazidis living in private homes for the purchase of food in nearby markets. Despite the goodwill of local Kurds, by 2018 most Yazidis, distrustful of the Turkish state, had either attempted to reach Europe or returned to Iraq. As a result, the majority of the refugee camps were closed that year.

The Killing of Abu Bakr al-Baghdadi

October 2019 was an exceptionally violent month in Syria. In addition to the clashes along the border, it also saw the death of the undisputed leader of the Islamic State. The coalition had lost track of al-Baghdadi when he slipped out of Baghuz prior to the battle. Several months later the SDF, working with the CIA, tracked him to an isolated compound in western Syria. It lay in the village of Barisha, three miles south of the Turkish border in Idlib province. Marine Corp General Frank McKenzie, who had assumed command of CENTCOM earlier in the year, was informed of the developments at his Tampa Bay headquarters. The general instructed the U.S. military to immediately assemble a strike force. On the morning of Saturday, October 26, General McKenzie gave the order to launch a mission later that night to "kill or capture" the elusive ISIS leader. The raid was code-named Operation Kayla Mueller, after the humanitarian aid worker who had been kidnapped by the terrorist group in 2013 and murdered a year and a half later.

That night, shortly after 11:00 p.m. Iraqi time, some 70 Delta Force soldiers and army Rangers lifted off from their staging area in eastern Syria. The special operations troops employed eight Chinook and Blackhawk helicopters for the one-hour flight to Barisha. Fighter aircraft and several drones were also dispatched to provide air cover and video feed of the mission. Both the Turks and Russians were notified of the operation so as to avoid any accidental interference with the U.S. force.

As the helicopters approached al-Baghdadi's location they came under fire from several militants on the ground. At the time, the Americans did not believe these fighters were members of ISIS (it is more likely that they were members of Hay'at Tahrir al-Sham). Nevertheless, since they were clearly hostile, they were killed by machine gun fire from the supporting choppers. It was estimated they numbered between 10 and 15 men. Once on the ground, the Americans surrounded, secured, and rapidly entered the compound. In Arabic, the soldiers called for all those inside the main house to peacefully surrender. Speaking at a press briefing at the Pentagon after the raid, General McKenzie stated: "Those who came out of the building were checked for weapons and moved away, U.S. forces detained and later released the noncombatants. The group was treated humanely at all times and included 11 children." He added that five people "did not respond to commands in Arabic to surrender and they continued to threaten the force. They were engaged by the raid force and killed: four women and a man."[15]

Al-Baghdadi himself slipped down into a tunnel as the Americans approached. He was accompanied by two of his children. As soon as he realized he was about to be captured, the terrorist leader detonated his suicide vest, killing himself and the children, both of whom were under 12 years of age. Following the explosion, a military working dog was sent in to find the body. For decades dogs, with their keen sense of smell, have been used by the army to locate humans, both living and deceased, under difficult battlefield conditions. After clearing the tunnel and recovering the remains of the self-proclaimed "caliph," the troops seized a large cache of ISIS material, including documents and electronics from the house. Two American soldiers were slightly wounded during the operation, as was Conan, the dog used in the operation. The Belgian Malinois was injured when he was exposed to live electrical cables in the tunnel but has since recovered.

The body of al-Baghdadi was placed aboard one of the helicopters. Once the force was airborne, the entire compound was destroyed by aircraft, so as to leave nothing that could be turned into a shrine to honor the ISIS leader. The entire raid lasted four hours. Al-Baghdadi's identity was soon confirmed by matching his DNA to a sample that had been taken while he was a prisoner at Camp Bucca in Iraq in 2004. His body was buried at sea. As much of the world, including the Yazidis, rejoiced at the news of al-Baghdadi's death, many wished he had been made to stand trial for his appalling crimes. The hundreds of thousands of men and women who suffered horrendous physical pain or emotional and psychological trauma at the hands of his minions or lost their lives due to his dictates must always be remembered. In his closing remarks General McKenzie stated: "We will not forget the victims of the atrocities he directed and inspired since 2014."[16]

6. A Complicated Part of the World

Justice for a Wronged Minority

After the collapse of the Islamic State the fate of captured militants along with their families had to be decided. There were many questions that needed to be answered. Should the jihadis be brought to trial for their crimes by the Kurds, the Syrian or Iraqi governments, or by an international tribunal? What of foreign nationals who had traveled to the Middle East to join ISIS? In what venue should they be made to answer for their actions? And what should be done with the families of these men? Fortunately, these issued were resolved relatively quickly. With regard to the wives and children of fighters, most were confined to SDF-run internment camps in Syria. The largest of these facilities was al-Hol, which, by November 2018, contained some seventy thousand people. The vast majority of internees were Iraqis or Syrians, but the camp also held citizens from dozens of other countries.

The process of releasing these civilians began in mid–2019, when a few hundred were allowed to return to their homes, although it was suspended due to the Turkish incursion that was launched later that year. The living conditions at al-Hol could only be described as harsh. The camp was overcrowded, and shortages of food and fresh water made life incredibly difficult. The Syrian Kurds had limited funds to spend to improve the living standards, and international humanitarian contributions were slow in coming. To make matters worse, some 40 people were murdered—and dozens more physically assaulted—within the camp by their own people. It was believed by the Kurdish authorities that these crimes were committed by diehard ISIS loyalists against those whose views may have softened during their time in captivity. Kurdish soldiers conducted sweeps through the camp and arrested 125 people for these offenses. Not surprisingly, many of those taken into custody had been members of the Hisbah (religious police) before the destruction of the caliphate.

During this period, negotiations between the SDF and the Iraqi government concerning the repatriation of the thirty thousand Iraqis held in al-Hol made some headway. Unfortunately, they ended when the Iraqis failed to erect their own holding facility in Nineveh province for the returnees. In April 2021, however, progress was made when the Kurds and the government in Baghdad agreed that 500 Iraqi families would be allowed to return to their home country. The SDF commander, Mazloum Abdi, called for other nations to retrieve their citizens, both fighters and family members, and place those who had joined ISIS on trial in their home countries. To date, most Western countries have been extremely reluctant

ISIS and the Yazidis

to take such action. Most have taken the position that trials should be held in the areas in which the crimes were committed, i.e., Syria or Iraq. A few nations have repatriated a handful of family members of ISIS fighters. Russia and Kazakhstan have accepted one thousand people, Uzbekistan has allowed 25 women and 73 children to return, and Germany and Finland have done the same with five women and 18 children.[17] International organizations such as Human Rights Watch that have interviewed internees have reported that dozens of women expressed their desire to return to their home countries. Their positions did not change even when informed that they may face criminal charges upon their return.

For years, al-Baghdadi had called for Muslims around the world to join him in the creation of a new "pure" state, one free of infidels and the corruption that has gripped the existing counties of the Middle East. Some chose to heed that call. ISIS counted jihadis from more than 120 nations within its ranks. From the West some five thousand Europeans and two hundred Americans made the journey to northwest Syria. With regard to U.S. citizens, it has been the policy of the Justice Department that these people should be returned to the United States to face criminal prosecution. To date, nine people have been charged with either "belonging to a terrorist organization," or "providing material support for a terrorist organization."[18]

On November 12, 2015, Mohammed Emwazi, one of the most feared and ruthless foreign members of ISIS, was killed in a U.S. drone strike. The British-born Emwazi, nicknamed Jihadi John, had beheaded multiple captives, including James Foley, Steven Sotloff, and Peter Kassig. Emwazi was one of a group of four British-born militants nicknamed "the Beatles" by hostages because of their accents. Other victims of these Islamic extremists included Alan Hemming, David Haines, and Kayla Mueller. Almost five years after Emwazi's death, two members of the notorious quartet, El Shafee Elsheikh and Alexanda Kotey, arrived in the United States to face terrorism charges in court. They had been captured by Kurdish forces in Syria and handed over to the U.S. Army in 2019. The pair were subsequently imprisoned at an American military base in Iraq. The British government stripped the two of their citizenship, but their extradition was delayed by a British court until the U.S. attorney general agreed not to seek the death penalty. Great Britain, after a long campaign beginning in 1965, abolished capital punishment in 1998. Once the Justice Department agreed to this demand, the United Kingdom provided crucial evidence against the accused terrorists.

The two men were indicted for multiple crimes, including conspiracy

6. A Complicated Part of the World

to provide material support to a foreign terrorist organization (which carries with it a life term should the act result in the death of a person), hostage taking resulting in death, and conspiracy to murder U.S. citizens outside the United States. The James Foley Legacy Foundation, on behalf of the American victims' families, issued a press release that stated: "James, Peter, Kayla and Steven were kidnapped, tortured, beaten, starved, and murdered by members of the Islamic State in Syria. Now our families can pursue accountability for these crimes against our children in a U.S. court." It continued: "Kotey and Elsheikh's extradition and trial in the United States will be the first step in the pursuit of justice for the alleged horrific human rights crimes against these four young Americans who saw the suffering of the Syrian people and wanted to help, whether by providing humanitarian aid or by telling the world about the evolving Syrian crisis."[19] Prosecutors claimed that the men, along with their two accomplices, murdered more than 27 people. On September 2, 2021, in a federal courtroom in Alexandria, Virginia, Kotey avoided a lengthy trial by pleading guilty to all charges. He faces life in prison. The fourth member of the group, Aine Davis, was captured in Turkey and is currently serving a seven-year sentence in that country.

In early 2020, frustrated that so few foreign governments were willing to repatriate their citizens, the Syrian Kurds announced that they would begin placing the militants in their custody on trial. The accused men included native Syrians, a large number of Iraqis, and hundreds of other foreign nationals. Interestingly, the officials of the semi-autonomous region declared that they would not impose the death penalty on ISIS members. Those convicted of being frontline fighters would receive sentences of up to 20 years in prison. To the east across the Euphrates, the followers of al-Baghdadi who were in Iraqi government custody also faced prosecution for their wartime actions.

By the time the Kurds began their judicial proceedings, Iraqi courts had already tried and convicted thousands of Islamic State fighters. The Iraqis had no compunction about handing out the death penalty to those convicted of belonging to a terrorist group. The defendants, captured on the battlefield weeks or months earlier, were tried under Iraq's broad counterterrorism law. While some applauded this swift form of justice, others, primarily human rights groups, argued that the trials were hasty affairs and incompatible with the concept of due process. They asserted that the courts made no distinction between men who were simply guilty of pledging their loyalty to ISIS and those who had actually committed war crimes and/or crimes against humanity. Often the accused were brought into court in groups, a lawyer having been appointed for each man only minutes earlier. This meant that the attorney had little time to review his client's file and mount a legal defense. Generally individuals plead not guilty to the charge of membership in a terrorist organization. Most also claimed that ISIS had forced them to remain in Syria, and that, had they tried to leave, they would have been seen as traitors and executed. Once evidence was presented, a panel of judges then quickly pronounced sentence.

Since most suspects were charged under the counterterrorism law the prosecution was under no obligation to add additional specific charges to an indictment. As a result, victims, including Yazidi women, were deprived of their day in court. In Iraq, traditionally women have been reluctant to speak out about rape. This hesitancy stems from the fear that the woman would be blamed for the assault and that such an incident would tarnish the family name. However, with regard to ISIS and the staggering number of women sexually abused by its members, attitudes have begun to change. Many Yazidi women have openly declared that it is necessary to testify against their attackers. In addition to serving justice, this act of testifying in court would, no doubt, provide a sense of closure for ISIS victims. One young Yazidi woman living in the Sharya camp in Kurdistan expressed her frustration: "This doesn't feel like justice yet, I want the men who took me, who raped me, to stand trial. And I want to have my voice heard in court."[20] Her feelings of anger and frustration are entirely understandable as she was only 14 when she and her sister were taken. The two girls were held for five months before they managed to escape.

What Yazidis have sought since the end of the caliphate is simple justice. The knowledge that ISIS fighters have been sent to prison or given the death sentence for belonging to a terrorist organization has provided many with some sense of satisfaction. Yet the Yazidi community as a whole will have closure only when the perpetrators who murdered their men and enslaved their women stand trial specifically for those crimes. In late February 2020, an event occurred that was clearly a step in the right direction. Alissa Rubin, the *New York Times* Baghdad bureau chief who survived the deadly helicopter crash on Mount Sinjar in the summer of 2014, covered a case that made judicial history in Iraq. For the first time a Yazidi woman, Ashwaq Haji Hamid Talo, testified in court against her ISIS kidnapper. The defendant, Mohammed Rashid Sahab, was found guilty of belonging to a terrorist organization and of abducting and raping Yazidi women. He was sentenced to death. At the conclusion of the trial Ms. Haji Hamid stated: "The most important thing to me is that my dream came true, and I was watching the one who raped me being sentenced to death.... I want

6. A Complicated Part of the World

my story to reach the whole world, so my message is heard by my friends and gives them the courage to do the same thing that I did."[21] Belkis Wille of Human Rights Watch commented: "This would be the first case I have come across in the last four years where a victim has had any meaningful role in the proceedings.... And it would be the first case where the charge of rape was added and addressed by the court, which is significant."[22]

Ms. Haji Hamid spent her childhood in the small town of Khana Sor, in northern Iraq. She came from a large family that included six sisters and 12 brothers; her father married twice. Her ordeal began when she and her sisters were captured. Each sister was sold separately to ISIS fighters for between $100 and $200. She herself was presented to Mohammed Sahab as a gift from his superiors since he had been wounded in battle. After several months Ms. Haji Hamid, along with other *sabaya*, slipped some sleeping pills into a meal they had prepared for Sahab and his companions. While the men slept, the women made good their escape. Eventually, her father was able to buy back five of his daughters for $15,000. Tragically the fate of one sister, Reham, remains unknown, as does that of five of the young woman's brothers. The family assumes that the men were murdered by ISIS in the first few days of the attack on Sinjar. At his trial Sahab refused to admit that he had done anything wrong and expressed no remorse for his actions.[23] While the trial and sentencing of Sahab can never erase the pain inflicted on this family, it did offer a small measure of justice to one Yazidi woman.

The international community has shown no desire to punish individual ISIS members for their deeds, leaving that job to the Iraqis and Kurds. Should the will to do so emerge, however, the means is available in the form of the International Criminal Court (ICC) in The Hague. Created by the United Nations, this unique international tribunal was established in 2002 after 60 nations ratified the Rome Statute of 1998. Its purpose has been to hold those accused of war crimes and crimes against humanity accountable when individual states cannot or will not do so. While its goal is laudable, the ICC has not been embraced by the governments of all countries. Today only 118 of the 193 member states of the United Nations have ratified the Rome Statute. Notable exceptions include Russia, India, China, and the United States.

Although the United States was the force behind the creation of both the Nuremburg and Tokyo war crimes trials in 1946, it, along with several other nations, expressed serious reservations when it came to supporting the new entity. These included the fact that the ICC is not directly accountable to the U.N. Security Council, and that the court could be politicized,

ISIS and the Yazidis

i.e., nations could use it to influence the foreign policy of others. To illustrate this point, in the past, American critics of the court have pointed to submissions to the ICC calling for the indictment of Bush administration officials for alleged war crimes in Iraq and Afghanistan. The most frequently cited reason for noncooperation, however, is that the ICC infringes upon national sovereignty. There are officials who feel that their national judicial systems alone, rather than an international body, should have the authority to punish their citizens should the need arise. When it comes to the two countries in the Middle East in which ISIS operated, neither Syria nor Iraq have ratified the Rome Statute.

Alleged war criminals, or those accused of violating human rights during a conflict, may be prosecuted by the ICC if cases are referred by a member state, or the U.N. Security Council. The ICC's prosecutor is also empowered to open cases on his own authority. The fact that dictators and tyrants can be held to an international standard when it comes to human rights gives hope to people all over the world who find themselves living under authoritarian regimes. A case in point involved Hassan Ahmad al-Bashir, the president of Sudan. Al-Bashir came to power in a coup in 1989. A brutal ruler, he immediately introduced Sharia law and eliminated any opposition. When a rebellion began in the Darfur region in 2003, he not only used the army but also sent in the Janjaweed (the term means "devils on horseback") to suppress the uprising. These Arab militias not only fought rebels but also raped, looted, and terrorized the local population. The conflict also included an ethnic component; the Janjaweed, which was controlled by the Sudanese government, was composed of Arab Muslims, while the victims in Darfur were primarily black African Christians. The fighting led to the deaths of some four hundred thousand people and the displacement of 2.5 million.[24] In 2008 the ICC issued a warrant for the arrest of President al-Bashir. He was charged with five counts of crimes against humanity, two of war crimes, and three counts of genocide. In 2019 the dictator was himself overthrown in a coup, convicted of corruption, and sent to prison. Once his current term is completed, the government of Sudan has pledged to hand him over to the ICC for prosecution of crimes committed in Darfur.

It is not only national leaders who can and should be held accountable for their genocidal actions but soldiers on the ground who carry out such acts. By obeying unjust orders, e.g., the murder of unarmed prisoners or women and children, these men become complicit in the crime. Following this logic, the ICC would be entirely justified in charging individual ISIS commanders and fighters for the myriad of crimes committed against

6. A Complicated Part of the World

the Yazidi people. Since the collapse of the Islamic State, thousands of ISIS militants who were not captured by the Kurds have quietly slipped back into communities in Syria or returned to their home countries. Should these former fighters travel to, or reside in, a nation that has ratified the Rome Statute, they could be arrested and sent to The Hague to stand trial. The prosecution of such men would serve as a powerful deterrent to those in the future who might consider taking part in war crimes and crimes against humanity.

Another way in which the extremists could be held accountable for implementing genocide against the Yazidis would be for the United Nations Security Council to create a special tribunal. There is precedent for such a move. Between 1991 and 1995, as Yugoslavia disintegrated, vicious fighting erupted in Bosnia between Serbs, Croats, and Bosnian Muslims. The majority of atrocities were committed by Bosnian Serbs and the Serbian army against Bosnian Muslims as part of a de facto "ethnic cleansing." It made no difference to Bosnian Serbs, who were striving to consolidate power, that their neighbors considered themselves Europeans first, that their families had lived in the Balkans for centuries, and that very few were observant Muslims. This civil war nearly destroyed Bosnia, as more than one hundred thousand soldiers and civilians were killed, including sixty-five thousand Bosnian Muslims. After enduring months of sieges and indiscriminate shelling of their homes, 1.3 million men, women, and children became refugees.[25] As part of the Serb strategy to terrorize and destroy the Muslim community, tens of thousands of Bosnian Muslim women were sexually assaulted by Serbian soldiers, many in aptly named "rape camps." In addition to this and other war crimes, in July 1995, Bosnian Serbs committed an outrageous act of mass murder when they shot to death some eight thousand unarmed Muslim men and boys on the outskirts of the city of Srebrenica. Nothing of the kind had been seen in Europe since World War II.

After more than three years the war finally ended through a combination of diplomacy and NATO airstrikes against Serbian military positions. In December 1995 peace returned to Bosnia. Responding to the undeniable human rights violations, the U.N.'s upper body had previously created the International Criminal Tribunal for the former Yugoslavia (ICTY) in 1993. The ICTY indicted 21 defendants for the Srebrenica massacre. The Serbian president, Slobodan Milošević, was also charged with genocide and complicity in the murders at Srebrenica. The ICTY, like the ICC today, was entirely dependent upon the cooperation of governments to arrest and hand over accused war criminals. In 2001 the Serb authorities arrested the former president and sent him to The Hague to stand trial. Unfortunately for the cause of justice, Milošević died of a heart attack on March 11, 2006, before the trial had concluded. Following his death the court found no evidence that tied him directly to the genocide, but the Serbian leader was found guilty of failure to prevent it and of not punishing those involved.

Aside from Milošević, two other notorious Serb leaders became associated with the Bosnian genocide: Radovan Karadžić, the president of the self-proclaimed Serbian republic, and Ratko Mladić, the ruthless general commanding the Bosnian Serb military forces. The two men made no secret of their goals of driving out and/or eliminating the Muslim population of Bosnia. They were both prosecuted under Article 7 of the ICTY Statute (which could serve as a model for future indictments against ISIS figures). The provision held that "a person who planned, instigated, ordered, committed, or otherwise aided and abetted, in the planning, preparation or execution of a crime [… genocide; crimes against humanity] … shall be individually responsible for the crime."[26]

When peace finally returned to the former Yugoslavia, Radovan Karadžić, aware that he was a wanted man, hid for years in Serbia under an assumed name. In 1995 he was indicted by the ICTY. Years later, on July 21, 2008, he was arrested and sent to stand trial. In 2016 he was found guilty of 10 of 11 charges and sentenced to 40 years imprisonment. Like his leader, General Ratko Mladić was also arrested and sent to The Hague to answer for his crimes. On November 22, 2017, the disgraced officer was sentenced to life in prison, having been convicted on 10 counts of genocide and human rights violations. On June 8, 2021, an appeals court refused to overturn his conviction. He will remain in prison for the rest of his life.

The Future of the Yazidis

Several years after the vicious attack upon Sinjar, the vast majority of Yazidis remain in internally displaced persons camps in Kurdistan. The Esyan camp in Duhok's Shekhan district, for example, is home to 13,400 people living in three thousand tents. Although most Yazidis would like to return to Sinjar City, that remains a difficult undertaking. Large parts of it remain in ruins. Neither the Iraqi government, the Kurdistan Regional Government, nor the United Nations has done much to aid reconstruction efforts. As in other cities in Iraq and Syria, almost all of Sinjar's infrastructure was destroyed by ISIS either during the initial attack or in the battle to retake the city. There are several reasons for the lack of movement on

6. A Complicated Part of the World

this issue, including the fact that the Iraqi economy has slowed, the impact of the COVID-19 pandemic, and the ongoing dispute between the central government and the KRG over which entity will control the area. Yazidis put it more simply: they believe no help has arrived because they are poor and have no political power.

The region's slow recovery has become intertwined in politics. Two years after the liberation of Sinjar, tensions between the national government and the KRG, which had always been contentious, grew worse. In 2017, Kurdistan's president, Masoud Barzani, called for a referendum on independence. The result was clear: 93 percent of Kurds voted in favor of separating from Iraq.[27] The vote enraged Iraqi Prime Minister Haider al-Abadi. Rather than allow the country to break apart, he sent troops north to reclaim territory then occupied by the Kurds. His forces moved into Kirkuk (with its rich oil fields) and Nineveh province, including Sinjar. Today Iraqi soldiers are in control of the city. The U.S. government, also not wishing to see Iraq divided, backed the prime minister's move. The State Department issued a statement that read: "The vote and the results lack legitimacy, and we continue to support a united, federal, democratic and prosperous Iraq."[28]

Even before Sinjar changed hands in 2017, it had been difficult for Yazidis to return. While ISIS had been driven from the city in November 2015, safety concerns prevented a large-scale movement of civilians from reclaiming their homes and property. Militants remained in the region, and Shia militias took up positions south of Sinjar. Adding to this complex situation was the fact that the PKK, which had been instrumental in breaking the siege of Mount Sinjar, was engaged in a power struggle with the KRG's Peshmerga. The two forces each held territory in and around Sinjar City. Though both armed groups were composed of Kurds and had a common enemy in ISIS, relations between the two remained cool. The situation became even more unstable when, in March 2018, Turkey threatened to move against its old enemy the PKK in Sinjar. The Iraqi government quickly redeployed troops north and warned President Erdoğan not to implement his plan. At the same time, Baghdad quietly applied diplomatic pressure to persuade the PKK to withdraw from the area. In late March, an agreement was reached, and the last five hundred fighters departed Sinjar. To date only 20 percent of Yazidis have returned to the region they once called home.[29]

Since the summer of 2014 thousands of Yazidis have moved abroad in search of safety. While many hoped to begin new lives in Europe, some have arrived in places as far away as Australia. In 2017 the government of

ISIS and the Yazidis

Canada, which has been very friendly to refugees in the past, granted asylum to twelve hundred Yazidis.[30] That number has since increased to fourteen hundred. It has also permitted thousands of Syrian refugees fleeing the civil war to remain within its borders. In the United States the Yazidi population numbers only some four thousand people. This may change in the future as the United States moves toward a more liberal policy on immigration. In spring 2021 President Joe Biden raised the yearly number of refugees to be admitted to 62,500. This marked a dramatic increase from the record low of fifteen thousand set by the Trump administration.

Unquestionably, Germany has been the most generous country when it comes to taking in displaced Yazidis. Approximately 150,000 have resettled in that nation. It is the largest Yazidi community in exile. In 2015 alone, the government approved 97 percent of asylum applications filed by Yazidis. By 2018 that figure had fallen to 60 percent as German authorities determined that Kurdistan was no longer threatened by ISIS and Yazidis could safely live in that part of Iraq.[31]

Faced with the choice of staying in crowded IDP camps in Iraqi Kurdistan or returning to an unsafe and uncertain future in Sinjar, it is no wonder some Yazidis have sought to emigrate. Lilah Salih spent three years in an IDP camp before immigrating, along with her husband, to the United States in 2017. In an interview with Voice of America (VOA) she echoed the feelings of many who have moved to Europe or the United States to begin new lives. She declared, "I feel safe here, I am not discriminated against because of my religion; I am respected."[32] Lilah has continued her education and is on track to become a nurse. Her desire is to one day use her medical skills to aid her fellow Yazidis.

In Sinjar City itself, public services have yet to be fully restored. Hospitals and schools in the region are only now beginning to reopen. For some people returning to Sinjar is not an option for another reason. The events of 2014 are still too traumatic, memories too fresh. Thoughts of how their Arab neighbors betrayed them and sided with the terrorists continue to trouble Yazidis. Whether these acts were done for profit or out of a sense of self-preservation is moot. The fact that, after years of living peacefully together, one group would sell out the other is hard to forgive. The question arises, can or should these people be trusted again?

Then there are the physical reminders of what happened, the empty shells of homes and businesses that were looted and destroyed. Worst of all, of course, are the memories of loved ones who will never return. Thousands of innocent people were murdered for no other reason than that they remained true to their faith. Yazda, the Yazidi advocacy organization, has

6. A Complicated Part of the World

confirmed there are 64 mass graves across the region that have yet to be examined.

For many, though, Sinjar has always been and will continue to be the Yazidi homeland. Rebuilding their lives there will be difficult but not impossible. The Nobel Peace Prize winner Nadia Murad has advised her fellow Yazidis to return to Sinjar. She believes this will send a clear message to the world that ISIS fanatics have failed in their plans to scatter and destroy her people. The activist has also stated that the Iraqi government must increase its efforts at de-mining the area, and she has consistently lobbied in favor of financial compensation for Yazidi survivors.

The political situation in Iraq remains unstable. Even though ISIS has been vanquished for the most part, the movement is not entirely dead. Although its adherents have gone underground, they continue to plague Iraqi society. On January 21, 2021, ISIS claimed responsibility for twin car bombings at a clothing market in central Baghdad that left 32 people dead and 110 injured. Iraq's U.S.-trained Counter Terrorism Service (CTS), along with the Iraqi Federal Police, still conduct raids in order to arrest suspected ISIS members. Recently there have been multiple skirmishes around the city of Kirkuk. The security forces must continue to be vigilant if they are to prevent a resurgence of this malevolent force.

Although the United States has continued to provide support to the Iraqi military, the current prime minister, Mustafa al-Kadhimi, has had trouble reassuring Iraqis that the government can protect its people and keep them safe. In addition to dealing with the remnants of ISIS, al-Kadhimi is struggling to root out corruption in the federal bureaucracy and disarm the various militias. The Shia have been particularly reluctant to cooperate with the national government. To add to the instability of the country, the economy has faltered and one in three Iraqis lives below the poverty line.

Since the defeat of the caliphate there has been a drawdown of U.S. personnel in Iraq. In November 2020, the Pentagon announced that by January 15, 2021, troop levels would be reduced from three thousand to twenty-five hundred (with a few hundred remaining in eastern Syria). This action was taken in conjunction with the withdrawal of troops from Afghanistan, set to be reduced from forty-three hundred to twenty-five hundred by the same date. The last American troops were scheduled to depart that country on September 11, 2021, exactly 20 years after the attacks of 9/11. President Joe Biden decided that no U.S. military personnel should remain in country and ordered all troops out by the end of August. The withdrawal of U.S. forces only emboldened the Taliban, leading it to

ISIS and the Yazidis

launch offensives against Afghan government forces throughout the country. Without American air and—equally important—moral support, the Afghan army began to disintegrate.

In one of the most catastrophic military collapses in history, the Afghan army melted away and, contrary to pundits' predictions that the army would fight on for months if not several years, the Taliban captured Kabul in only 11 days. Anyone who had opposed the terrorists, including thousands of translators and guides who had aided U.S troops over 20 years, was now in grave danger. These brave men and women, along with their families, would surely be labeled as traitors and executed now that the militants had returned to power. In a gallant effort, some 123,000 Afghan civilians were airlifted out from Kabul airport in the final days of the American presence in Afghanistan. The last Americans departed the capital a few minutes past midnight on Tuesday, August 31, 2021. While it is clear that nations must themselves take on a large measure of responsibility in dealing with extremist groups within their own borders, the debacle in Afghanistan has given the U.S. government pause. With regard to Iraq, for the time being the small contingent of American troops will remain to assist the Iraqi army and advise the government.

The Iraqis who would like to see the last twenty-five hundred American military advisors leave the country claim that ISIS is no longer a threat. Those who wish to see them remain point out that the militants have been driven underground but could easily reemerge. The Kurds continue to view the United States as their most powerful ally, and most hope the Americans will maintain a small contingent of troops in Erbil and Baghdad. In the north, the dispute between the national government and the KRG over disputed territory has only benefited ISIS. The mountainous areas south of Erbil between Iraqi army and Peshmerga positions has become a haven for the remnants of the terrorist army. Recently the Iraqi military launched a two-week operation in the region in which 30 jihadis were killed and one hundred hideouts destroyed. In addition to dealing with what remains of ISIS, U.S. troops on Iraqi army bases have also come under rocket assault by Shia militias. Since the killing of Iran's General Soleimani, these powerful groups have demanded that the United States withdraw all its forces from Iraq and continue to press Prime Minister al-Kadhimi on the issue.

In the years since Operation Inherent Resolve began in late 2014, American casualties have mounted. While the Kurds and the Iraqi army bore the brunt of the ground fighting in the war against ISIS, the United States has suffered losses in Iraq and Syria. To date, 102 American

6. A Complicated Part of the World

soldiers have lost their lives in the struggle against the terrorist group.[33] Twenty-one military personnel have been killed in action.[34] Eighty-one have died in other ways while deployed (these include illness, accidents, and suicide) and 230 have been wounded in action.

Today the word "hero" is overused in daily conversation, but the soldiers who rescued the Yazidis trapped on Mount Sinjar in the summer of 2014 were truly heroic. The fighters of the YPG, YPJ, and PKK performed admirably as they broke the ISIS lines and led frightened men, women, and children to safety. A debt of gratitude is also owed to the Iraqi army and Peshmerga that drove ISIS from Iraq and the Kurdish forces that pressed the attack in Syria in order to destroy the caliphate. Those soldiers who fell did not die in vain as they helped rid the world of a ruthless, blood-stained regime based on a twisted interpretation of Islam. The fact that scores of countries agreed to participate in the Global Coalition to Defeat ISIS demonstrates that nations can set aside their differences and work together for the common good of humanity. In the face of such a threat the countries of the coalition each contributed what they could toward the destruction of a heinous entity.

The American effort to resupply and defend the Yazidis on Mount Sinjar was truly a shining moment for the United States. This action undoubtedly saved men, women, and children from dying of thirst and exposure. In addition, it also bought time for Kurdish units to reach the tens of thousands of survivors on the mountain. Following the successful evacuation of the Yazidis, President Obama made a short speech in which he praised the efforts of the U.S. armed forces. He stated: "Because of the skill and professionalism of our military—and the generosity of our people—we broke the ISIL (ISIS) siege of Mount Sinjar; we helped vulnerable people reach safety; and we helped save many innocent lives." The President continued: "As Commander-in-Chief, I could not be prouder of the men and women of our military who carried out this humanitarian operation almost flawlessly. I'm very grateful to them and I know that those who were trapped on that mountain are extraordinarily grateful as well."[35] As for the Yazidi people themselves, they have weathered the ISIS storm that threatened to annihilate their culture. There is no doubt that they will continue to endure as they have for over thirty-five hundred years.

Chapter Notes

Chapter 1

1. Haider E., telephone interview by author, May 4, 2020.
2. Birgul Acikyildiz, *The Yezidis: The History of a Community, Culture and Religion* (New York: I.B.Tauris, 2010), 71.
3. *Ibid.*, 86.
4. Even though the United States was a major Allied power, it focused its manpower and resources on the war in Europe and for the most part left the Middle East theater to Great Britain and France.
5. Elizabeth Schmermund, *ISIS and the Yazidi Genocide* (New York: The Rosen Publishing Group, 2018), 9.
6. Angela Adams, *The War Against ISIS* (New York: Cavendish Square Publishing, 2018), 6.
7. Editors, "Qusay and Uday Hussein Killed," *History*, February 9, 2010, www.history.com/this-day-in-history/qusay-and-uday-hussein-killed, retrieved July 15, 2020.
8. Matthew White, *The Great Big Book of Horrible Things: The Definitive Chronicle of History's 100 Worst Atrocities* (New York: W.W. Norton, , 2012), 512.
9. One American commander obviously had a good sense of humor: As his armored unit moved forward, he played the song "Rock the Casbah" by the Clash from a loudspeaker mounted on his tank.
10. White, 515.
11. Schmermund, 12.
12. Saddam Hussein's three daughters—Raghad, Rana, and Hala—fled with their children to Jordan in 2003.
13. Montenegro and Kosovo became independent nations in 2006 and 2008, respectively.
14. Michael Weiss and Hassan Hassan, *ISIS Inside the Army of Terror* (New York: Regan Arts, 2015), 6.
15. *Ibid.*, 14.
16. *Ibid.*, 28.
17. Kennedy Hickman, "Iraq War: Second Battle of Fallujah," *ThoughtCo.*, March 25, 2018, www.thoughtco.com/Iraq-war-second-battle-of-fallujah-2360 957, retrieved July 17, 2020.
18. Weiss and Hassan, 56.
19. *Ibid.*, 65.
20. U.S. Commission on International Religious Freedom, December 2008, Report of the United States Commission on Religious Freedom on Iraq, 22. www.uscirf.gov/sites/default/files/resources/iraq%20report%20final.pdf#page=20, retrieved July 17, 2020.
21. *Ibid.*, 20.
22. *Ibid.*
23. Yitzhak Felsher, interview by author, Las Vegas, Nevada, August 14, 2014.
24. Najim Abed Al-Jabouri and Sterling Jensen, "The Iraqi and AQI Roles in the Sunni Awakening," *PRISM: A Journal of the Center for Complex Operations* 2, no. 1 (December 2010): 1.
25. *Ibid.*, 9.
26. *Ibid.*
27. In Arab culture it is considered an insult to show the soles of your shoes to someone. That is why, when the large statue of Saddam Hussein was pulled down, the world saw images of men and boys hitting it with their shoes.
28. Weiss and Hassan, 79.
29. Some people, including President Barack Obama, used the term ISIL, which stands for the Islamic State of Iraq and the Levant. The Levant refers to the lands of the eastern Mediterranean.

Notes—Chapter 2

Chapter 2

1. *Frontline: Once Upon a Time in Iraq*, directed by James Bluemel (Boston: PBS, WGBH, July 14, 2020), www.pbs.org/wgbh/frontline/once-upon-a-time-in-iraq/, retrieved November 10, 2020.
2. Ibid.
3. Jared Keller, "ISIS has just as many fighters in Iraq and Syria as it did 4 years ago," *Task & Purpose*, August 15, 2018, www.taskandpurpose.com/bulletpoint/-number-isis-fighters-iraq-syria, retrieved July 8, 2020.
4. Major Adam Scher, "The collapse of the Iraqi army's will to fight: A lack of motivation, training, or force generation?" *Army U Press*, February 19, 2016, www.armyupress.army.mil/Portals/7/Army-Press-Online-Journal/documents/16-8-Scher-19Feb16.pdf, retrieved August 10, 2020.
5. Ibid., 2.
6. The Old Testament book of Ezra–Nehemiah relates the story of how the two men led the Jews back to Jerusalem to rebuild the Temple and reestablish their community after the fall of Babylon in 539 BC.
7. Susan Shand, *Sinjar: 14 Days that Saved the Yazidis from the Islamic State* (Guilford, CT: Lyons Press, 2018), 59.
8. Haider E. interview.
9. Cathy Otten, *With Ash on Their Faces: Yezidi Women and the Islamic State* (New York: OR Books, 2017), 58.
10. Shand, 61.
11. Office of the High Commissioner for Human Rights, "Report on the Protection of Civilians in the Armed Conflict in Iraq: July 6 to September 10, 2014," 14, www.ohchr.org/sites/default/files/Documents/Countries/IQ/UNAMI_OHCHR_POC_Report_FINAL_6July_10September2014.pdf, retrieved August 14, 2020.
12. Ibid.
13. Shand, 56.
14. Schmermund, 19.
15. Winstonchurchill.org/resources/speeches/1940-the-finest-hour/be-ye-men-of-valor/, accessed October 10, 2022.
16. Ben Kiernan, *Blood and Soil: A World History of Genocide and Extermination from Sparta to Darfur* (New Haven: Yale University Press, 2007), 10.
17. U.N. Human Rights Council, "'They came to destroy': ISIS crimes against the Yazidis," June 15, 2016, www.reliefweb.int/report/syrian-arab-republic/they-came-destroy-isis-crimes-against-yazidis-human-rights-council, retrieved September 29, 2020.
18. The magazine was named for the small Syrian town that, according to a hadith, will serve as the location for a massive battle between the followers of Islam and infidels that will end in the destruction of the world. It has been likened to the Christian concept of Armageddon in the Book of Revelation.
19. Jessica Stern and J. M. Berger, *ISIS: The State of Terror* (New York: HarperCollins, 2015), 216.
20. Otten, 16.
21. United Nations Independent International Commission of Inquiry on the Syrian Arab Republic, "The Yazidi Genocide," *The Cairo Review of Global Affairs* (Fall 2016), www.thecairoreview.com/essays/the-yazidi-genocide/, retrieved August 8, 2020.
22. Otten, 112.
23. "The Yazidi Genocide," 10.
24. "'They came to destroy': ISIS crimes against the Yazidis," 14.
25. Otten, 190.
26. Emma Graham-Harrison, "'I was sold seven times': Yazidi women welcomed back into the faith," *The Guardian*, July 1, 2017, www.theguardian.com/global-development/2017/jul/01/i-was-sold-seven-times-yazidi-women-welcomed-back-into-the-faith, retrieved August 25, 2020.
27. "Report on the Protection of Civilians in the Armed Conflict in Iraq: July 6 to September 10, 2014," 13.
28. Shand, 77.
29. Chris Dunker, "Letter from Representative Jeff Fortenberry to President Barack Obama," *Lincoln Journal Star*, August 5, 2014, journalstar.com/letter-from-rep-jeff-fortenberry-to-president-barack-obama/pdf_017f3b8b-7798-5230-99fe-67764662fc42.html, retrieved January 20, 2020.
30. Ibid.

Notes—Chapter 3

31. Bridget Johnson, "Rep. Wolf to Obama: 'You will come to sincerely regret your failure to stop the genocide,'" *PJ Media*, August 8, 2014, pjmedia.com/tatler/2014/08/07/rep-wolf-to-obama-you-will-come-to-sincerely-regret-your-failure-to-take-action-to-stop-the-genocide-n194677, retrieved January 20, 2020.
32. *Ibid.*
33. Haider E. interview.
34. The other Yazidi member of the national legislature, an elderly man, rarely attended sessions or voted on bills.
35. YouTube, video uploaded by Syrian Perspective, August 7, 2014, www.youtube.com/watch?v=bnqedigxi8w, retrieved August 30, 2020.
36. Abigail Haworth, "'If they capture me, they will execute me at once': Meet the Iraqi woman standing up to ISIS," *Marie Claire*, January 8, 2015, www.marieclaire.com/politics/news/a12989/iraqs-most-wanted-woman/, retrieved August 31, 2020.
37. Shand, 128.
38. Dan Froomkin, "How many U.S. soldiers were wounded in Iraq? Guess again," *HuffPost*, January 30, 2011, www.huffpost.com/entry/iraq-soldiers-wounded_b_1176276, retrieved August 27, 2020.
39. www.Obamawhitehouse.archives.gov/pressoffice/2014/08/07/statement-president, retrieved September 8, 2020.
40. Shand, 135.
41. "New UK aid supplies delivered to Iraq," August 14, 2014, www.gov.uk/governemnt/news/new-uk-aid-supplies-delivered-to-iraq, retrieved September 9, 2020.
42. "Speeches and Selected Remarks of Secretary of Defense Chuck Hagel February 2013-February 2015," Press conference on Iraq: August 8, 2014, Archives and Special Collections, University of Nebraska, Omaha.
43. *Ibid.*
44. Martin Chulov, "U.S. forces bomb ISIS militant positions in northern Iraq," *The Guardian*, August 8, 2014, www.theguardian.com/world/2014/aug/08/us-iraq-air-strikes-isis-irbil, retrieved September 10, 2020.
45. "U.S. forces land on Mount Sinjar in Iraq," *Irish Times*, August 13, 2014, www.irishtimes.com/news/world/middle-east/us-forces-land-on-mount-sinjar-in-iraq-1.1895602, retrieved September 14, 2020.
46. Haider E. interview.
47. Associated Press, "Defense Secretary Hagel says 130 more military advisors going to Iraq," *KPBS*, August 12, 2014, www.kpbs.org/news/2014/aug/12/-hagal-hold-town-hall-camp-pendleton/, retrieved September 17, 2020.
48. Shand, 168.
49. Shand, 171.
50. The Editorial Board, "Preventing a slaughter in Iraq," *The New York Times*, August 8, 2014, www.nytimes/2014/08/08/opinion/preventing-a-slaughter-in-iraq.html, retrieved September 18, 2020.
51. Alissa J. Rubin, "On a helicopter going down: Inside a lethal crash in Iraq," *The New York Times*, August 16, 2014, www.nytimes.com/2014/08/16/world/middleeast/Iraq-alissa-j-rubin-a-times-correspondent-recounts-fatal-helicopter-crash-in-kurdistan.html, retrieved September 20, 2020.
52. *Ibid.*, 4.
53. Schmermund, 23.
54. Shand, 195.
55. *Ibid.*, 196.
56. Dan Lamothe, "Marines planned massive evacuation on Iraq's Mount Sinjar," *The Washington Post*, October 8, 2014, www.washingtonpost.com/news/checkpoint/wp/2014/10/08/marines-planned-massive-evacuation-on-iraqs-mount-sinjar/, retrieved September 27, 2020.
57. "Transcript: President Obama's Speech on Combating ISIS and Terrorism," CNN, September 10, 2014, www.cnn.com/2014/09/10/politics/transcript-obama-syria-isis-speech/index.html, retrieved December 26, 2020.
58. *Ibid.*
59. Adams, 22.

Chapter 3

1. Though taxes were high, the Romans did provide vital services. In an amusing

Notes—Chapter 3

scene from the film *Monty Python's Life of Brian*, which is set in Judea, one rebel asks, "What have the Romans ever done for us?" The others shout out numerous Roman contributions, to which the first rebel responds, "But apart from the sanitation, medicine, education, wine, public order, irrigation, roads, the freshwater system, and public health, what have the Romans ever done for us?"

2. A Roman legion was composed of 10 cohorts of 500 men each, totaling five thousand men plus auxiliaries.

3. White, 50.

4. Flavius Josephus, *The works of Flavius Josephus, the learned and authentic Jewish Historian and Celebrated Warrior* (Cincinnati : E. Morgan and Company, 1847), 543.

5. *Ibid.*

6. *Ibid.*, 562.

7. *Ibid.*, 573.

8. White, 51.

9. Elon Gilad, "The Bar Kochba Revolt: A Disaster Celebrated by Zionists on Lag Ba'Omer," *Haaretz*, October 4, 2018, www.haaretz.com/jewish/.premium-bar-kochba-revolt-utter-disaster-1.5358629, retrieved October 25, 2020.

10. *Ibid.*, 7.

11. White, 52.

12. David M. Crowe, *War Crimes, Genocide, and Justice* (New York: Palgrave Macmillan, 2014), 18.

13. White, 99.

14. Terence Wise and G. A. Embleton, *Armies of the Crusades* (London: Osprey Publishing, 1978), 5.

15. David Nicolle, *The First Crusade 1096–1099: Conquest of the Holy Land* (Oxford: Osprey Publishing, 2003), 56.

16. *Ibid.*, p. 69.

17. *Ibid.*, 69.

18. *Ibid.*, 80.

19. *Ibid.*

20. Crowe, 19.

21. An impressive statue of Richard the Lionheart on horseback with a raised sword has stood outside the houses of Parliament in London since the middle of the nineteenth century.

22. Peter Balakian, *The Burning Tigris: The Armenian Genocide and America's Response* (New York: Perennial, 2003), 106.

23. Kennedy Hickman, "Hitler and the Armenian Genocide," *Genocideeducation*, 2014, the Genocide Education Project, www.genocideeducation.org/background/hitler-and-the-armenian-genocide/, retrieved December 12, 2019.

24. White, 353.

25. Pasha is an honorary title given to high-ranking officials and military officers equivalent to a British lord.

26. This attack ultimately proved disastrous for the Allies. In January 1916, after suffering nearly 250,000 casualties, Allied troops were forced to withdraw. Politically, the defeat cost the future British Prime Minister Winston Churchill his position as First Lord of the Admiralty.

27. Balakian, 187.

28. Kiernan, 409.

29. *Ibid.*, 411.

30. Balakian, 336.

31. Kiernan, 412.

32. Balakian, 184.

33. *Ibid.*, 194.

34. Crowe, 107.

35. Henry Morgenthau, *Ambassador Morgenthau's Story: A Personal Account of the Armenian Genocide* (New York: Doubleday, Page and Company, 1918), 38.

36. Balakian, 243.

37. Jay Winter, ed., *America and the Armenian Genocide of 1915* (Cambridge: Cambridge University Press, 2003), 160.

38. *Ibid.*, 243.

39. *Ibid.*, 244.

40. *Ibid.*, 249.

41. In January 1917 Arthur Zimmermann, the German foreign minister, dispatched a cable to the German ambassador in Mexico City. The message, which was intercepted by the British and passed along to the Americans, revealed a plan to form an alliance with Mexico if the United States declared war on Germany. The telegram stated that in exchange for Mexican participation, Germany was prepared to aid that country in recovering Texas, New Mexico, and Arizona, lands that had been lost to the U.S. in the mid-nineteenth century.

42. Morgenthau, 256.

43. Crowe, 111.

44. Martine Madden, "Armin Wegner, the German who stood up to genocide of

Notes—Chapter 4

both Armenians and Jews," *Irish Times*, May 7, 2015, www.irishtimes.com/culture/books/armin-wegner-the-german-who-stood-up-to-genocide-of-both-armenians-and-jews-1.2201998, retrieved December 9, 2019.

45. Balakian, 258.

46. "The virtually unknown genocide of Yazidis by the Turks along with the Armenians, Assyrians and Greeks," *Ihgjlm* (Institute on the Holocaust and Genocide in Jerusalem), www.ihgjlm.com/the-virtually-unknown-genocide-of-yezidis-by-the-turks-along-with-the-armenians-assyrians-and-greeks/, retrieved November 20, 2019. Originally published in *Genocide Prevention Now*, Special Issue 5, Winter 2011.

47. Maria Six-Hohenbalken, "The 72nd Firman of the Yezidis: A 'Hidden Genocide' during WWI?" *Genocide Studies International* 13, no. 1 (Spring 2019): 67.

48. *Ibid.*

49. Morgenthau, 224.

50. *Ibid.*, 228.

51. *Ibid.*, 229.

52. *Ibid.*, 236.

53. Crowe, 112.

54. In 1934 Mustafa Kemal was given the surname "Atatürk," meaning "father of the Turks," to honor his many accomplishments.

Chapter 4

1. Faisal I., interview by author, Lincoln, Nebraska, November 6, 2019.

2. Ahmed M., interview by author, Lincoln, Nebraska, November 6, 2019.

3. Omar R., interview by author, Lincoln, Nebraska, November 7, 2019.

4. Mesur H., interview by author, Lincoln, Nebraska, November 8, 2019.

5. Falah R., interview by author, Lincoln, Nebraska, November 7, 2019.

6. Amel H., interview by author, Lincoln, Nebraska, November 8, 2019.

7. Shahab B., interview by author, Lincoln, Nebraska, November 9, 2019.

8. Amnesty International, "Ethnic Cleansing on a Historic Scale: Islamic State's Systematic Targeting of Minorities in Northern Iraq," 2014, https://www.amnesty.org/en/wp-content/uploads/2021/06/mde140112014en.pdf, retrieved January 10, 2021.

9. *Ibid.*

10. Dana J. H. Pittard and Wes J. Bryant, *Hunting the Caliphate: America's War on ISIS and the Dawn of the Strike Cell* (New York: Post Hill Press, 2019), 71.

11. Command Sergeant Major Mark A. Millare, "Defeating ISIS in Iraq: A Race Against Time," *Army U Press*, 3, January 2019, www.armyupress.army.mil/portals/7/nco-journal/docs/2019/january/-defeating-isis/defeating-isis-in-iraq.pdf, retrieved January 9, 2021.

12. *Ibid.*

13. Pittard and Bryant, 97.

14. "Battle for Sinjar, Iraq," Threat Action Report, April 2016, 4, www.info.publicintelligence.net/usarmy-battleforsinjar.pdf, retrieved January 10, 2020.

15. Schmermund, 35.

16. "Mass grave of Yazidi women executed by ISIS found in Iraq," *Al Arabiya English*, November 4, 2015, english.alarabiya.net/News/middle-east/2015/11/14/Mass-grave-of-Yazidi-women-executed-by-ISIS-found-in-Iraq, retrieved July 6, 2018.

17. Stephen Losey, "As Mosul battle neared end, anti-ISIS airstrikes reached new peak," *Air Force Times*, July 10, 2017, www.airforcetimes.com/news/your-air-force/2017/07/10/as-mosul-battle-neared-end-anti-isis-airstrikes-reached-new-peak/, retrieved February 2, 2021.

18. *Ibid.*

19. Pittard and Bryant, 207.

20. David Cenciotti, "U.S. B52 Bombers have dropped 3,419 weapons on Daesh targets since April 2016," *The Aviationist*, February 21, 2017, www.theaviationist.com/2017/02/21/u-s-b-52-bombers-have-dropped-3419-weapons-on-daesh-targets-since-april-2016, retrieved January 31, 2021.

21. Pittard and Bryant, 215.

22. Jeremy Bender, "ISIS Militants Captured 52 American-Made Weapons That Cost $500,000 Each," *Business Insider*, July 15, 2014, www.businessinsider.com/isis-has-52-american-weapons-that-can-hit-baghdad-2014-7, retrieved January 5, 2021.

23. Alistair Pope, "The Rise and Fall of ISIS Armor," *Modern War* #46 (March–April 2020).

24. *Ibid.*
25. Millare, 5.
26. Ralph Ellis, "Enormous Resources on Rescue Attempt for Kayla Mueller, Obama Says," CNN, February 12, 2015, www.cnn.com/2015/02/12/middleeast/mueller-rescue-attempts/, retrieved February 16, 2020.
27. Pittard and Bryant, 135.
28. Weiss and Hassan, 234.
29. *Ibid.*
30. General Joseph Votel, telephone interview by author, June 23, 2020.
31. *Ibid.*
32. *Ibid.*
33. Gayle Tzemach Lemmon, *The Daughters of Kobani: A Story of Rebellion, Courage, and Justice* (New York, Penguin Press, 2021), 89.
34. *Ibid.*, 90.

Chapter 5

1. Weiss and Hassan, 127.
2. *Ibid.*, 130.
3. "Houla: How a massacre unfolded," *BBC*, June 8, 2012, www.bbc.com/news/world-middle-east-18233934, retrieved February 25, 2021.
4. *Ibid.*
5. Fawaz A. Gerges, "Syria war: Tide turns Assad's way amid ceasefire push," *BBC*, February 13, 2016, www.bbc.com/news/world-middle-east-35562943, retrieved, June 3, 2020.
6. Pittard and Bryant, 272.
7. Jack Stubbs, "Four-fifths of Russia's Syria strikes don't target Islamic State: Reuters analysis," Yahoo, October 21, 2015, www.ca.news.yahoo.com/four-fifths-russias-syria-strikes-dont-target-islamic-150239086.html, retrieved March 1, 2021.
8. *Ibid.*
9. Human Rights Watch, "World Report 2019: Syria," 3, www.hrw.org/world-report/2019/country-chapters/syria#, retrieved February 25, 2021.
10. *Ibid.*, 2.
11. Lemmon, 63.
12. General Votel interview.
13. "Islamic state and the crisis in Iraq and Syria in maps," *BBC*, March 28, 2018, www.bbc.com/news/world-middle-east-27838034, retrieved June 12, 2020.
14. The Week Staff, "Life under the ISIS caliphate," *The Week*, August 22, 2015, www.theweek.com/articles/572910/life-under-isis-caliphate, retrieved February 16, 2020.
15. *Ibid.*
16. Noah Rayman, "ISIS manifesto depicts its grim vision of the role of women," *Time*, February 5, 2015, www.time.com/3696956/isis-manifesto-role-of-women/, retrieved April 17, 2021.
17. "Islamic state and the crisis in Iraq and Syria in maps," *BBC*, retrieved June 12, 2020.
18. Weiss and Hassan, 273.
19. Father Patrick Desbois and Costel Nastasie, *The Terrorist Factory: ISIS, the Yazidi Genocide, and Exporting Terror* (New York: Arcade Publishing, 2018), 82.
20. "'They came to destroy': ISIS crimes against the Yazidis," 19.
21. freeyezidi.org, accessed October 7, 2022.
22. Farida Khalaf and Andrea C. Hoffmann, *The Girl Who Escaped ISIS* (London: Vintage, 2016), 62.
23. *Ibid.*, 63.
24. Lemmon, 144.
25. In some cases middlemen and families were later reimbursed by the Kurdistan Regional Government's Office of Kidnapped Affairs.
26. Dunya Mikhail, *The Beekeeper: Rescuing the Stolen Women of Iraq* (New York: New Directions Books, 2018), 21.
27. Abigail Haworth, "Vian Dakhil: Iraq's only female Yazidi MP on the battle to save her people," *The Guardian*, February 8, 2015, www.theguardian.com/world/2015/feb/08/vian-dakhil-iraq-isis-yazidi-women, retrieved December 7, 2020.
28. Shand, 217.
29. Jane Arraf, "Freed from ISIS, Yazidi Mothers Face Wrenching Choice: Abandon Kids or Never Go Home," *NPR*, May 9, 2019, www.npr.org/2019/05/09/721210631/freed-by-isis-yazidi-mothers-face-wrenching-choice-abandon-kids-or-never-go-home, retrieved April 6, 2021.
30. *Ibid.*
31. Tim Lister, "Battle for Raqqa:

Notes—Chapter 6

Seven things you need to know," *CNN*, June 6, 2017, www.cnn.com/2017/06/06/middleeast/raqqa-great-battle-begins-tim-lister/, retrieved April 11, 2021.

32. "Massive military reinforcements from the Coalition arrive to the Syria Democratic Forces and head to take part in the grand battle of Al-Raqqah," Syrian Observatory for Human Rights, July 6, 2017, www.syriahr.com/en/69491/, retrieved April 12, 2021.

33. Lemmon, 190.

34. Barbara Starr, "Top U.S. general says defeat in Syria wouldn't mean the end for ISIS," *CNN*, February 11, 2019, www.cnn.com/2019/02/11/politics/votel-isis-syria/index.html, retrieved April 9, 2021.

35. Jane Arraf, "Freed from ISIS, Few Yazidis Return to Suffering Families, Many Remain Missing," *NPR*, March 14, 2019, www.npr.org/2019/03/14/702650912/-freed-from-isis-few-yazidis-return-to-suffering-families-many-remain-missing, retrieved May 22, 2020.

Chapter 6

1. John Bolton, *The Room Where It Happened: A White House Memoir* (New York: Simon & Schuster, 2020), 195.

2. Ibid., 200.

3. Ibid., 206.

4. Nisan Ahmado, "Hundreds of Yazidis Displaced Amid Turkey's Incursion in Northern Syria," *VOA News*, October 16, 2019, www.voanews.com/extremism-watch/hundreds-yazidis-displaced-amid-turkeys-incursion-northeast-syria, retrieved April 25, 2021.

5. Andrew Solender, "Trump Said He's Cozier With 'Tougher And Meaner' Dictators, Calls Them Smarter Than Biden," *Forbes*, September 14, 2020, www.forbes.com/sites/andrewsolender/2020/09/14/trump-said-hes-cozier-with-tougher-and-meaner-dictators-calls-them-smarter-than-biden/, retrieved April 27, 2021.

6. Jay Nordlinger, "Trump and Dictators," *National Review*, October 20, 2020, www.nationalreview.com/2020/10/trump-and-dictators/, retrieved April 27, 2021.

7. "Statement from the Press Secretary," October 6, 2019, www.trumpwhitehouse.archives.gov/briefings-statements/-statement-press-secretary-85/, retrieved April 26, 2021.

8. "Trump Makes Way for Turkey Operation Against Kurds in Syria," *BBC*, October 7, 2019, www.bbc.com/news/-world-middle-east-49956698, retrieved April 20, 2021.

9. "Statement from President Donald J. Trump Regarding Turkey's Actions in Northeast Syria," October 14, 2019, www.trumpwhitehouse.archives.gov/-briefings-statements/statement-president-donald-j-trump-regarding-turkey's-actions-northeast-syria/, retrieved April 26, 2021.

10. Phillip Rucker and Jenna Johnson, "Trump on Turks and Kurds: 'Like two kids in a lot, you've got to let them Fight,'" *The Washington Post*, October 17, 2019, www.washingtonpost.com/politics/trump-on-turks-and-kurds-like-two-kids-in-a-lot-youve-got-to-let-them-fight/2019/10/17/bf37283c, retrieved April 29, 2021.

11. Bolton, 212.

12. General Joseph Votel, interview by author.

13. Bethan McKernan, "Syrian Refugees Return to Hometowns in 'Safe Zone' Despite Dangers," *The Guardian*, December 18, 2019, www.theguardian.com/world/2019/dec/18/syrian-refugees-return-to-home-towns-in-safe-zone-despite-dangers, retrieved May 1, 2021.

14. Nurcan Baysal, "Yazidis in Turkey are still awaiting their fate," *Ahval*, September 26, 2018, www.ahvalnews.com/yazidis/yazidis-turkey-are-still-awaiting-their-fate, retrieved November 20, 2019.

15. Liam, ed., "Video shows Special Forces in al-Baghdadi Raid," *Warfare Today*, October 31, 2019, www.warfare.today/2019/10/31/video-shows-special-forces-in-al-baghdadi-raid/, retrieved May 4, 2021.

16. "CENTCOM Commander General McKenzie Briefing on Baghdadi Raid," *C-Span*, October 31, 2019, www.c-span.org/video/?465918-1/centcom-commander-general-mckenzie-briefs-reporters-baghdadi-raid, retrieved May 7, 2021.

Notes—Chapter 6

17. Scott Lucas, "Updates: UN Officials Tell Countries—Repatriate 27,000 Children from al-Hol Camp in NE Syria," *EA World View*, February 9, 2021, www.eaworldview.com/2021/02/un-officials-tell-countries-repatriate-27000-children-from-al-hol-camp-in-ne-syria/, retrieved May 11, 2021.

18. *Frontline: Return from ISIS*, directed by Josh Baker (Boston: PBS, WGBH, December 15, 2020), www.pbs.org/wgbh/frontline/film/return-from-isis/, retrieved February 20, 2021.

19. "Foley, Kassig, Mueller and Sotloff Families Welcome Move to Try 'Beatles' in the United States," *James Foley Foundation*, October 7, 2020, www.jamesfoleyfoundation.org/press-releases-1/2020/10/6/foley-kassig-mueller-and-sotloff-families-welcome-move-to-try-the-isis-beatles-in-the-united-states, retrieved May 15, 2021.

20. Reuters, "For Yazidis, Baghdadi's Death 'Doesn't Feel Like Justice Yet,'" *VOA*, October 29, 2019, www.voanews.com/a/middle-east_yazidis-baghdadis-death-doesnt-feel-justice-yet/6178495.html, retrieved March 10, 2020.

21. Alissa J. Rubin, "She Faced Her ISIS Rapist in Court, Then Watched Him Sentenced to Death," *The New York Times*, March 2, 2020, www.nytimes.com/2020/03/02/world/middleeast/isis-iraq-trial, retrieved May 11, 2021.

22. *Ibid.*
23. *Ibid.*
24. Crowe, 381.
25. *Ibid.*, 342.
26. *Ibid.*, 346.
27. Shand, 216.
28. *Ibid.*, 217.

29. Seth J. Frantzman, "After pivotal role saving Yazidis from ISIS, PKK leaves Sinjar," *The Jerusalem Post*, April 4, 2018, www.Jpost.com/middle-east/after-pivotal-role-saving-yazidis-from-isis-pkk-leaves-sinjar-547874, retrieved May 21, 2020.

30. Adams, 40.

31. Dan Froomkin, "Germany turning away more Yazidi refugees," *Deutsche Welle*, September 2, 2019, www.dw.com/en/germany-turning-away-more-yazidi-refugees-/a-47438698, retrieved May 27, 2021.

32. Nisan Ahmado, "Yazidis in U.S. Mark IS Genocide Anniversary," *VOA News*, August 4, 2018, https://www.voanews.com/a/yazidi-in-us-mark-anniversary-of-is-genocide/4513899.html, retrieved November 21, 2019.

33. "U.S. Military Casualties-Operation Inherent Resolve (OIR) Military Deaths," *Defense Casualty Analysis System*, May 27, 2021, www.dcas.dmdc.osd.mil/dcas/pages/report_oir_deaths.xhtml, retrieved May 28, 2021.

34. The service losses are as follows: Army 11, Navy 5, Marines 4, Air Force 1.

35. "Statement by the President," August 14, 2014, www.obamawhitehouse.archives.gov/the-press-office/2014/08/14/-statement-president, retrieved March 2, 2018.

Bibliography

Interviews

Shahab B., Lincoln, Nebraska, November 9, 2019.
Haider E., telephone, May 4, 2020.
Amel H., Lincoln, Nebraska, November 8, 2019.
Mesur H., Lincoln, Nebraska, November 8, 2019.
Faisal I., Lincoln, Nebraska, November 6, 2019.
Ahmed M., Lincoln, Nebraska, November 6, 2019.
Falah R., Lincoln, Nebraska, November 7, 2019.
Omar R., Lincoln, Nebraska, November 7, 2019.
General Joseph Votel, telephone, June 23, 2020.

Government Documents

"New UK aid supplies delivered to Iraq." August 14, 2014. www.gov.uk/government/news-uk-aid-supplies-delivered-to-iraq.
"Speeches and Selected Remarks of Secretary of Defense Chuck Hagel February 2013–February 2015." Press Conference on Iraq: August 8, 2014. Archives and Special Collections, University of Nebraska, Omaha.
"Statement by the President." August 7, 2014. www.obamawhitehouse.archives.gov/pressoffice/2014/08/07/statement-president.
"Statement by the President." August 14, 2014. www.obamawhitehouse.archives.gov/the-press-office/2014/08/14/-statement-president.
"Statement from President Donald J. Trump Regarding Turkey's Actions in Northeast Syria." October 14, 2019. www.trumpwhitehouse.archives.gov/briefings-statements/statement-president-donald-j-trump-regarding-turkey's-actions-northeast-syria.
"Statement from the Press Secretary." October 6, 2019. www.trumpwhitehouse.archives.gov/briefings-statements/-statement-press-secretary-85/.

United Nations and Non-Governmental Organizations Documents

Amnesty International. "Ethnic Cleansing on a Historic Scale: Islamic State's Systematic Targeting of Minorities in Northern Iraq." 2014. https://www.amnesty.org/en/wp-content/uploads/2021/06/mde140112014en.pdf.
Human Rights Watch. "World Report 2019: Syria." www.hrw.org/world-report/2019/country-chapters/syria.
Office of the High Commissioner for Human Rights. "Report on the Protection of Civilians in the Armed Conflict in Iraq: July 6–September 10, 2014." www.ohchr.org/sites/default/files/Documents/Countries/IQ/UNAMI_OHCHR_POC_Report_FINAL_6July_10September2014.pdf.
U.N. Human Rights Council. "'They came to destroy': ISIS Crimes against the Yazidis." June 15, 2016. www.reliefweb.int/report/syrian-arab-republic/they-came-destroy-isis-crimes-against-yazidis-human-rights-council.
U.S. Commission on International Religious Freedom. "Report of the United

Bibliography

States Commission on Religious Freedom on Iraq." December 2008. http://www.uscirf.gov/sites/default/files/resources/iraq report final.pdf.

Documentaries

Baker, Josh, dir. *Frontline: Return from ISIS*. Boston: PBS, WGBH, December 15, 2020. www.pbs.org/wgbh/frontline/film/return-from-isis/.

Bluemel, James, dir. *Frontline: Once Upon a Time in Iraq*. Boston: PBS, WGBH, July 14, 2020. www.pbs.org/wgbh/frontline/once-upon-a-time-in-iraq/.

Books

Acikyildiz, Birgul. *The Yezidis: The History of a Community, Culture and Religion*. New York: I.B. Tauris, 2010.

Adams, Angela. *The War Against ISIS*. New York: Cavendish Square Publishing, 2018.

Balakian, Peter. *The Burning Tigris: The Armenian Genocide and America's Response*. New York: Perennial, 2003.

Bolton, John. *The Room Where It Happened: A White House Memoir*. New York: Simon & Schuster, 2020.

Crowe, David M. *War Crimes, Genocide, and Justice*. New York: Palgrave Macmillan, 2014.

Desbois, Father Patrick, and Costel Nastasie. *The Terrorist Factory: ISIS, the Yazidi Genocide, and Exporting Terror*. New York: Arcade Publishing, 2018.

Josephus, Flavius. *The Works of Flavius Josephus, the Learned and Authentic Jewish Historian and Celebrated Warrior*. Cincinnati: E. Morgan and Company, 1847.

Khalaf, Farida, and Andrea C. Hoffmann. *The Girl Who Escaped ISIS*. London: Vintage, 2016.

Kiernan, Ben. *Blood and Soil: A World History of Genocide and Extermination from Sparta to Darfur*. New Haven: Yale University Press, 2007.

Lemmon, Gayle Tzemach. *The Daughters of Kobani: A Story of Rebellion, Courage, and Justice*. New York: Penguin Press, 2021.

Mikhail, Dunya. *The Beekeeper: Rescuing the Stolen Women of Iraq*. New York: New Directions Books, 2018.

Morgenthau, Henry. *Ambassador Morgenthau's Story: A Personal Account of the Armenian Genocide*. New York: Doubleday, Page and Company, 1918.

Nicolle, David. *The First Crusade 1096–1099: Conquest of the Holy Land*. Oxford: Osprey Publishing, 2003.

Otten, Cathy. *With Ash on their Faces: Yezidi Women and the Islamic State*. New York: OR Books, 2017.

Pittard, Dana J. H., and Wes J. Bryant. *Hunting the Caliphate: America's War on ISIS and the Dawn of the Strike Cell*. New York: Post Hill Press, 2019.

Schmermund, Elizabeth. *ISIS and the Yazidi Genocide*. New York: The Rosen Publishing Group, 2018.

Shand, Susan. *Sinjar: 14 Days that Saved the Yazidis from the Islamic State*. Guilford, CT: Lyons Press, 2018.

Stern, Jessica, and J. M. Berger. *ISIS: The State of Terror*. New York: HarperCollins, 2015.

Weiss, Michael, and Hassan Hassan. *ISIS Inside the Army of Terror*. New York: Regan Arts, 2015.

White, Matthew. *The Great Big Book of Horrible Things: The Definitive Chronicle of History's 100 Worst Atrocities*. New York: W.W. Norton, , 2012.

Winter, Jay, ed. *America and the Armenian Genocide of 1915*. Cambridge: Cambridge University Press, 2003.

Wise, Terence, and G.A. Embleton. *Armies of the Crusades*. London: Osprey Publishing, 2003.

Journal Articles and Online Sources

Ahmado, Nisan. "Hundreds of Yazidis Displaced Amid Turkey's Incursion in Northern Syria." *VOA News*, October 16, 2019. www.voanews.com/extremismwatch/hundreds-yazidis-displaced-amid-turkeys-incursion-northeast-syria.

———. "Yazidis in US Mark IS Genocide Anniversary." *VOA News*, August 4, 2018. www.voanews.com/a/yazidi-in-

Bibliography

us-mark-anniversary-of-is-genocide/4513899.html.

Al-Jabouri, Najim Abed, and Sterling Jensen. "The Iraqi and AQI Roles in the Sunni Awakening." *PRISM: A Journal of the Center for Complex Operations* 2, no. 1 (December 2010). cco.ndu.edu/Portals/96/Documents/prism/prism_2-1/-Prism_3-18_Al-Jabouri_Jensen.pdf.

Arraf, Jane. "Freed from ISIS, Few Yazidis Return to Suffering Families, Many Remain Missing." *NPR*, March 14, 2019. www.npr.org/2019/03/14/702650912/freed-from-isis-few-yazidis-return-to-suffering-families-many-remain-missing.

———. "Freed from ISIS, Yazidi Mothers Face Wrenching Choice: Abandon Kids or Never Go Home." *NPR*, May 9, 2019. www.npr.org/2019/05/09/721210631/freed-by-isis-yazidi-mothers-face-wrenching-choice-abandon-kids-or-never-go-home.

Associated Press. "Battle for Sinjar, Iraq." Threat Action Report. April 2016, www.info.publicintelligence.net/usarmy-battleforsinjar.pdf.

———. "Defense Secretary Hagel Says 130 More Military Advisers Going to Iraq." *KPBS*, August 12, 2014. www.kpbs.org/news/2014/aug/12/hagel-hold-townhall-camp-pendleton.

Baysal, Nurcan. "Yazidis in Turkey Are Still Awaiting Their Fate." *Ahval*, September 26, 2018. www.ahvalnews.com/yazidis/yazidis-turkey-are-still-awaiting-their-fate.

Bender, Jeremy. "ISIS Militants Captured 52 American-Made Artillery Weapons That Cost $500,000 Each." *Business Insider*, July 15, 2014. www.businessinsider.com/isis-has-52-american-weapons-that-can-hit-baghdad-2014-7.

Cenciotti, David. "U.S. B-52 Bombers have dropped 3,419 weapons on Daesh targets since April 2016." *The Aviationist*, February 21, 2017. www.theaviationist.com/2017/02/21/u-s-b-52-bombers-have-dropped-3419-weapons-on-daesh-targets-since-april-2016.

"CENTCOM Commander General McKenzie Briefing on Baghdadi Raid." *C-Span*, October 31, 2019. www.c-span.org/video/?465918-1/centcom-commander-general-mckenzie-briefs-reporters-baghdadi-raid.

Chulov, Martin. "US forces bomb ISIS militant positions in northern Iraq." *The Guardian*, August 8, 2014. www.theguardian.com/world/2014/aug/08/us-iraq-air-strikes-isis-irbil.

Dunker, Chris. "Letter from Representative Jeff Fortenberry to President Barack Obama." *Lincoln Journal Star*, August 5, 2014. journalstar.com/letter-from-rep-jeff-fortenberry-to-president-barack-obama/pdf_017f3b8b-7798-5230-99fe-67764662fc42.html.

The Editorial Board. "Preventing a slaughter in Iraq." *New York Times*, August 8, 2014. www.nytimes.com/2014/08/08/opinion/preventing-a-slaughter-in-iraq.html.

Editors. "Qusay and Uday Hussein killed." *History*, February 9, 2010. www.history.com/this-day-in-history/qusay-and-uday-hussein-killed.

Ellis, Ralph. "Enormous Resources on Rescue Attempt for Kayla Mueller, Obama says." *CNN*, February 12, 2015. www.cnn.com/2015/02/12/middleeast/mueller-rescue-attempts/.

"Foley, Kassig, Mueller, and Sotloff Families Welcome Move to Try 'Beatles' in the United States." *James Foley Foundation*, October 7, 2020. www.jamesfoleyfoundation.org/press-releases-1/2020/10/6/foley-kassig-mueller-and-sotloff-families-welcome-move-to-try-the-isis-beatles-in-the-united-states.

Frantzman, Seth J. "After pivotal role saving Yazidis from ISIS, PKK leaves Sinjar." *The Jerusalem Post*, April 4, 2018. www.jpost.com/middle-east/after-pivotal-role-saving-yazidis-from-isis-pkk-leaves-sinjar-547784.

Froomkin, Dan. "Germany turning away more Yazidi refugees." *Deutsche Welle*, September 2, 2019. www.dw.com/en/-germany-turning-away-more-yazidi-refugees-/a-47438698.

———. "How many U.S. soldiers were wounded in Iraq? Guess again." *Huffpost*, January 30, 2011. www.huffpost.com/entry/iraq-soldiers-wounded_b_1176276.

Gerges, Fawaz A. "Syria war: Tide turns Assad's way amid ceasefire push."

Bibliography

BBC, February 13, 2016. www.bbc.com/news/world-middle-east-35562943.

Gilad, Elon. "The Bar Kochba Revolt: A Disaster Celebrated by Zionists on Lag Ba'Omer." *Haaretz*, October 4, 2018. www.haaretz.com/jewish/.-premium-bar-kochba-revolt-utter-disaster-1.5358629.

Graham-Harrison, Emma. "'I was sold seven times': Yazidi women welcomed back into the faith." *The Guardian*, July 1, 2017. www.theguardian.com/global-development/2017/jul/01/-i-was-sold-seven-times-yazidi-women-welcomed-back-into-the-faith.

Haworth, Abigail. "'If they capture me, they will execute me at once': Meet the Iraqi woman standing up to ISIS." *Marie Claire*, January 8, 2015. www.marieclaire.com/politics/news/a12989/iraqs-most-wanted-woman/.

———. "Vian Dakhil: Iraq's only female Yazidi MP on the battle to save her people." *The Guardian*, February 8, 2015. www.theguardian.com/world/2015/feb/08/vian-dakhil-iraq-isis-yazidi-women.

Hickman, Kennedy. "Hitler and the Armenian Genocide." *Genocideeducation*, 2014, the Genocide Education Project, www.genocideeducation.org/background/hitler-and-the-armenian-genocide/.

———. "Iraq War: Second Battle of Fallujah." *ThoughtCo.*, March 25, 2018. www.thoughtco.com/iraq-war-second-battle-of-fallujah-2360957.

"Houla: How a massacre unfolded." *BBC*, February 13, 2016. www.bbc.com/news/world-middle-east-18233934.

"Islamic state and the crisis in Iraq and Syria in maps." *BBC*, March 28, 2018. www.bbc.com/news/world-middle-east-27838034.

Johnson, Bridget. "Rep. Wolf to Obama: 'You will come to sincerely regret your failure to stop the genocide.'" *PJ Media*, August 8, 2014. pjmedia.com/tatler/2014/08/07/rep-wolf-to-obama-you-will-come-to-sincerely-regret-your-failure-to-take-action-to-stop-the-genocide-n194677.

Keller, Jared. "ISIS has just as many fighters in Iraq and Syria as it did 4 years ago." *Task & Purpose*, July 8, 2020. www.taskandpurpose.com/bulletpoint/-number-isis-fighters-iraq-syria.

Lamothe, Dan. "Marines planned massive evacuation on Iraq's Mount Sinjar." *The Washington Post*, October 8, 2014. www.washingtonpost.com/news/checkpoint/wp/2014/10/08/marines-planned-massive-evacuation-on-iraqs-mount-sinjar/.

Liam, ed. "Video shows Special Forces in al-Baghdadi Raid." *Warfare.Today*, October 31, 2019. www.warfare.today/2019/10/31/video-shows-special-forces-in-al-baghdadi-raid/.

Lister, Tim. "Battle for Raqqa: Seven things you need to know." *CNN*, June 6, 2017. www.cnn.com/2017/06/06/middleeast/raqqa-great-battle-begins-tim-lister/.

Losey, Stephen. "As Mosul battle neared end, anti–ISIS airstrikes reached new peak." *Air Force Times*, July 10, 2017. www.airforcetimes.com/news/your-air-force/2017/07/10/as-mosul-battle-neared-end-anti-isis-airstrikes-reached-new-peak/.

Lucas, Scott. "Updates: UN Officials Tell Countries—Repatriate 27,000 Children from al-Hol Camp in NE Syria." *EA World View*, February 9, 2021. www.eaworldview.com/2021/02/un-officials-tell-countries-repatriate-27000-children-from-al-hol-camp-in-ne-syria/.

Madden, Martine. "Armin Wegner, the German who stood up to genocide of both Armenians and Jews." *Irish Times*, May 7, 2015. www.irishtimes.com/culture/books/armin-wegner-the-german-who-stood-up-to-genocide-of-both-armenians-and-jews-1.2201998.

"Mass grave of Yazidi women executed by ISIS found in Iraq." *Al Arabiya English*, November 4, 2015. english.alarabiya.net/News/middle-east/2015/11/14/-Mass-grave-of-Yazidi-women-executed-by-ISIS-found-in-Iraq.

"Massive military reinforcements from the Coalition arrive to the Syrian Democratic Forces and head to take part in the grand battle of Al-Raqqa." Syrian Observatory for Human Rights, July 6, 2017. www.syriahr.com/en/69491/.

McKernan, Bethan. "Syrian Refugees

Bibliography

Return to Hometowns in 'Safe Zone' Despite Dangers." *The Guardian*, December 18, 2019. www.theguardian.com/world/2019/dec/18/syrian-refugees-return-to-home-towns-in-safe-zone-despite-dangers.

Millare, Command Sergeant Major Mark A. "Defeating ISIS in Iraq: A Race Against Time." *Army U Press*, January 2019. www.armyupress.army.mil/portals/7/nco-journal/docs/2019/january/defeating-isis/defeating-isis-in-iraq.pdf.

Nordlinger, Jay. "Trump and Dictators." *National Review*, October 20, 2020. www.nationalreview.com/2020/10/trump-and-dictators/.

Pope, Alistair. "The Rise and Fall of ISIS Armor." *Modern War* #46 (March-April 2020).

Rayman, Noah. "ISIS manifesto depicts its grim vision of the role of women." *Time*, February 5, 2015. www.time.com/3696956/isis-manifesto-role-of-women/.

Reuters. "For Yazidis, Baghdadi's Death 'Doesn't Feel Like Justice Yet.'" *VOA*, October 29, 2019. www.voanews.com/a/-middle-east_yazidis-baghdadis-death-doesnt-feel-justice-yet/6178495.html.

Rubin, Alissa J. "She Faced Her ISIS Rapist in Court Then Watched Him Sentenced to Death." *The New York Times*, March 2, 2020. www.nytimes.com/2020/03/02/world/middleeast/isis-iraq-trial.

———. "On a helicopter going down: Inside a lethal crash in Iraq." *The New York Times*, August 16, 2014. www.nytimes.com/2014/08/16/world/middleeast/iraq-alissa-j-rubin-a-times-corrrespondent-recounts-fatal-helicopter-crash-in-kurdistan.html.

Rucker, Phillip, and Jenna Johnson. "Trump on Turks and Kurds: 'Like two kids in a lot, you've got to let them fight.'" *The Washington Post*, October 17, 2019. www.washingtonpost.com/politics/trump-on-turks-and-kurds-like-two-kids-in-a-lot-youve-got-to-let-them-fight/2019/10/17/bf37283c.

Scher, Major Adam. "The collapse of the Iraqi army's will to fight: A lack of motivation, training, or force generation?" *Army U Press*, February 19, 2016. www.armyupress.army.mil/Portals/7/Army-Press-Online-Journal/documents/16-8-Scher-19Feb16.pdf.

Six-Hohenbalken, Maria. "The 72nd *Firman* of the Yezidis: A 'Hidden Genocide' during World War I?" *Genocide Studies International* 13, no. 1 (Spring 2019): 52–76.

Solender, Andrew. "Trump Said He's Cozier With 'Tougher And Meaner' Dictators, Calls Them Smarter Than Biden." *Forbes*, September 14, 2020. www.forbes.com/sites/andrewsolender/2020/09/14/trump-said-hes-cozier-with-tougher-and-meaner-dictators-calls-them-smarter-than-biden/.

Starr, Barbara. "Top U.S. general says defeat in Syria wouldn't mean the end for ISIS." *CNN*, February 11, 2019. www.cnn.com/2019/02/11/politics/votel-isis-syria/index.html.

Stubbs, Jack. "Four-fifths of Russia's Syria strikes don't target Islamic State: Reuters analysis." *Yahoo*, October 21, 2015. www.ca.news.yahoo.com/four-fifths-russias-syria-strikes-dont-target-islamic-150239086.html.

"Transcript: President Obama's Speech on Combating ISIS and Terrorism." *CNN*, September 10, 2014. www.cnn.com/2014/09/10/politics/transcript-obama-syria-isis-speech/index.html.

"Trump Makes Way for Turkey Operation Against Kurds in Syria." *BBC*, October 7, 2019. www.bbc.com/news/world-middle-east-49956698.

"US forces land on Mount Sinjar in Iraq." *Irish Times*, August 13, 2014. www.irishtimes.com/news/world/middle-east/us-forces-land-on-mount-sinjar-in-iraq-1.1895602.

"US Military Casualties-Operation Inherent Resolve (OIR) Military Deaths." *Defense Casualty Analysis System*, May 27, 2021. www.dcas.dmdc.osd.mil/dcas/pages/report_oir_deaths.xhtml.

"The virtually unknown genocide of Yazidis by the Turks along with the Armenians, Assyrians and Greeks." *Ihgjlm* (Institute on the Holocaust and Genocide in Jerusalem). www.ihgjlm.com/the-virtually-unknown-genocide-

Bibliography

of-yezidis-by-the-turks-along-with-the-armenians-assyrians-and-greeks/. Originally published in *Genocide Prevention Now*, Special Issue 5, Winter 2011.

The Week Staff. "Life under the ISIS caliphate." *The Week*, August 22, 2015. www.theweek.com/articles/572910/life-under-the-isis-caliphate.

United Nations Independent International Commission of Inquiry on the Syrian Arab Republic. "The Yazidi Genocide." *The Cairo Review of Global Affairs* (Fall 2016). www.thecairoreview.com/essays/the-yazidi-genocide/.

YouTube. Video uploaded by *Syrian Perspective*. August 7, 2014. www.youtube.com/watch?v=bnqedigxi8w.

Index

Numbers in **_bold italics_** indicate pages with illustrations

Acre, Israel 73
Afghanistan 19, 57, 58, 126; U.S. war in 1, 16, 154; U.S. withdrawal from 159–160
Africa 144, 154; North 46, 67, 118
al-Abadi, Haider 44, 106, 157
al-Assad, Bashir 117–121, 122–123, 142; Americans and Kurds oppose 124; Ankara government opposes 141; dictatorship of 22; forces threaten Kurdish civilians 53; Kurdish military seeks alliance with 145; rebellion against 27, 136; regime crushes rebellion 140; Syrian refugees fear 146
Alawites 119
al-Baghdadi, Abu Bakr 112, 124; extreme interpretation of Islam 125; flees Baghuz 139; followers 110, 150, 151; killing of 147–148; leads al-Qaeda 27; proclaims Islamic caliphate 29, 37, 107; treatment of Kayla Mueller 115
Aleppo, Syria 39, 71, 113; in Armenian genocide 78, 80, 82, 83, 84; chlorine gas unleashed on 122; falls to al-Assad's forces 140; shelling of 121; Turkish army shells YPG positions in 141
al-Kadhimi, Mustafa 160
al Kateab, Waad 121
al-Khansaa Brigade 126, 127
al-Maliki, Nouri 26–27, 44
al-Nusra Front 27
al-Qaeda in Iraq (AQI) 21, 23, 24, 27, 42
al-Sadr, Muqtada 21–22
al-Zarqawi, Abu Musab 18, 19–21, 23–24
Anatolia/Asia Minor 69, 82, 87; eastern 76, 77, 78, 80, 146
Ankara, Turkey 78, 123, 141, 144, 145
AQI (al-Qaeda in Iraq) 21, 23, 24, 27, 42
Arab Spring 118
Armenians 70, 74–80, 82–92, 100; see also genocide, Armenian
Arminius 65
Asia: central 46; southeast 50
Asia Minor/Anatolia see Anatolia/Asia Minor

Ataturk (Kemal, Mustafa) 92, 167n54
Azerbaijan 12

Ba'athists 14, 20, 21, 25
baba sheikhs 10, 133, 134
Baghdad, Iraq 29, 51, 70, 97, 157; al-Maliki press conference in 26; bombings in 20, 22, 159; Dana Pittard arrives in 103; government in 11, 32, 43, 50, 149; Iraq Museum in 127; Muqtada al-Sadr from 21; *New York Times* Baghdad bureau 152; railway 81; Sheikh Adi studies in 9; U.S. advisors in 45, 50, 160; U.S. troops enter 17
Baghuz, Syria 139, 147
Bahrain 11, 23, 118
Bar Kochba 66–67
Barzani, Masoud 33, 99, 100, 157
beheadings 33, 45, 73, 113, 139; of James Foley 114; of Kayla Mueller 115; of Khaled al-Asaad 129; of Nicholas Berg 21; of Peter Kassig 114; of Steven Sotloff 150
ben Matityahu (Flavius Josephus) 62, 63, 64, 67
Berg, Nicholas 21
Biden, Joe 158, 159
bin Laden, Osama 16, 58
bombers (aircraft) 108, 109, 120
Bosnia/Bosnians 17, 155, 156
Bremer, L. Paul 20
Bush, George, H.W. 15
Bush, George, W. 16–17, 20, 26–27, 50, 154

C-130 Hercules 46, **_46_**
caliphates 31, 125, 126, 132, 152; al-Baghdadi's 29, 30, 107, 124; Al-Zarqawi wishes to establish 20; boys fight for 39, 129; capital of 145; defeat of 159; destruction of 131, 138, 139, 149; forces of 34; France bombs 112; Iraqi army's role in destroying 161; ISIS fighters celebrate **_29_**; ISIS territorial 143; receives money 127; of seventh and eighth centuries 1; 2014 military defeat 59; U.S. seeks to destroy 115

177

Index

Canada 42, 57, 144, 158
car bombs 20, 93, 97, 108, 136, 159
CENTCOM (U.S. Central Command) 46, 49, 51, 103; McKenzie commands 147; Votel commands 115, 123, 138
China 153
Christians 10, 33, 113, 142; in Armenian genocide 74, 76, 82, 87–89, 100; Assyrian Christian militias 136; in Crusades 68–73; in Darfur 154; in Iraq 95; ISIS attacks 42; ISIS considers second class 1; ISIS targets in Mosul 23, 31; in Ottoman Empire 130; protest Yazidis genocide in U.S. 48; Sunni extremist groups target 18; victimize Jews 67
CIA (Central Intelligence Agency) 30, 50, 147
Committee of Union and Progress (CUP) 74, 79
Constantinople, Turkey 69, 78, 80, 83, 87; Armenians send pleas for help to 86; boycott against Christians in 82
Counter Terrorism Service (CTS) 103, 159
counterterrorism 56, 151, 152
crimes against humanity 151, 153, 155, 156; al-Bashir charged with 154; ISIS charged with 36; Saddam charged with 17
Crusades 5, 60, 68–73
CUP (Committee of Union and Progress) 74, 79

Dabiq (online magazine) 37, 164n18
Daesh 28, 31, 57, 104, 116
Dakhil, Vian 43–44, 51–52, 57
Daraa, Syria 118
Davis, Leslie A. 82–84
decapitation *see* beheadings
Deir-ez-Zor, Syria 77, 86, 113, 115
Delta Force 56, 113, 115, 147
Democratic Party of Kurdistan (KDP) 12, 32, 43
Dempsey, Martin 44
drones 23, 47, 108, 110, 147, 150

Egypt 19, 23, 64, 70, 108, 118, 143
England *see* Great Britain
enslavement 1, 5, 58, 95, 106, 127, 139; of Nadia Murad 34; by Ottoman Empire 130; by Romans 62, 63, 64; standing trial for 152; Wadi 135; of Yazidi women 36–40
Erbil, Kurdistan 43, 48, 55, 56, 160; ISIS attacks 44, 45, 47, 107; Ministry of Peshmerga Affairs in 32; U.S. advisors in 50
Erdogan, Recep Tayyip 106, 123, 140–146, 157
Eshoo, Anna 41
Europe 53, 84, 102, 128, 163n4; armies 130; Bosnian civil war 17, 155–156; in Crusades 69–73; against Erdoğan 144; Global Coalition to Defeat Daesh (ISIS) 57; Holocaust 74; ISIS attacks in 111–112; ISIS fighters from 125, 150; Jews of 36, 40, 67, 75; refugees to 97, 122, 135, 146–147, 157, 158; religion 13, 68; World War I 76, 85
extremists 2, 6, 24, 36, 37, 97, 132; of al-Nusra Front 27; attack in Paris 112; Bin Laden and 16; capture heavy weapons 110; dealing with 160; holding accountable for genocide 155; in Iraq 93; Israel retaliates against 31; kill homosexuals 126; northern Iraq falls to 33; in possession of Mosul Dam 114; puritanical way of living 26; retaliate against translators 99; from Russia 125; seek strict society 1; Sunni Muslim 18; thrive on hate 95; use civilians as human shields 107; victims of 150; *see also* fanaticism/fanatics

F/A-18 Hornets 47, **49**, 108, 109, **138**
Fallujah, Iraq 21, 23, 29, 104
fanaticism/fanatics 14, 27, 29, 36, 49, 73; Arab tribesmen 87; attack Christians in Europe 68; behead James Foley 114; brutality of 95; in Crusades 72; destroy ancient artifacts 128; fail to annihilate Yazidis 159; fight to the death 37, 105; genocide based on 5; Iraqi military intimidated by 7; Janissaries 130; seek martyrdom 24; *Shabiha* 119, 120; Sunni Muslims 18; well-armed 98, 102, 110; YPJ against 116, 136; zealots 19, 61–65; *see also* extremists; suicide attacks
First World War *see* World War I
Flavius Josephus 62, 63, 64, 67
Foley, James 113, 114, 150, 151
For Sama (documentary) 121
Fortenberry, Jeff 41, 42
France 99, 108, 112, 116, 163n4; citizens join ISIS 125; in Crusades 69; mandate over Syria and Lebanon 91; 1920 Treaty of Sevres 11; in Triple Entente 76

Gaddafi, Muammar 45, 109, 118
gas: chlorine 122; mustard 12; nerve 14; sarin 122
genocide 2, 36, 67, 68, 70, 154–156
genocide, Armenian 5, 60, 74–79, 80, 81, 82–90, 100; arrest of Armenian men in Mezre **78**
genocide, Bosnian 17, 155–156
genocide, Jewish 5, 36, 74, 75, 80, 154–156; in Crusades 67, 68, 70
genocide, Rwandan 42
genocide, Yazidi 2, 5, 18; enslavement of

Index

women 36–40; latest to occur 60, 155; Obama speaks on 58; U.S. prevents 2, 3, 44–49; Wolf cautions Obama about 42

George H.W. Bush, USS 47, **48**

Germany 11, 76, 81, 86, 150; accepts Yazidi refugees 97, 99, 135, 136, 158; Battle of the Teutoburg Forest 65; Crusaders ravage 69; Nazi 3, 74; Syrians flee to 122; Wilson declares war with 85, 166n41

Global Coalition to Defeat ISIS 57, 161

Great Britain 76, 91, 116, 163n4; abolishes capital punishment 150; citizens join ISIS 125; establishes no-fly zone 12; in Global Coalition to Defeat Daesh (ISIS) 57; 1920 Treaty of Sevres 11

Hadrian 66, 67
Hagel, Chuck 47, 50
Haines, David 113, 114, 150
Harput, Turkey 82, 83, 84
Hay'at Tahrir al-Sham (Organization for the Liberation of the Levant) 122, 146, 148
Hemming, Alan 113, 150
Hercules, C-130 46, **46**
Herod the Great 61, 64
Hezbollah 122
Hisbah 125, 149
Hitler, Adolf 14, 75, 87
Holocaust 5, 36, 42, 74, 80
holy war *see* jihad
homosexuals 126
Hornets, F/A-18 47, **49**, 108, 109, **138**
Human Rights Watch 119, 150, 153
humanitarianism 45, 47, 122, 151, 161; aid workers 113, 115, 147; airdrops 50; international 42, 149; to prevent genocide 2
Hussein, Saddam 19, 26, 163n12, 163n26; abuses Yazidis 96, 97; al-Abadi opposes 44; Anfal campaign 11; Arabization campaign 34; dictatorship of 10; fall of 12, 14–18, 20; Kurds help overthrow 51; Shias oppose 21, 22, 27

India 47, 153
internally displaced persons (IDP) camps 135, 156, 158
International Criminal Court (ICC) 37, 153–155
Iran 21, 70, 126, 160; al-Assad's ally 117, 122; Iran-Iraq War 11, 97; Iranian revolution 13, 14, 22; against ISIS 105; Kurdish militias receive arms from 50; Kurdish population of 10; Kurds forced to ally with 142; Peshmerga buys arms from 32; Saddam fought 15; Shia majorities of 12; Sunni leaders see as threat 25; Yazidis living along border 7
Iraqi army 96, 111, 116; in battle for Mosul 106; Camp Justice base 17; dismantled 18; drives ISIS from Iraq 161; ineffective 103; kills Kurds 11; in Operation Desert Storm 15; reclaims Mosul Dam 114; reorganizes 21; retreats from ISIS 30, 32, 110; U.S. trains and equips 104; U.S. troops assist 160

Iraqi government 30, 94, 151, 159; agrees to U.S. troop withdrawal 26; cannot defeat ISIS 1; corruption of 18, 124; deploys troops against Turkey 157; fears Turks will attack Kurds 106; ISI asked to cooperate with 25; negotiations with SDF 149; in reconstruction efforts 156; requests U.S. help for Yazidis 45; U.S. favors al-Abadi to head 44

Iraqi Security Forces (ISF) 23, 50, 103, 108

Iraqis 30, 99, 151, 153, 159, 160; destroy Saddam paintings/posters 17; in internment camps 149; under Operation Desert Storm 15; Petraeus works with 25; under Saddam 16; in struggle for Fallujah 21; vilify Jews 31

ISIL (Islamic State of Iraq and the Levant) 33, 46, 58, 161, 163n28

ISIS-controlled territory **6**, 104, 133

ISIS female militia 126, 127

ISIS's religious police 125, 149

Islamic State of Iraq (ISI) 23, 25–28

Islamists 76, 122, 123, 124, 137

Israel 19, 87, 119, 142; ancient 66, 67; Hamas and Islamic Jihad attacks 25; modern state created 31, 68; part of Ottoman Empire 11

Jackson, Jesse B. 82, 83–84
Janissaries 130
Jerusalem, Israel 9, 66, 67, 164n6; during Crusades 70, 71–73; fall of 64; under Rome 61, 62, 63
Jews 19, 88, 164n6; in Anatolia 82; during Crusades 69; in Iraq 31; ISIS considers second class 1; journey to New York City 40; in Nazi Germany 74–75, 87; people of the Book 33; Roman-Jewish wars 5, 60–68; view Jerusalem as holy city 9, 71; *see also* genocide, Jewish
jihad 16, 25, 30, 76, 130
jihadis 123, 160; al-Zarqawi 19; atrocities spur people to join 120; bulldoze Yazidi homes 35; call Yazidi men dogs 132; destroy ancient artifacts 128; destroy Mosul Museum 127; enslave females 37; ex-government employees become 20; face criminal prosecution 149–150; from foreign countries 26; Hay'at Tahrir al-Sham 146; impregnate Yazidi females 134; Iraqi and Kurdish security forces fight 104; Jihadi John 150; lose Baghuz 139;

Index

lose Raqqa 136, 137; punish women 133; slaughter Yazidis 33; threatened YPJ 116; torture homosexual men 126
jizyah 31
Jordan 18, 20, 108, 125; airstrike on Raqqa 115; government 19, 114; in Ottoman Empire 11; Saddam's daughters flee to 163n12; Syrian refugees in 122
Josephus 62, 63, 64, 67

Kabul, Afghanistan 160
Kassig, Peter 113, 114, 150
KDP (Democratic Party of Kurdistan) 12, 32, 43
Kemal, Mustafa 92, 167n54
Khalaf, Farida 131
Kirkuk, Iraq 11, 157, 159
Knights Hospitallers 72
Knights Templars 72
Kobani, Syria 116, 123, **124**, 144
Kocho, Iraq 33, 34
Koran 25, 129, 130
KRG (Kurdistan Regional Government) *see* Kurdistan Regional Government (KRG)
Kurdish militias 59, 95, 141, 145; aid U.S. 17; in Baghuz 139; base at Fishkilbur 51; in siege of Mount Sinjar 53, 56, 57; U.S. supplies with weapons 50; units of 105; wish to defeat ISIS 123–124
Kurdish security forces 104
Kurdish semiautonomous region *see* Kurdistan region
Kurdistan Democratic Party (KDP) 12, 32, 43
Kurdistan region 24, 39, 51, 151
Kurdistan Regional Government (KRG) 32, 41, 96, 168n25; disputes with national government 156, 160; established 12; runs refugee camps 55
Kurdistan Workers Party (PKK) 11, 105, 141, 142; close ties to YPG 123, 140; in siege of Mount Sinjar 52–54, 157, 161; supports Resistance Units 57
Kurds 24, 106, 116, 132, 135, 155; attacks on 18; capture terrorists 150; consider U.S. ally 160; desire autonomy 9–12, 157; growing power 141–143; help protect Yazidis 6; ISIS considers second class 1; jihadi crimes against 149; put ISIS militants on trial 151, 153; rescue Yazidis 94, 161; resent al-Maliki 27; retreat from ISIS 32–33; Saladin 72; semi-autonomous status 21, 145–147; Turkish military attack 140; U.S. supplies with weapons 49–53; Yazidis are ethnic Kurds 7; *see also* Kurdish militias; Kurdistan Workers Party (PKK); People's Defense Units (YPG); Peshmerga
Kuwait 12, 15, 17, 27, 57, 122

Lalish 9, 10, 134
Lebanon 9, 11, 70, 91, 113, 122, 126
Lemkin, Raphael 36
Libya 39, 45, 108, 118, 125
Lincoln, Nebraska 40, 41, 42

Mahdi Army 22
Masada 64, 65
mass graves 106, 137, 138, 159
mass murder 5, 30, 74, 75, 77, 79, 155
McKenzie, Frank 147, 148
Melek Taus 8
Milley, Mark 145
Morgenthau, Henry 88, 89, **89**, 90; in Armenian genocide 84–86; works with Taalat and Enver 81–83
mortars 32, 47, 119, 136, 142
Mosul, Iraq 9, 17, 37, 43; al-Qaeda attacks 21; battle to retake 107, 116, 136; Christians and Yazidis attacked in 23–24; during Crusades 70; falls to ISIS 29–31, 34, 95, 101, 103–104; ISIS destroys ancient artifacts of 128; ISIS destroys Mosul Museum 127; ISIS fighters from 7; ISIS occupies 114; ISIS supply route 105, 106; Petraeus commands in 25
Mount Sinjar **54**, 98, 100, 101; helicopter crash on 51, 152; siege of broken 52–58, 157; strikes on ISIS near 47, 50, 107, 108; Yazidi women unable to reach 37; Yazidis find refuge near 88; Yazidis led from **55**, **56**; Yazidis on rescued 123, 161; Yazidis take refuge on 1, 5, 34–36, 94; Yazidis trapped on 40–44, 45, 96
Mueller, Kayla 113, 115, 150
Muhammad 13, 19, 33, 72, 128
Mujahedeen *see* al-Qaeda in Iraq (AQI)
Mukhabarat 119
Murad, Nadia 34, 159

Obama, Barack 48, 116, 161; airstrikes against ISIS 96; Fortenberry requests aid to Yazidis 41–42; informs Congress of ISIS fight 49; "One Iraq" policy 50; orders Yazidi aid 2–3, 5, 44–45; speech on ISIS 57–58; uses term ISIL 163n28; Yazidi rescue plan 56
Ocalan, Abdullah 52, 53–54
Oman 122
Operation Desert Storm 15
Operation Ezra and Nehemiah 31
Operation Inherent Resolve 57, 106, 109, 160
Operation Kayla Mueller 147
Operation Peace Spring 141, 147
Ospreys, V-22 56, 57
Ottoman Empire 80, 82, 86, 130; Armenians live in 74, 75; collapse of 19, 91, 92; defeated

Index

in WWI 11; joins Central Powers 76; Kurds in 10; partners with Germany 85

Palestine 70, 91
Palmyra, Syria 39, 128, 129
Party of God 122
Pasha, Enver 77, *81*
Pasha, Talaat 77, *90*
Patriotic Union of Kurdistan (PUK) 12, 32
Peacock Angel 8
People's Defense Units (YPG) 105, 124, 130; aids Yazidis 94, 161; in battle for Baghuz 139; in battle for Raqqa 136–137; in battle to retake Mosul 116; fights ISIS 98–99, 101; formed to defend Kurds 11; helps Yazidis on Mount Sinjar *54*; proven fighting ability 117; in siege of Mount Sinjar 52–59; Turkey attacks 140–145; U.S. partnership with 123
Persian Gulf 47, 107, 108
Peshmerga 31–35, 96, 98, 160; abandoned their posts 7, 94, 95, 100, 102; in anti–ISIS coalition 105; corruption among 99; drove ISIS from Iraq 161; hostility with Iraqi army 104; internal issues 103; interrogates ISIS prisoners 130; KRG's military force 12; power struggle with PKK 157; prepares to attack ISIS 50–51; in retaking Sinjar 105, 106; in siege of Mount Sinjar *54*; works with Iraqi army 114
Petraeus, David 25
Pittard, Dana 103, 105
PKK (Kurdistan Workers Party) *see* Kurdistan Workers Party (PKK)
poison gas *see* gas
Pope Urban II 68–69
Publius Quinctilius Varus 65–66
PUK (Patriotic Union of Kurdistan) 12, 32
Putin, Vladimir 120, 143, 145

Qahtaniya, Iraq 24, 93
Qatar 109, 122
Quran 25, 129, 130

Ramadi, Iraq 104
rape 117, 133, 134, 153, 154; by Arab brigands 83; attitudes toward 152; of girls 38; of Kayla Mueller 115; by military guards 80; as punishment 39, 58; rape camps 155; by secret police 119; Uday Hussein 14; as weapon of war 34; of Yazidi slaves 129; of Yazidi women 152
Raqqa, Syria 40, 112–115, 130, 136–138; ISIS supply route 105; ISIS takes 29; Kremlin's soldiers in 145; Yazidi women taken to 37
Reagan, Ronald 108
religious minorities 1, 5, 18, 41, 58, 146
Richard the Lionheart 72, 73, 166n21

Roman-Jewish wars 5, 60–68
Rome (empire) 60–61, 63–67, 153–155
Rome Statute 153, 154, 155
Roosevelt, Franklin D. 81, 102
Roosevelt, Theodore 84, 85
Royal Air Force 47
Rubin, Alissa 51, 52, 57, 152
Russia 105, 143, 145–147, 153; Air Force 120, 121; in Armenian genocide 74, 76; assists al-Assad 122; Muslim extremists from 125; opposes ISIS 117; repatriates family members of ISIS 150; Russian Orthodox Church 68; weapons and aircraft 50, 51, 108, 111, 121
Russian Armenia 82, 88
Russians 88, 120, 121, 146, 147; invade eastern Anatolia 77; in Raqqa 145; relations with Armenians 76

Saladin 72, 73
Samarra, Iraq 104
Saudi Arabia 15, 39, 119, 143; citizens join ISIS 125; death penalty for gays in 126; in Ottoman Empire 11; rivalry with Iran 122; Sunni dominant in 14; supply opposition groups in Syria 123; Wahhabism in 19
Sayyaf, Abu 115
Second World War *see* World War II
sexual violence/assault *see* rape
Shabiha militias 119, 120
sharia law 34, 38, 113, 125, 154
Sheikh Adi 8, 9
Shero, Hemoye 88
Shia 101, 125, 128, 159; al-Zarqawi pressures 21; considered heretics 19; executed 30; flee to Kurdistan 95; ISIS considers second class 1; as majority 12; martyrs 15; militias 27, 104, 105, 116, 122, 157, 160; occupy top government positions 18; origin 13; rivalry with Sunni 17, 20, 22; in Syria 119
Sinjar City, Iraq 1, 5, 101, 158; ISIS assault on 7; ISIS captures 34–36; ISIS defenses in 107; ISIS occupies 56, 100; PKK and KRG hold territory in 157; Yazidis flee 49; Yazidis want to return to 156
snipers 21, 105, 136, 142
Soleimani, Qasem 22, 160
Sons of Iraq 25
Sotloff, Steven 113, 114, 150
Sudan 154
suicide attacks 14, 111, 112, 114, 148; bombers 24, 25, 26, 105, 130, 136
Sunni 1, 30, 101, 122; alliance with Kurds 123; under al-Maliki 27; in anti–ISIS coalition 105; child soldiers 39, 129; dominate Saudi Arabia 14; insurgency in Iraq 21; in majority 12, 119; origin 13; resent ISI fighters 26; rivalry with Shia 17, 20, 22;

181

Index

under Saddam 18; side with Islamists 124; U.S. pays 25; view of Wahhabism 19
Syria, eastern 77, 145, 147, 159
Syria, northern 124, 137, 142, 143; under al-Baghdadi's control 30; ISIS conquers territory in 1, 29; Turk-YPG rivalry in 123
Syria, western 147
Syrian Democratic Forces 123, 132, 136, 137, 143
Syrians 53, 55, 122, 141, 146, 149, 151

Tal Afar, Iraq 37
Taliban 16, 126, 128, 159, 160
terrorism 19, 150
Tikrit, Iraq 17, 29, 30, 104
Titus 61, 62, 63, 64
torture 36, 135, 151; by Crusaders 71; of homosexuals 126; ISIS threatens own with 110; of Kayla Mueller 115; of Khaled al-Asaad 129; by Nazis 87; by Shia militias 22
translators 40, 42, 94, 95, 97, 99, 160
Trump, Donald 140–145, 158
Tunisia 118, 125
Turkey 86, 117, 120, 144, 145; in Armenian genocide 75, 82, 83, 100; during Crusades 69; Davis captured in 151; Kurdish movement in 11; Kurdish population of 10; Kurds view as threat 142; NATO ally 51; not charged with war crimes 92; Ocalan directs operations against 53; Ocalan imprisoned in 52; operation into northern Syria 143; Syrian refugees in 122, 123, 140, 141, 146; threatens PKK 157

UNHCR (United Nations High Commissioner for Refugees) 98, 122
UNICEF (United Nations International Children's Emergency Fund) 40, 55
United Arab Emirates (UAE) 107, 108, 123
United Kingdom *see* Great Britain
United Nations 137, 153, 156; al-Zarqawi bombs 20; defines genocide 36; imposes economic sanctions 15
United Nations Assistance Mission for Iraq (UNAMI) 33
United Nations Educational, Scientific and Cultural Organization (UNESCO) 107
United Nations High Commissioner for Refugees (UNHCR) 98, 122
United Nations Human Rights Council 36
United Nations International Children's Emergency Fund (UNICEF) 40, 55

United Nations Security Council 155
U.S. Air Force 23, 46, 48, 57, 107, 109, 136
U.S. Army 26, 42, 97, 99, 150; Delta Force 56, 115; Rangers 113; Special Forces soldiers 45; Threat Action Report 105
U.S. Central Command (CENTCOM) *see* CENTCOM (U.S. Central Command)
U.S. Marine Corps 21, 26, 57, 147
U.S. military 6, 57, 113, 120, 147; airstrikes in Iraq and Syria 59; ordered out of Afghanistan 159; ordered to aid Yazidis 2, 5; searches for al-Zarqawi 23; in siege of Mount Sinjar 45, 49, 98; track al-Afri 24; translators 40, 95
U.S. Navy 47, 54, 57, 108; SEALs 113; *see also* F/A-18 Hornets

V-22 Ospreys 56, 57
Vespasian 61, 62, 64
Votel, Joseph 115, 116, 123, 138, 145

war crimes 91, 153, 154, 155; ISIS committed 36, 151
War Powers Act of 1973 49
weapons of mass destruction (WMDs) 16, 17
Wegner, Armin T. 86, 87
Western hostages 111–116
Wilson, Woodrow 84, 85
Wolf, Frank 41, 42
Women's Protection Units (YPJ) **55**, 139, 161; executed 142; formation of 53; lead Yazidis from Mount Sinjar **55**; not intimidated by Islamic fanatics 116; protect Yazidis 54; rescue Yazidi girls 132; in Syrian Democratic Forces 136
World War I 86, 111; Armenian genocide in 74, 76; Near East Relief founded 84; Ottoman Empire broken up 11, 91
World War II 3, 14, 107, 155; death marches 75; ethnic cleansing in 17; genocide in 36; war crimes 92; *see also* Holocaust

Yazda 49, 158
Yazidi genocide *see* genocide, Yazidi
Yemen 118
YPG (People's Defense Units) *see* People's Defense Units (YPG)
YPJ (Women's Protection Units) *see* Women's Protection Units (YPJ)

zealots 19, 61, 62, 63, 64, 65

www.ingramcontent.com/pod-product-compliance
Lightning Source LLC
Chambersburg PA
CBHW032047300426
44117CB00009B/1218